Honoring the fallen at Volgograd.

By Edwin P. Hoyt

Nonfiction

199 Days: The Battle for Stalingrad
The U-Boat Wars
Defeat at the Falklands
The Kamikazes
The Invasion Before Normandy
Hitler's War

Fiction

The Last Stand

199 Days

The Battle for
Stalingrad

Edwin P. Hoyt

A Tom Doherty Associates Book
New York

199 Days: The Battle for Stalingrad

Copyright © 1993 by Edwin P. Hoyt

This book is printed on acid-free paper.

A Forge Book
Published by Tom Doherty Associates, Inc.
175 Fifth Avenue
New York, NY 10010

Forge® is a registered trademark of Tom Doherty Associates, Inc.

Maps by Ellisa Mitchell, with the exception of the eight maps on pages 34, 80, 84, 97, 104, 231, and 278, which originally appeared in *War Maps* by Simon Goodenough; published by Macdonald & Co. Ltd.

All photographs used in this book are © by NOVOSTI PRESS AGENCY (APN), Moscow.

Library of Congress Cataloging-in-Publication Data

Hoyt, Edwin Palmer.
199 days : the battle for Stalingrad / Edwin P. Hoyt.
p.   cm.
"A Tom Doherty Associates Book."
ISBN 0-312-86853-7 (acid-free paper)
1. Stalingrad, Battle of, 1942-1943. I. Title. II. Title: One hundred and ninety-nine days.
III. Title: Battle for Stalingrad.
D764.3.S7H69   1993
940.54'21785—dc20
92-42576
CIP

First Tor hardcover edition: February 1993
First Tor mass market edition: February 1994
First Forge trade paperback edition: February 1999

Printed in the United States of America

0 9 8 7 6 5 4 3 2 1

ACKNOWLEDGEMENT

I owe an enormous debt to Robert Gleason, editor-in-chief of Tor Books. He gave me the idea for the Stalingrad book in the first place and helped with many suggestions about the finding of research materials and the management of the book. His editing was perspicacious all the way through. He found a copy of Guy Sajer's *The Forgotten Soldier*, which is probably the best war narrative to come out of any army after the Second World War.

TABLE OF CONTENTS

INTRODUCTION

The American writer Edwin P. Hoyt, who wrote this excellent book, lives and works in Japan. God only knows why Russian history is better seen by an American scholar from the Land of the Rising Sun than from America; maybe because Stalingrad is closer to Tokyo than to Washington.

Whatever the reason, the manuscript lost nothing by being produced on Japanese turf and imported to the U.S.A. Unlike good wine, good manuscripts are not spoiled by traveling across the sea.

What's more, this kind of import will be dearly welcomed in America. And not only in America, it seems to me. Because the book is a serious research project, of such a large caliber and long range that military terms are justified here, it will undoubtedly become a formidable contribution to the continuing, fifty-year-old battle waged by military historians for the true role and place of Stalingrad in World War II.

Alas, Stalingrad is even today an area of misunderstanding, cold war prejudices, stereotypes ("General Winter" defeated the Nazis, to name one), and plain ignorance. That's why Edwin Hoyt's honest book is so important.

Hoyt is remarkable in his portrayal of the Red Army at Stalingrad. He correctly perceives that the entire edifice of the German strategy crumbled on November 19, 1942, under the heavy blows of the Red Army's amazing counteroffensive.

Hoyt is correct in showing that the battle served as a turning point in the war, that for the first time the Nazi leaders faced the prospect of a final defeat.

The Soviet people paid a high price for the victory at Stalingrad, which, they say, was a modern-day Cannae. But even Cannae was never like this extended, exhausting fight to the finish. The Germans seemed to bring down all the iron of the Ruhr, Lorraine, Lapland and Biscay upon the narrow strip of land along the Volga: An average of 1,250 shell, bomb and mine fragments hit each yard of the land for which 800,000 Soviets gave their lives.

Stalingrad was called "the contemporary Cannae" also because the encirclement there—the most formidable in the history of wars— emulated the skillful encirclement by Hannibal of 80,000 Roman legionaires under the command of consul Emilius Paullus. Many centuries after that, German generals dreamed of a victories of such a scale, and believed that only they were capable of doing that. When the Red Army executed a pincers movement of their own around the 330,000-strong Sixth Army of Friedrich Paulus (what ironic coincidence!), the Wehrmacht generals, taken by surprise, could not believe that the Russians had outsmarted them.

On the news of Paulus's surrender the bells of the Moscow Kremlin were rung for the first time since October 1917.

The Soviet people paid a high price at Stalingrad—the 400-year-old city virtually ceased to exist.

Joseph Davies, President Roosevelt's personal envoy and close friend, went to Stalingrad four months after the battle was over. In his plane he flew over the tortured and devastated city several times. The picture stunned everyone in the plane into dead silence. Upon landing, Davies observed that there was no point in rebuilding Stalingrad. He thought a new city would have to be built five miles down or up from the old site.

President Roosevelt and Prime Minister Churchill also suggested that Stalingrad's rubble be preserved intact so that the ruins, like the ruins of Carthage, would forever remain a monument to human endurance and suffering.

But the Russian reasoning was different: Not the horrible lifeless ruins, but a city raised from the rubble would be a monument to the victory of the Stalingraders. It was a hard job to restore it to life, but the whole nation helped to do it.

An American delegation arrived in Stalingrad in July 1943. One of the guests wondered: Do you really expect to smelt metal here so soon? To answer that question, the delegates were invited to the Red October Plant. Its half-destroyed shops had no roof as yet, but an open-hearth furnace was already pouring out steel.

Forty-three years later, on July 16, 1986, Professor William Folger of Denver, Colorado, stood on the Volga bank right near that plant and wept. With other American World War II veterans, he participated in a peace cruise down the Volga. Professor Folger said: "I wept at Stalingrad. I wept tears of sorrow. I thought of the thousands of brave Soviet soldiers who died here. That stark, terrible statistic—eight hundred thousand Soviet dead—is beyond human comprehension. Eight hundred thousand! That is more than twice the present population of Buffalo, New York, where I worked on the morning daily newspaper. That stark, tragic figure—eight hundred thousand—is thirty-two times the number of men, women and children in the small city of my birth—Lockport, New York.

"On that historic hill called Mamayev Kurgan, I saw a man wipe a tear from his eyes. A veteran of that bloody battle, he told of the death of his military unit—he was the only survivor of it."

A couple of years ago, an Afghan war five-year veteran paratrooper, without wounds and unscratched, returned to his native Stalingrad only to meet his death on Mamayev Kurgan—he stepped on a German anti-infantry mine of 1942 vintage. . . .

These visions of the past are conjured up by this magnificent book.

VLADIMIR BELYAKOV
Russian Embassy to the United States
Washington, D.C.
October 25, 1992

CAST OF CHARACTERS

ADOLF HITLER—Dictator of Germany who planned and executed Operation Barbarossa, the invasion of Soviet Russia

JOSEPH STALIN—Dictator of Soviet Russia who, six months before the invasion, secured appointment by the Politburo as chief of state so that he could rule by fiat

VYACHESLAV M. MOLOTOV—Commissar of foreign affairs of the USSR and leader of Russia's "war party," as opposed to Stalin's "peace party"

JOACHIM VON RIBBENTROP—Foreign minister of Germany whose plans for pacification and alliance with nationality groups in the USSR were overruled by Hitler

ALFRED ROSENBERG—Philosophical leader of the Nazi movement who found justification for the Nazis' "Aryan" policies and wanted control of the Russian people

HERMANN GOERING—Head of the German air force and economic czar of Germany; quarreled with Rosenberg, Himmler, and Bormann over control of the Russian people; was heir apparent to Hitler's mantle as leader of the Third Reich

HEINRICH HIMMLER—Head of the SS, Gestapo, and conquered-peoples sections of the German government; he advocated enslavement of the Russian peoples

WILHELM KEITEL—Field marshal and chief of staff of Oberkommandowehrmacht, the German high command over all the armed forces and the instrument through which Hitler ran the war

ALFRED JODL—Director of operations of OKW

WALTHER VON BRAUCHITSCH—German field marshal and commander

in chief of the army, whom Hitler later dismissed in the winter of 1941 in favor of himself

FRANZ HALDER—Chief of staff of Oberkommando des Heeres, the German land army, whom Hitler dismissed in September 1942 at the height of the Battle of Stalingrad

SEMYON TIMOSHENKO—War commissar of the Soviet Union, first commander of the Stavka (field headquarters), and field marshal

GEORGI ZHUKOV—Stalin's best general, chief of staff of Russian armies, and originator of the plan for victory at Stalingrad

KLIMENT VOROSHILOV—Russian field marshal and member of the State Defense Committee

LAVRENTI P. BERIA—Head of Security Bureau (NKVD) and member of the State Defense Committee

GEORGI MALENKOV—Political commissar and member of the State Defense Committee

NIKITA KHRUSHCHEV—Political commissar in the defense of Stalingrad

SEMYON M. BUDENNY—Field marshal and drinking companion of Stalin

KONSTANTIN K. ROKOSSOVSKY—Russian general, rehabilitated after having been purged by Stalin in the 1930s as a student of the hated Marshal Mikhail Tukhachevsky, who was given the task of destroying the German 6th Army

ANDREI YEREMENKO—Russian general given the task of saving Stalingrad in the summer of 1942, but later discarded by Stalin

ALEXANDER M. VASILEVSKY—Marshal and Russia's second chief of staff, who served during the Battle of Stalingrad

VASILI CHUIKOV—General and commander of the Russian 62nd Army who fought the Battle of Stalingrad from September 12, 1942 to end

GERD VON RUNDSTEDT—German field marshal, commander of Army Group South in Operation Barbarossa, and the first German general to leave the Eastern Front after quarreling with Hitler

FRIEDRICH VON PAULUS—General and later field marshal, commander of the German 6th Army

EWALD VON KLEIST—General, commander of Army Group A during the Battle of Stalingrad, and Paulus's immediate superior

HEINZ GUDERIAN—General and leading armored-warfare expert who stood up to Hitler and was dismissed from the Eastern Front

FEDOR VON BOCK—German field marshal and commander of Army

Group B, who was dismissed by Hitler at the beginning of the
Stalingrad campaign

WOLFRAM VON RICHTHOFEN—Luftwaffe general and commander of the
4th Luftflotte in the Battle of Stalingrad

ERIC VON MANSTEIN—German field marshal and commander of Army
Group Don, which undertook to rescue the German 6th Army from
the Stalingrad pocket

INVASION of POLAND · SEPT. 1940

PROLOGUE

PART I

A few minutes before midnight on June 21, 1941, a fleet of limousines drove out of the Kremlin, crossed Red Square, and moved swiftly out of Moscow on the Kuntsevo road. Soon they stopped at a villa and the party got down from the limousines. Stalin had arrived at his hideaway, as he came every night to get away from the cares of the Kremlin.

It was Saturday, and the next day Russians would enjoy their Sunday holiday from work. Stalin had spent the evening fending off warnings that the German army was about to attack the Soviet Union. He did so with his usual abrupt and angry denials of what he did not want to believe. He had made a nonaggression pact with the Germans in 1939, thus freeing Hitler's eastern flank and allowing him to proceed with the war against Poland that swiftly erupted into World War II. But Stalin had used Hitler's preoccupation with war in the west to grab large chunks of territory from Poland and the Baltic States. While Hitler was fighting in the west, Stalin had moved heavy concentrations of troops to the frontier between Germany and Russia, angering Hitler, who in the summer of 1940 told his intimates that he planned to attack Russia. "In the course of this contest, Russia must be disposed of," Hitler said. "Spring 1941. The quicker we smash Russia the better."

But in Moscow on June 21, the war in Europe still seemed far away. On June 14 all Soviet newspapers and radio stations had carried a Tass announcement in which informed persons instantly recognized Stalin's handiwork.

"Despite the obvious absurdity of rumors about a forthcoming war, responsible circles in Moscow have authorized a statement that according to evidence in the possession of the Soviet Union both Germany and the

Soviet Union are fulfilling to the letter the terms of the Soviet Non-aggression Pact. German troop movements in the eastern and northern parts of Germany are explained by other motives that have no connection with Soviet-German relations. It is false to state that the Soviet Union is preparing for a war with Germany."

On Saturday morning the front pages of *Pravda* and *Izvestia* were filled with news of production achievements in Kazakhstan and a long report on the Moscow conference of the Communist Party, which had been held that week. The news of the war was back on page 5. General Erwin Rommel was winning battles in North Africa, and the British offensive called Operation Battleaxe had just failed. Journalists were speculating that Hitler might now be prepared to move through Spain against Gibraltar. Russian newspaper readers were much more interested in the sports pages, and the announcement that an exhibition of aquatic sports was to open in Moscow on Sunday.

On Saturday, however, the War Commissariat received confirmation of earlier reports that said the Germans would attack on the night of June 22. Stalin had expressed his disbelief when the reports reached him, as had Comrades Georgi Malenkov and Andrei Zhdanov. But the reports were not stilled by Stalin's derision.

The evidence continued to mount. A German deserter informed a Russian frontier commander that his unit was to go into action against the Russians at dawn. Armed with this information, War Commissar Marshal Semyon Timoshenko and Chief of Staff General Georgi Zhukov came to see Stalin at five o'clock in the afternoon, with a prepared order to put all Russian border units on war alert.

"Just a provocation," Stalin snorted. But the generals were serious and very insistent. Stalin grumbled, but he had authorized the alert, stating that he expected a series of provocations, and adding: "The main task of our armies is not to be taken in by any provocations."

It was after eleven o'clock that this was hashed out, and orders were sent by telegram to the field units: "Have all units battle ready. No other measures are to be employed without special orders."

After midnight the orders went out, and at 2:25 A.M. they began arriving at the field headquarters. And what were the commanders to do? "No other measures without special orders." What did that mean? If the Germans came, were they to shoot at them? In some cases, such as the Baltic district, the commander ordered his men not to fire when provoked by the Germans. In Moscow, at two o'clock, General Ivan Tyulenev, commander of the Moscow defense district, had a call from Stalin telling him to have his antiaircraft defenses at 75 percent of war readiness. Tyulenev said, "Yes, sir," and got off the phone to think about what that meant. So fearful were the generals of Stalin—the purges of the army having eliminated the top 30 percent of officers—that they would do nothing to provoke their leader, whom they called the All-Highest. If they shot, they might be shot.

At precisely 3:15 on the morning of June 22 the Germans struck with Teutonic precision.

At four o'clock, General Zhukov telephoned the dacha and insisted to the nervous policeman who answered the telephone that Stalin had to be awakened immediately. Stalin was awakened, and he hurried back to Moscow and the Kremlin. But he still clung to his "provocation" theory, although generals were calling from Odessa to Murmansk with reports of bombing and artillery fire and advancing German troops all along the line.

Stalin insisted on his theory even yet. Did they not remember the Japanese, who in 1938 had attacked on the Mongolian border? Provocation. On two occasions the Japanese had been beaten off and had ceased military operations. This might well be the same, the idea of the German generals. For it was the German generals, not Hitler, that Stalin distrusted. He often said that the generals were trying to push Hitler into attack.

Foreign Minister Molotov arrived at the Kremlin after an interview with German Ambassador Count Friedrich Schulenberg. Germany had finally declared war formally.

Even then Stalin did not believe it was real. He gave orders: German attacks were to be repelled but not returned. No Soviet troops would cross the frontier until further orders.

It was noon before the men in the Kremlin pulled themselves together enough to announce to the people of Russia that they were at war. Even then Stalin did not have the courage to make the statement, and it was Molotov who told the people of Germany's "faith-breaking."

Late that evening, Stalin and several other members of the Politburo arrived at the Commissariat of Defense, and there Marshal Timoshenko showed them the situation map. Three German army groups had cut deeply into the Soviet Union, led by armored columns. The Russian air defense was already shattered, and twelve hundred planes had been destroyed, eight hundred on the ground.

Stalin exploded in rage. Why were the Russian troops retreating? They were to begin advancing immediately. Immediately! By June 24 they must advance sixty to ninety miles in the north and seize strategic points in Germanized Poland.

The orders were given, and the Soviet armored divisions were called into action. It was all premature: not one of the divisions was ready for action. Personnel were on leave, many vehicles were under repair. Some of the units were not completely equipped. But into action they went.

Stalin left the Commissariat of Defense that night of June 22 and returned to his dacha at Kuntsevo. No orders were given, no word came from the dacha. Stalin was completely paralyzed with shock and incapable of action. For a week he hid in his country retreat and abandoned all his responsibilities, and the government was run by Marshal Timoshenko and General Zhukov.

What was Stalin thinking about in his seclusion?

What he should have been thinking about was what he had done to the Soviet armed forces in the Great Terror of 1937 and 1938 when twenty million people died. The assault on the army began in June 1937 with the trial and execution of what historian Robert Conquest called "the flower of the Red Army Command." The leading figure was Marshal Mikhail Tukhachevsky, deputy commissar of defense, who had begun to build a modern efficient army. He and all the men around him, eight generals, were tried one day and shot the next. Immediately afterward a wholesale purge of the army was conducted by the NKVD, and thousands of officers were arrested and executed or imprisoned. The navy was also purged. In the summer of 1938 another purge was conducted. As a result the Soviet defense system was damaged to the point of incompetence, and the fear in which high officers lived thereafter precluded them from taking any initiatives.

THE RED ARMY PURGE

In 1937 and 1938, to protect his own power Stalin had purged the army. He thus eliminated

3 of the 5 marshals
13 of the 15 army commanders

(continued next page)

(*continued from preceding page*)
8 of the 9 senior admirals
50 of the 57 corps commanders
154 of the 186 divisional commanders
16 of the 16 army commissars
25 of the 28 corps commissars
58 of the 64 divisional commissars
36,000 army officers
3,000 navy officers

The most competent and trained officers had been removed from the service. A 1940 survey showed that at a meeting of 226 division commanders, there was not one graduate of the Frunze Academy (the Russian West Point). The result was that when the Germans struck in June 1941, the Russian armies were commanded by incompetents and they lost battle after battle.

On June 23 the Russian newspapers all carried Molotov's war announcement and a big picture of Stalin. The war communiqué said the Germans were being repulsed and that the Luftwaffe had suffered heavy losses while the Russian air force had lost only seventy-six planes.

By June 24 the Germans had moved more than one hundred miles inside Russia at some point, and large Russian forces had been encircled, entrapped, and destroyed, with hundreds of thousands of Russian troops captured. By June 29 the Germans had seized most of Lithuania and a large part of Belorussia, and Stalin was still out of action. He did not come back until July 1, when it was announced that he had taken over as chairman of a new State Defense Committee in company with Marshal Klimenti Voroshilov, State Security Director Lavrenti Beria, and Georgi Malenkov. Two days later Stalin addressed the nation and called for a relentless struggle against the German enemy, a scorched-earth policy, partisan activity behind the German lines, and ultimate victory. A few weeks later Stalin took over the Commissariat of Defense personally.

He was a very bad general, surrounded by sycophants and incompetents. He proceeded to divest himself of his best general, Georgi Zhukov, who was sent to the Leningrad Front. The Russian armies suffered one defeat after another in a campaign where Stalin plunged enormous numbers of men into operations, time and again. Biographer Adam Ulam put it this way:

> The first six weeks of the war eroded most of the varnish of propaganda and uniformity which Stalin's rule had imposed upon the life of the nation. In the first shock, soldiers either fled or died bravely, civilians either cursed the regime or volunteered to fight "for the country, for Stalin." But when the German pressure slackened temporarily, the initial panic and then resolution were succeeded by realization of the appalling truth: the system under which they lived was grotesquely inefficient, to the point that the war made it appear unreal, yet as before the man who had built and epitomized this system was exempt from criticism. Only a few of his immediate circle knew that Stalin's stubbornness in the face of expert advice was costing hundreds of thousands of lives, that decisions to extricate and save whole armies or to evacuate valuable supplies were not being made because Stalin said he was too busy to come to the telephone. But for the Soviet citizen, whether soldier or civilian, there was simply the shattering realization of yet another and fatal aspect of his country's life: he was governed by Stalin, the Party, and the NKVD, but he was now more than ever a slave of rules and documents. In a situation which called for enterprise and initiative, he was alone, bound hand and foot by regulations that made little or no sense.

The Russian armies reeled from one catastrophe to another for a year and a half. The Wehrmacht was defeated before Moscow in December 1941, but it did not lose its mastery of the field. The Red Army did not really recover, either physically or psychologically, until the Battle of Stalingrad.

The story of the Battle of Stalingrad is one of the great stories of World War II. This battle marked the turning point of Adolf Hitler's campaign in Russia. Before Stalingrad he had a chance to achieve victory. After Stalingrad there was none, and the war would quickly begin to go the other way.

But until Stalingrad, Stalin had not mastered his job as generalissimo of the armies. Until Stalingrad, the leadership of the Russian armies was almost uniformly incompetent and produced almost uniformly disastrous results. Stalin's best general, Georgi Zhukov, found himself moved from one place to another, his advice unheeded, and the defeats piling up. It was Stalingrad that changed it all, including Zhukov's fortunes.

PART II

From the standpoint of the Germans, why Hitler attacked Russia is one of the anomalies of history, certainly the greatest of Hitler's. His basic motivation had to be a combination of fear and greed, which quite marred a judgment that was so accurate in his appraisal of his western European enemies. On the face of the matter, it was insanity for a nation of 80 million people to undertake the conquest of a nation of more than 200 million, living in a vast landmass that spanned two continents. But Hitler's fear of Communism was very real and so was his determination that Communism and Naziism could not coexist on the same planet. But his announced fear that Russia would attack Germany was totally faked, manufactured to impress his generals.

Stalin's attitude toward Naziism was to welcome it as a revolutionary movement whose greatest value was its destruction of western capitalism. Following the tenets of Marxist-Leninist theory, he expected to see the ultimate victory of Communism in Germany, and meanwhile he was quite comfortable with Naziism as a neighbor.

The fact is that Hitler and Stalin admired and learned from each other. Hitler, for his part, admired Stalin's use of power. On one occasion he told Field Marshal Wilhelm Keitel of his admiration, and said he wished that he had the absolute exercise of power that his adversary enjoyed.

Stalin felt the same way about Hitler, for in all his purging of his enemies, Stalin operated in two ways: either to have them killed secretly or to have them tried publicly on charges so substantial, though often faked, that there was no escape. The need to operate with such trappings was considered by Stalin to be a diminution of his power, from which Hitler did not suffer.

Many eminent historians, including B. H. Liddell Hart, have speculated on the cause of Hitler's decision to invade Russia in the spring of 1941, when he had already conquered continental western Europe and had only Britain to contend with. Sometimes the decision has been ascribed to the Nazi desire for a slave empire. In spite of Stalin's deep-seated belief that the war was the product of the Prussian military mind, the German generals, most of whom knew nothing about the Hitler plan until about six months before its execution, were almost uniformly opposed to the adventure. From the outset they advised against a two-front war. Later Hitler was to claim that his advisors had misled him as to the strength of the Russian army. The generals denied that charge.

Field Marshal Paul von Kleist had this to say:

> We did not underrate the Red Army as it is commonly imagined. The last German military attaché in Moscow, General Ernst Koestring—a very able man—had kept us well informed about the state of the Russian army. But Hitler refused to credit that information.

On a lower level, Hitler complained that General Heinz Guderian, the armor expert, had misled him as to the strength of Russian armored forces, a charge Guderian denied.

Guderian knew that the Russians had twenty thousand tanks but feared that the number would not be believed in German military circles. So Guderian wrote in a book that the Russian had ten thousand tanks, and Hitler attacked that number as highly exaggerated.

Some of the generals knew of the plan as early as July 1940. What Hitler told them was that the Russians were planning to strike Germany and they must strike first in self-defense. Field Marshal Gerd von Rundstedt, for one, did not believe that story. He saw no evidence of Russian planning for war.

> In the first place the Russians seemed to be taken by surprise when we crossed the frontier. On my front we saw no signs of offensive preparations in the forward zone, though there were some farther back. They had twenty-five divisions in the Carpathian sector, facing the Hungarian frontier, and I had expected they would swing around and strike at my right flank as it advanced. Instead they retreated. I deduced from this that they were not in a state of readiness for offensive operations, and hence that the Russian command had not been intending to launch an offensive at an early date.

As the generals were informed of Hitler's plans, virtually all the German high command opposed the decision: Field Marshal Keitel, Walther von Brauchitsch, Franz Halder, Alfred Jodl, all those concerned intimately with the operations of the army.

Hitler paid no attention to their objections. In 1935, when he was planning the march into the Rhineland to defy the western Allies and junk the Versailles Treaty, his generals counseled against the move. If the French marched, or even the British, the Germans would be forced to beat a quick and ignoble retreat. Hitler said the Allies would not march, and carried out his Rhineland plan. He was right: the western Allies did nothing. From that point on Hitler was contemptuous of the timidity of his generals and had small use for their advice.

From Hitler's point of view the Nazi-Soviet nonbelligerency pact was never more than a tactical gesture, designed to preserve his eastern flank while he destroyed Poland. From the very beginning he had meant to break it as soon as it was expedient for him. From the outset he was furious with having to make huge territorial concessions to the Russians to secure their agreement. He had to give them a free hand in Finland, and in Estonia, Latvia, and Lithuania, all of which had large populations of ethnic Germans. The concession was a total abnegation of Hitler's highly touted pan-Germanism. The thought of it made Hitler grit his teeth, but he could console himself because he knew that the situation was only temporary.

As far as Russia was concerned, since the Vienna days Hitler had been obsessed with a feeling that he must destroy Communism, lest it destroy him. At first the feeling had been largely inchoate, linked closely with his obsession with the Jews. In the lean years the Communists of Germany had been a convenient whipping boy for whom the Nazis could blame many of their excesses and justify others.

Hitler's feeling about Communism was that it was the one political element that offered a real threat to Naziism, not because of any innate virtue in the economic system, but because it was the one system that adopted Hitler's own thesis that struggle was the essence of existence. Force was Hitler's first law of existence, as it was Stalin's. Hitler respected Stalin because he had succeeded so well in bringing the 200 million people of the Soviet Union under the Communist thumb. One of the reasons he was to adopt the policy of total ruthlessness was that he had seen Stalin succeed so admirably in it.

What the westerners did not understand was that Hitler and Stalin understood each other thoroughly. Nearly half a century after his death it seems obvious that Stalin never believed in the ideal of communism, the utopian dream of a people's commune. To Stalin the Communist Party was an instrument of power, just as was the Red Army, and these instruments were to be exploited to maintain Stalin in power. He never forgot that the Bolsheviks, with a tiny political base, stole the Russian Revolution from the Social Democrats. Hitler recognized this and the essential single-mindedness of Stalin even when some of Stalin's associates credited him with kindness that did not exist. Stalin was Hitler's "kind of guy." He called him "the cunning Caucasian." What he really admired was Stalin's cunning in using Bolshevism "as only a means to, a disguise designed to trick the Germanic and Latin people."

Hitler admired Stalin's methods, and the Gulag and the NKVD had quickly become models for his own concentration camps and Secret Police.

Above all, Hitler understood that it made no difference how puerile his ideas might be in fact; the trick was to get the people to accept those ideas without realizing that their purpose was to perpetuate the leader in power.

As for Stalin, he admired Hitler as he did no other living man, and he took some of his ideas from the Hitler style. Stalin observed with great interest the Hitler purge of Ernst Roehm and the Sturmabteilung, the original gang of bullyboys whom Hermann Goering had welded into a private army and then turned over to Roehm. Three years later Stalin began the purge of the Red Army and the Communist Party to the same end, the creation of his own impregnable position, by killing all the potential threats.

Stalin believed that he could deal with Hitler in his own good time, and in the 1930s he was patient when Hitler began his rise to power. Stalin forced the German Communists to cooperate with the Nazis against the Social Democrats, which they did in the Prussia referendum of 1931 and the transport strike of 1932. He devised the concept of Hitler as the forerunner of the Communist Revolution. Let Hitler have the ball, he said, and run the field, and then ultimately the Communists would take over and convert the Nazis, who would then make valuable agents in the coming Communist world.

In fact, in the middle 1930s Moscow overtly sided with the Nazis and the Fascists as being fellow "have-nots." The embarrassment of the Spanish Civil War, which saw the Soviets and the Fascists on opposite sides of the fence, was one of these anomalies that Stalin handled without a tremor. In his negotiations with the Germans he simply ignored that conflict.

In 1936 Stalin began putting out feelers to the Germans for a nonaggression pact. He had always feared western encirclement, and he knew by 1936 that the USSR was vulnerable. He also had the advantage of knowing what he was going to do inside Russia that would make it more vulnerable. So in attempting to disarm Hitler, he was protecting his flank.

The attempt did not work very well, and it was not until 1938, when Hitler could see in a Soviet-Nazi pact some advantage to himself, that Berlin began taking it seriously.

PART III

When Hitler began his war in Poland, within the first week the Polish army was destroyed. At this point, Stalin, knowing Hitler, feared that Hitler would not live up to the secret protocol that gave the Russians the eastern half of the country.

Bickering began immediately over borderlines, and Stalin ordered troops to the area.

Hitler told close associates that he intended to deal with Stalin as quickly as possible. This could not have been a new idea. Although the Germans had agreed in principle to allowing the Russians a free hand with Estonia, Latvia, and Lithuania, when it came right down to it, it shocked Hitler to know that Stalin had moved so quickly. He had been thinking in terms of spheres of influence, and suddenly Stalin had moved to take 100,000 ethnic Germans into the Soviet Union.

When Hitler had written *Mein Kampf* back in the 1920s, he had referred to his coming *Drang nach Osten*—drive to the East—and he had never forgotten his intention of taking the German Empire to the Pacific. From his point of view the only question was when the Soviet-Nazi pact had served its purpose and kept the Russians quiescent while Hitler took over Poland. It had been unfortunate that so much of Poland had been given to the Russians, but that had been the price of the moment, and because Hitler intended to get it all back anyhow, he had not caviled at the Russian demand for more than half the Polish territory.

At this point he was annoyed with Stalin's aggressiveness and made the decision that Russia would be dealt with just as soon as possible. When the Germans and Russians drank champagne at the state banquet on September 28, 1939, to celebrate the redrawing of the map of Europe, Hitler was already turning over plans in his mind of the strike against Russia.

Early in 1940 he began the *Aufbau Ost*—Buildup East. The Germans began the buildup of their forces along the twenty-five-hundred-mile border from the Baltic to the Black Sea, and it was so well camouflaged the Russians had no knowledge of it.

Hitler believed that Stalin was vulnerable militarily, and he was determined to exploit that vulnerability. Keitel, who was Hitler's chief military planner, reported that spring that the Russians had 155 divisions in European Russia while the Germans could muster only 121. Still Hitler was undeterred. He would rely on the superior quality of the German army, he said.

At the time of the invasion, the Germans could muster only six hundred tanks, and the Russians in the southern sector alone had twenty-four hundred tanks. But again Hitler was undismayed. He believed in the superior quality of the German tanks (and for the moment he was right) and thought this would overcome the Russian superiority in number.

As British historian and armored expert Liddell Hart said, the facts justified Hitler's faith. It was only after the first year of war, when the Russians improved both their quality and their quantity, that they began to win battles.

PART IV

In the spring of 1941 Hitler also believed that the USSR was vulnerable politically. He was sure the USSR's persecuted peoples and captive nations were waiting for the chance to rebel. He based his idea on his observation of the purges of the mid-1930s. The continued economic failures in Russia and the Soviets' inability to adequately supply the Republicans in Spain had given the Germans some added clues as to Stalin's internal instability.

Not that Hitler had any plans for liberating these captive peoples. Just as Stalin had done, he said, he would rule with the steel gauntlet.

"It is the kindest way," he said to his generals when he announced his plans that spring at the Reich Chancellery.

He expected the Russian commissars to launch a campaign of terror against the German rear and vowed to fight terror with terror.

The other matter on which Hitler was adamant was that his armies could conquer Russia in a matter of weeks. Having studied the relative strengths and the weaknesses, and knowing from that most intelligent of military attachés, General Koestring, that Stalin had destroyed the nucleus of his military command, he was supremely confident. As Field

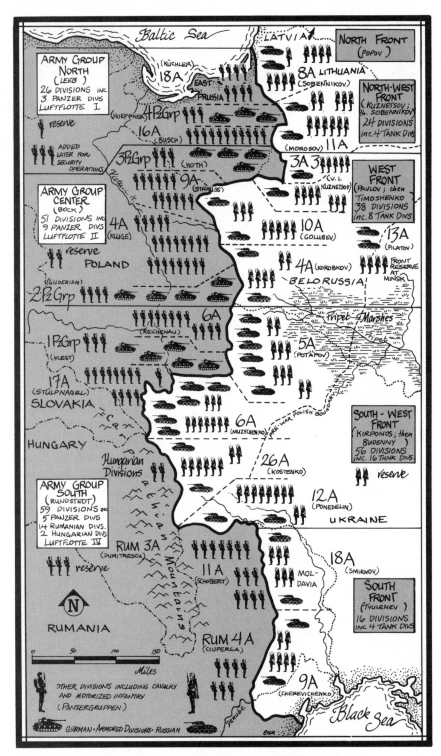

MILITARY BUILDUP • JUNE, 1941

General Kleist later recalled: "There were no plans for a prolonged struggle. Everything was based on the idea of decisive result before the autumn of 1941."

As it turned out, Hitler was right in his assessment. Had the Germans continued steadily toward Moscow that summer and early fall, they would have seized the Soviet capital. Moscow captured, the Soviet Union would simply cease to exist as a politically viable entity, for Moscow was the center of communications and government, to a far greater degree than the capital in any other country in the world. Moscow gone, the USSR would be brain-dead.

The war, however, was decided not in Moscow but in Stalingrad. On the road to Stalingrad, Hitler faced many problems—some military, some political, some personal. In the light of history, many of these problems would later seem insoluable. But at the time—to Adolf Hitler—they appeared not as problems, but as golden, glittering opportunities.

PART I
THE ROAD TO HELL

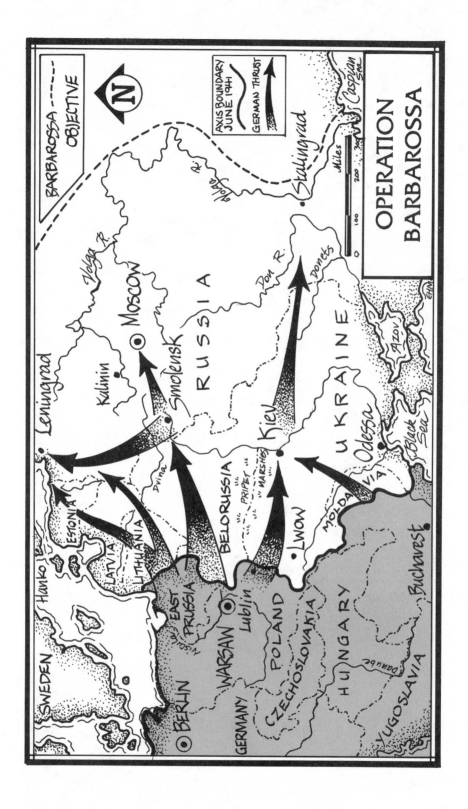

OPERATION BARBAROSSA

BARBAROSSA --- OBJECTIVE

AXIS BOUNDARY JUNE 1941
GERMAN THRUST

Miles
0   100   200   300

1

A few months before the beginning of Operation Barbarossa, the attack on the Soviet Union, Hitler called his generals together. This was not going to be an ordinary war, he told them. It was to be conducted with the utmost ferocity. The Soviet Union was to be destroyed and replaced by a group of colonies which would serve the Third Reich. The Russian people would be enslaved, and Russia would become a breadbasket and an oil sump for the Third Reich. All that Russia produced would be placed at the service of Germany.

Hitler summed up his policy toward Russia in three words:

Conquer.

Rule.

Exploit.

On June 22, 1941, the German war machine began its race through western Russia. The panzers were moving forty miles a day. In a week they had moved three hundred miles and conquered Minsk on the sixth day of the war. Before the month was out Wilhelm Kube, a Nazi member of the Reichstag, had been installed in Minsk as general commissar for Belorussia, the vital sector of the front, and the Nazi terror had begun. On one day the SD, the Nazi Party's security arm, took 280 civilian prisoners from the Minsk jail, led them to a ditch, and shot them. Because there was still more room in the ditch, they brought another thirty prisoners and shot them, too, including one man who had been arrested for violating the curfew and twenty-three Polish skilled workers who had been quartered in the jail because there was no other place to house them. The terror was wild and disorganized, with various elements of the Nazi government working against one another.

In Berlin, where it was predicted that the war in Russia would be over in six weeks, Reichsmarschall Goering, Martin Bormann, Heinrich Himmler, and Alfred Rosenberg quarreled about who should manage the Russian people. Foreign Minister Joachim von Ribbentrop had a plan to encourage separatist movements in Russia: the Ukraine, Belorussia, the Baltic States, and other national groups would be granted "independence" within the framework of the new German empire.

This plan was discarded in favor of forced labor and repression. Torture, murder, and systematic starvation became the Nazi policy toward Russia. The Germans soon found that as they defeated the Red Army and occupied the territory, their troubles mounted. As if haunted by a death wish, the Nazis had adopted the single policy in Russia that would unite the people against them.

2

For the enemy and his accomplices unbearable conditions must be created in the occupied territories. They must be pursued at every step and destroyed and their measures must be frustrated.

—Stalin

As soon as the Germans began to occupy parts of Russia, partisan bands became a major adjunct of the Red Army, and nothing could stop them. Since before the war started, the Soviet government had made preparations for partisan activity.

The Communist Party set up destruction battalions that consisted of about two hundred men who were not eligible for military service, supervised by the NKVD, the State Security bureau and ancestor of the KGB. Their tasks were to fight enemy parachutists, arrest deserters, hunt down counterrevolutionaries and enemy agents, and shoot at enemy aircraft. Later the best of these civilians would be chosen to fight as partisans.

PARTISANS

The partisans of Russia were an official part of the Russian war effort. By the end of 1941, ninety thousand partisans were operating behind the German lines. By 1944 the number was 250,000. The official history of the partisan movement claims that partisans killed nearly a million enemy soldiers, including forty-seven generals and Reichskommissar Wilhelm Kube, who was killed by a time bomb placed in his bed by his Belorussian partisan mistress. They also claimed to have destroyed 110,000 railroad cars, 5,000 locomotives, 14,000 tanks and armored cars, 1,100 aircraft and 65,000 vehicles. In 1942 the German army had to divert twenty-four divisions to fight the partisans, and eventually many divisions had a battalion assigned to antipartisan operations.

The partisans operated out of fixed bases covering small areas. The strongest partisan activity began in the west, White Russia and Belorussia, where unbroken forest and swampland stretch from the Pripyat Marshes to Lake Ilmen.

The Shmyrev detachment was typical. Formed in Surazh, thirty miles northeast of Vitebsk in eastern Belorussia, its first recruits were the employees of a cardboard factory in the village of Pudoti. Mihay Filipovich Shmyrev, the director of the factory, was chosen as leader. His political commissar was Vasil Shkredo, the party secretary of the factory. In early July 1941 the men built a camp in the woods. On the night of July 13, retreating Soviet troops gave them weapons and warned that the Germans were very close. The next day Germans entered the town of Surazh. That day, eight Soviet army stragglers and two local men joined the partisan group. On July 17 six local policemen and members of a destruction battalion that had broken up in Surazh also joined.

The detachment saw its first action on July 25, when it surprised a party of German cavalry bathing in a river and killed twenty-five of them without any casualties. The next day as a column of Germans passed through Pudoti, they fired on the last four trucks, destroying one of them and damaging the others. In the first week of September a dozen Soviet soldiers came to the camp and delivered four heavy machine guns and fifteen thousand rounds of ammunition, a heavy mortar, and a light mortar. With these weapons the partisans and the soldiers attacked Surazh on September 13, killing Germans and collaborators. The Soviet government issued a press release and used this attack as a publicity base for encouraging the partisans and frightening the Germans. The Germans made efforts to find them, and to persuade collaborators to betray them, but they did not succeed.

A PARTISAN REMEMBERS

In the autumn of 1942 we learned that the Germans were preparing a punitive operation against our partisan unit. The bridge across a nearby river had to be blown up so the tanks and armored personnel carriers would not get through. But the bridge was closely guarded.

My twelve-month-old daughter was with me in the partisan hideout, and when I went scouting I always left her with my mother who was with us there. On learning that several attempts to mine the bridge had failed I went to the commander and volunteered to do the job. I wrapped the small but powerful time bomb in a bundle with my daughter, took a basketful of apples and set out for the market in the nearby village. The way to the market lay across the bridge. The guard at one end of the bridge checked to see what was in my basket and took almost half of my apples but let me through. In the middle of the bridge I stopped to change my daughter's diaper. . . . Swiftly and deftly I attached the mine to a girder. At the other end of the bridge the Germans checked my basket again and left me a few apples but let me go. The bridge blew up three hours later. It took the Germans a month to repair it.

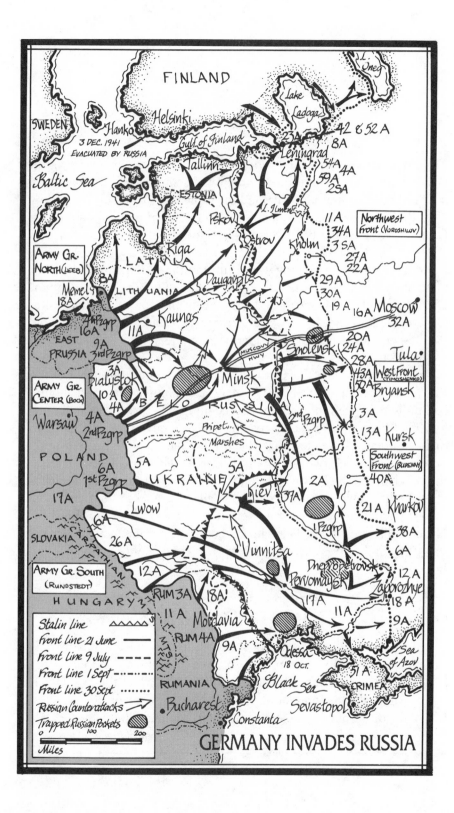

FINLAND

SWEDEN

Hanko
3 DEC. 1941
EVACUATED BY RUSSIA

Helsinki

Lake Ladoga

Gulf of Finland

Baltic Sea

Tallinn

ESTONIA

Leningrad

23A   42 & 52 A
8A
54A 4A
59A 2 SA

L. Ilmen

Pskov

Ostrov

Kholm

11 A
34A
3 SA

Northwest front (Voroshilov)

ARMY GR. NORTH (LEEB)

8A

Riga

LATVIA

Daugavpils

27A
22A

29A
30A

19 A 16A Moscow
32A

Memel

18A

LITHUANIA

Kaunas

4th Pzgrp
16A
9A
3rd Pzgrp

11A

EAST PRUSSIA

MOSCOW HWY

Smolensk

20A
24A
28A
43A
50A

Tula

West Front (TIMOSHENKO)

Bryansk

3A
Bialystok
10A
4A

ARMY GR. CENTER (BOCK)

Minsk

BELORUSSIA

2nd Pzgrp

3 A

Warsaw
4A
2nd Pzgrp

Pripet
Marshes

13A Kursk

POLAND
6A
1st Pzgrp

5A

5A

UKRAINE

Kiev 37A

2A

40A

Southwest Front (BUDENNY)

17A

Lwow

26A

SLOVAKIA

1 Pzgrp

21 A Kharkov
38A
6A

Vinnitsa

12A

ARMY GR. SOUTH (RUNDSTEDT)

RUM 3A 18A

Dnepropetrovsk

Pervomaysk

17A

12 A
Zaporozhye
18 A

HUNGARY

11 A Moldavia

11A

9A

RUM 4A

Stalin Line ∧∧∧∧∧
Front Line 21 June ——
Front Line 9 July – – –
Front Line 1 Sept –·–·–
Front line 30 Sept ·······
Russian Counterattacks →
Trapped Russian Pockets ▨

9A

Odessa
18 Oct.

Sea of Azov

51 A
CRIMEA

RUMANIA

Black Sea

Sevastopol

0   100   200

Miles

Bucharest

Constanta

GERMANY INVADES RUSSIA

3

The Germans attacked Russia with three army groups, one heading north toward Leningrad, one heading through the center toward Moscow, and the third heading south for Kiev and the Caucasus. By the middle of July 1941 the German front ran on a north-south line from the mouth of the Dniester River on the Black Sea to Narva on the Estonian frontier.

Hitler's dream was to replace the Red Flag with the Swastika. The new world that he was envisioning would run from the French Atlantic coast to Vladivostok. It would link with the Japanese empire at Manchuria. China would be conquered, and the Axis would control all that world from the western edge of Europe to Australia. Germany would get her old Pacific colonies back, and the German empire would be the greatest empire in the world.

Steadily and swiftly the German juggernaut rolled through western Russia. By September 1941 the Germans had captured Kiev, and another half million prisoners of war were loaded into cattle cars and open flatcars to begin their journey west to serve the Reich. By that time, the German high command estimated that the armies had captured 2.5 million prisoners and killed twice as many Russians. They had taken eighteen thousand tanks and twenty-two thousand field guns, and had destroyed fourteen thousand Russian aircraft. Leningrad was isolated from the rest of the USSR and seemed ripe for the picking. As far as the Donets River the Ukraine's black earth was German. So confident was the German general staff that planning was already begun for the withdrawal of eighty divisions from the Eastern Front.

STALIN'S EARLY GENERALS

At the outset of the war, Stalin relied almost completely on his old drinking companions, who had survived the purges of the 1930s because of their personal friendship with him. Two of these generals were Marshal Klimenti Voroshilov and Marshal Semyon Budenny.

At the outset of war, Budenny was put in command in the south and

(*continued next page*)

(*continued from preceding page*)
Voroshilov in the north. Hopelessy incompetent, both were advocates of the warfare of the past, like Stalin himself.

One day late in the summer, Marshal Budenny disappeared from his headquarters suddenly. Stalin was worried and he sent Zhukov out to find him. Zhukov finally tracked Budenny down in a town that had been abandoned and was about to be invested by the Germans. The marshal did not seem to be concerned.

"Where are you coming from?" he asked Zhukov.

"From Konev's headquarters."

"Well, how are things from Konev? It has been two days since I lost contact with him. Yesterday I was at 43rd Army Headquarters. In my absence my staff for the southern front has moved and now I don't know where it is."

This was the commander of an entire front. Lost, wandering around the front, in a car with a driver and no one else to accompany him. Out of touch, he was still in command of a million men.

In his account of the war, Edwin Erich Dwinger wrote of his wonderment at the Russian soldiers he was killing and maiming in the service of his Fuehrer. Observing the wounded, he sensed something almost superhuman about them.

Several of them, burnt by flamethrowers, had no longer the semblance of human faces. They were blistered, shapeless bundles of human flesh. A bullet had taken the lower jaw of one man. The scrap of flesh which sealed the wound did not hide his trachea, through which breath escaped in bubbles.

Five machine-gun bullets had shredded into pulp the shoulder and arm of another man, who was without any bandages. The Germans offered no medical help to their prisoners.

Not a cry or a moan escaped the lips of these wounded, who were seated on the grass. Hardly had the distribution of food begun than the Russians, even the dying, rose and moved forward. The man without a jaw could hardly stand. The man with one arm clung with his arm to a tree trunk. Half a dozen of them rose, holding their entrails in with one hand.

They do not cry. They do not groan. They do not curse. There is something mysterious, inscrutable, about their stern stubborn silence.

* * *

Already in three months of battle the Russians had learned to hate. The hatred was deep and terrible in its silence, as though they recognized and had to accept the inhuman core of the German soul. The prisoners regarded themselves as dead men; they knew they could expect no mercy from their enemies. They continued to go through the motions of life because there was nothing else to do.

The hatred grew as the German oppression spread. The killing of civilians had become a sport with them. On the slightest pretext the German soldiers would organize manhunts, entering towns and villages and capturing and killing anyone they saw. They usually lined up the civilians and shot them below the waist, which meant a lingering death in a recently dug pit.

Even before Operation Barbarossa began, Hitler had issued his "Order Concerning Military Justice in the Barbarossa Area," which gave German troops immunity from prosecution for atrocities they might commit. As the armies moved east, administration of the captured areas fell into the hands of special Reichskommissariat forces and the SS. The latter were particularly infamous, organizing "task groups" whose mission simply was to kill. Toward the front, each army had responsibility for policing its own area, and each corps assigned one motorized company to hunting down partisans.

The Russians began to retaliate in kind. Partisan groups ignored the rules of warfare and set their minds on exterminating Germans. On one occasion they derailed a hospital train and went into the cars and burned the German wounded to death with paraffin. On another occasion partisans poisoned the water supply of a German barracks.

Almost from the beginning this fierce German policy turned potential allies into enemies. The Russian people rallied around a government some of them detested, greeting one another with the fervor of lost relatives. The most famous war song of the people was "The Sacred War."

> Arise, vast land, in awesome might!
> For mortal combat gird
> Against the evil powers of night,
> The fascist hordes accursed!
> Let storms of indignation rage
> And righteous wrath outpour!
> This is a sacred war we wage,
> A people's sacred war.

4

The Germans continued to be supremely confident. In September 1941 many generals of the Oberkommandowehrmacht (the high command) and the army were saying that they would spend the winter in Moscow. Field Marshal Rundstedt was almost the single dissenter, telling all the others that the German army was overextended and should stand on the Dnieper River line until the spring of 1942. But Hitler made the decision on September 15 to destroy the "Timoshenko Army Group," the major Russian force in the south. Three-quarters of the German army on the Eastern Front was to be committed to this task. That included all the panzer divisions except Field Marshal Kleist's group, which would continue to clear the Ukraine.

The bulk of the German force would be used in the vicinity of Vyazma and Bryansk, south of Smolensk. Field Marshal Fedor von Bock's army group was ready for a totally renewed tank drive. General Werner Kempf's panzer corps had been brought north from Army Group South and assigned to General Heinz Guderian. General Erich Hoepner's panzer group had been brought down from Army Group North. This powerful force faced the last of the great Russian mass armies with which the Russian high command had started the war.

The German offensive began on September 30 near Bryansk, 150 miles southwest of Moscow. The Germans hit first at the link between General Andrei Yeremenko's troops and those of the Western Front, commanded by General Ivan Konev. On October 2 the German offensive widened to include all three fronts west of Moscow: the Western Front, the Reserve Front, and the Bryansk Front. The Russians had twelve armies in the fronts, with four armies in reserve. They had concentrated 40 percent of their troops and 35 percent of their tanks to meet the expected German assault.

Three days into the offensive the Germans had broken the Russian line. One day later the panzers caught the Russians off guard when they entered Orel, where machine tools and other supplies were stacked on railroad sidings, ready for shipment to the Urals. In the center, Hoepner had broken the Russian line, forcing the mass of Konev's front around against the upper Dnieper into the path of the German armies of Field

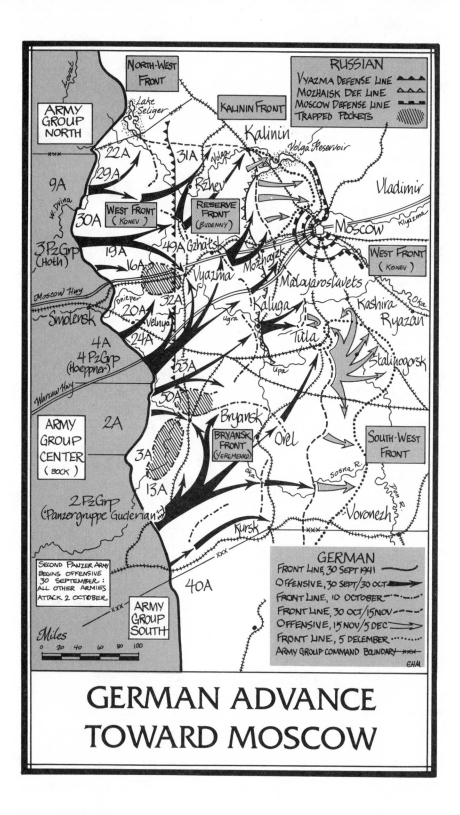

GERMAN ADVANCE
TOWARD MOSCOW

Marshal Guenther von Kluge and General Adolf Strauss. Farther north, General Hermann Hoth had moved down Vyazma-Gzhatsk highway to get behind the Russian infantry. A half million Russian soldiers were trapped in two pockets, and the way was clear for the Germans to attack Moscow. German confidence was high.

On the night of October 4 Moscow lost all contact with the Western Front.

At nine o'clock on the morning of October 5 word came that the Germans had broken through at the hinge of the Russian 43rd and 24th armies just south of Yelnya, and were moving east toward Moscow. Three hours later a reconnaissance plane reported a fifteen-mile-long German armored column moving along the Warsaw-Moscow highway, one hundred miles southwest of Moscow. There were no Russian troops in their path.

In Berlin, Propaganda Minister Joseph Goebbels told a press conference that the Russians were finished. "The annihilation of Timoshenko's army group has definitely brought the war to a close," he announced.

On October 6 Stalin telephoned General Zhukov in Leningrad and ordered him to come and try to save Moscow. Zhukov arrived at Moscow Central Airport at dusk on October 7 and went immediately to the Kremlin. There he found Stalin in his apartment, suffering from a case of influenza. The dictator greeted his general with a nod and turned to the situation map.

"Look," he said, "we're in serious trouble on the Western Front. Yet I can't seem to get a detailed report about what's going on."

He asked Zhukov to leave for the front immediately, to examine the situation. He was to telephone anytime, day or night.

"I'll be waiting for your call," Stalin said.

A quarter of an hour later, Zhukov was in the office of Marshal Boris Shaposhnikov, the chief of the general staff, for briefing. He ordered up a situation map from intelligence, to show the situation in the west as of noon that day, October 7. Shaposhnikov pointed at the map.

"Western Front headquarters is now where the Reserve Front had its headquarters in August, when you were conducting your operation against the Yelnya salient," he said.

Tea was brought, and they drank it. In this critical battle the marshal had been at his desk day and night and he appeared to be exhausted. There were almost no troops in the area. The volunteers, mostly workers, put into uniform by the State Defense Committee and the Party Central

Committee, were almost all they had. They were building defense lines in the Mozhaisk area and also near Moscow.

After the briefing, Zhukov left for Western Front headquarters by car. As they drove he studied the map by flashlight. He began to get drowsy, for he, too, had been up for a long time without sleep. He told the driver to stop and he jogged for two hundred yards to wake up.

Late that night the car reached the headquarters. The Military Council was then meeting. Generals Konev, Nikolai Bulganin, and Vasili Sokolovsky were meeting with Lieutenant General G. K. Malandin, the operations chief. The room was almost dark, lighted by a few candles.

Zhukov announced his mission. Bulganin said he had just spoken to Stalin by telephone. Stalin had demanded information, but Bulganin could give him no information because they did not have any.

Questioning Malandin, Zhukov began to get the picture, and at 2:30 in the morning he telephoned Stalin to report.

"The principal danger now is that the road to Moscow is almost entirely unprotected. The fortifications along the Mozhaisk line are too weak to halt a breakthrough by German armor. We must concentrate forces on the Mozhaisk defense line as soon as possible from wherever we can."

"Where are the 16th, 19th, and 20th armies?" Stalin asked. Zhukov told him that those armies and the Bodin group of the Western Front and the 24th and 32nd armies of the Reserve Front were all encircled west of Vyazma.

"What do you intend to do?"

First, Zhukov said, he had to find Marshal Budenny, commander of the Reserve Front.

The problem was that there was no information and he did not know where Budenny was. He made a guess and headed for Obninskoye, seventy miles from Moscow. He found the headquarters with some difficulty early on October 8. It was drizzling and a dense fog lay close to the ground. But Budenny was not there, and his chief of staff did not know where he was. He had left to visit the 43rd Army on October 7 and had not come back.

Zhukov went on and found Budenny at Maloyaroslavets. It was obvious to Zhukov that Budenny did not know what was going on. He left Budenny and visited several units. He learned that the Germans held Yukhnov, and were near Kaluga. He was still collecting information when a staff officer caught up with him on October 9 to tell him that he had been appointed commander of the Western Front.

On October 10, when Zhukov reached Western Front headquarters near Mozhaisk, the situation was indeed critical.

So what was Zhukov to do? He was Russia's most experienced field commander. In 1939 he had fought the Japanese at Nomonhan, on the Mongolian-Manchurian border, and defeated them, thus bringing to an end a Japanese threat against Russia.

On the basis of that experience he had early in 1941 been brought to Moscow as chief of staff of the Soviet high command and number two man to his friend Semyon Timoshenko, the commissar of defense at the time of the German attack. Timoshenko had taken over the disaster of September when Marshal Budenny lost Kiev to the Germans, and Zhukov had commanded the Reserve Front one hundred miles east of Smolensk in the Rzhev-Vyazma area. In July Timoshenko had begun and had halted the German advance there by September 5. A week later Zhukov had been sent to Leningrad to stop the Germans, replacing Marshal Voroshilov.

Zhukov arrived at Leningrad at the high point of the German attack. In a week the Germans would begin shifting their armor southward for the assault that was to begin against Moscow. Zhukov had stopped the Germans at Leningrad. Could he now do the same at Moscow?

First Zhukov concentrated on the Mozhaisk line outside Moscow because between Mozhaisk and Moscow lay a dense network of highways and railroads for troop movement. A whole series of defense lines of earthworks and antitank ditches could be installed, along the Lama, Moskva, Kolocha, Luzha, and Sukhodrev rivers.

By October 11 he had concentrated the command along the Mozhaisk line under the 5th Army and given command to General Dmitry Lelyushenko. Two days later the Germans took Kaluga, south of Moscow.

The Germans were still advancing toward Kalinin, north of Moscow. By October 15 the defensive strength of the Russians was only ninety thousand men, so few that the defense could not be continuous but had to be concentrated in sectors.

Panic set in at Moscow on that day. The Party Central Committee fled to Kuibyshev, taking state treasures with it and the diplomatic corps. The trains were jammed to overflowing, and long strings of limousines of the powerful and panicky clogged the roads. Apparently many of the Communist leaders agreed with the Germans that the war was over.

Stalin was furious. He announced that he was remaining in Moscow and ordered a state of siege four days later. Shamefacedly the officials of the Soviet government and the Communist Party who had fled in panic began to creep back to Moscow.

On the Western Front Zhukov's forces began to slow the Germans down as they approached Moscow. Late in October General Guderian's panzers headed for Tula and expected an easy victory. On October 30 they were stopped there, largely by workers with grenades and Molotov cocktails, which were bottles filled with gasoline and stuffed with a rag that became the fuse.

In October's and November's critical days, the working people of Moscow provided five divisions of volunteers. It was not yet winter, but the autumn rains slowed the Germans down. There was mud everywhere, and the tanks and trucks bogged down in it.

On November 6 Stalin proclaimed the twenty-fourth anniversary of the October Revolution and pledged his government to fight on to victory in this war. He recapitulated the German successes: occupation of most of the Ukraine, Belorussia, Moldavia, and Estonia, the penetration of the Don basin, the threat to Leningrad, and the menace to Moscow.

Admitting to the Red Army setbacks, he said the Germans had miscalculated. They had believed that the Soviet government was so unstable that it would collapse, and the opposite was happening.

"Advancing inland into our country, the German army is getting far away from the German rear, is compelled to act in hostile surroundings, is compelled to create a new rear in a foreign country, a rear which, moreover, is being undermined by our partisans, who are utterly disorganizing the supplies of the German army. This compels it to fear its own rear and kills its faith in the firmness of its position, at a time when our army, operating in its native surroundings, enjoys the uninterrupted support of its rear, is ensured of its supply of manpower, munitions and foodstuffs, and is firmly confident."

He alluded to the nature of this war and of his enemy, first quoting Hitler: "When politics require it," Hitler said, "it is necessary to lie, betray, and even to kill."

Stalin also reminded the Russians of Goering's words: "Kill everyone who is against us. Kill and kill again; I and not you bear the responsibility for it. Therefore kill."

Stalin epitomized the nature of the struggle by reading German military orders to the troops. One, dated September 25, found on the body of a dead German, said: "I order firing at every Russian as soon as he appears within 600 meters distance. The Russian must know that he is faced with a resolute enemy from whom he cannot expect any lenience."

Another order found on a dead German lieutenant: "You have neither heart nor nerves; they are not needed in war. Free yourselves from your feelings of compassion and sympathy—kill every Russian, every Soviet person. Don't stop, whether you have an old man, a woman, a girl, or a boy before you—kill!"

And, having set the mood, Stalin forecast the future that would lead to Stalingrad and beyond:

"The Germans want a war of extermination against the peoples of the USSR. Well, if the Germans want a war of extermination they shall have it. Henceforth our task consists of annihilating to the last man all Germans who penetrated the territory of our country. Death to the Germans. . . ."

REPRISALS

By the time the Germans reached the outskirts of Moscow, the Russians had learned a great deal about their enemies and about modern warfare. The Germans should have. Rommel was facing something of the same problems of place and people in Africa. Rommel had trouble with his Italian allies, whose officers and men too often interfered with the Arab women. The Arabs killed these Italian soldiers, and the Italians thought the way to solve the problem was to take reprisals. Said Rommel:

"There are always people who will invariably demand reprisals in this sort of situation—for reason, apart from anything else, of expediency. Such action is never expedient. The right thing to do is to ignore the incidents, unless the real culprits can be found."

So, too, it was in Russia, but there the SS was in charge. As German atrocities mounted, Russian hatred for the Nazis soared. By the winter of 1941 the Russians not only wanted to fight their enemy; in the snows of Moscow they had learned how.

5

In the second week of October Hoepner crossed the Ugra River northeast of Vyazma and faced Moscow with his panzers. The Germans might now turn to the right, to Kaluga. Or they might head straight for Moscow, which was about one hundred miles away. Or they might wheel north and join General Hoth.

In the center the Germans faced three Russian infantry divisions that had no tanks, no artillery, and very little cavalry. Eighty miles north another depleted Russian force was facing General Hoth's army and was falling back on Gzhatsk. This was the Russian front before Moscow. The Russians had only about eight hundred tanks left, and not many of them were T-34s, the only ones capable of defeating German panzer units.

In Moscow the Communist Party Secretariat was organizing "workers battalions." They had five thousand rifles to dispense. A battalion of 675 men would have 295 rifles, 120 hand grenades, 9 machine guns, 145 revolvers, and 2,000 Molotov cocktails. Only one fresh division of trained troops, the 310th Motorized Division, was on its way from Siberia.

6

On November 7, 1941, Stalin began his demand on the western Allies for a second front, but at the moment he would have to rely on another important ally who had not yet appeared on the scene, although he had given warning already: Old Man Winter. The Germans had heard of the "terrible Russian winter," but they had not yet felt it. They had experienced the Russian fall rains, which made mud seas of the plains and mud tracks of the roads. Now the rays of the sun were flat and tepid, low on the horizon. Each night dark black clouds would build up in the north, high above the plain. But each morning the clouds were gone, only to reappear in the twilight. It seemed that they were waiting for something.

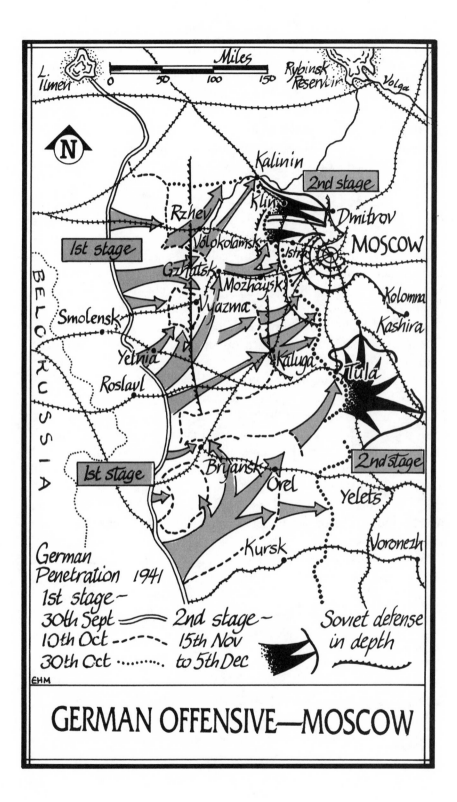

GERMAN OFFENSIVE—MOSCOW

Winter came early in November when the snow began to fall on the Moscow Front. At first it seemed a great relief to the Germans to have the temperatures fall to fourteen degrees. The endless seas of mud solidified and the panzers could move again.

But as they moved, the people of Moscow built their fortifications. A hundred thousand workers, mainly women, built gun emplacements, antitank ditches, seventy-five miles of barbed-wire entanglements.

By November 15 the Germans were driving on Kashira and Tula, which had given them so much trouble. The Germans employed fifty-one divisions. This was Hitler's belated acceptance of his generals' demand that Moscow be taken. It was called Operation Typhoon. At first the Germans moved fast, although they took heavy casualties from the Russian artillery. They broke through on the right side of the Kalinin Front. The situation by November 19 was so desperate that Stalin asked Zhukov if he really believed he could hold Moscow.

With two more armies and two hundred tanks he could do it, said Zhukov.

Stalin promised him the armies, but was at a loss for the tanks, because so many had been lost in recent weeks.

"As soon as possible" was the best he could promise.

In spite of ever more valiant Russian resistance, plus the growing cold, the Germans were confident of quick victory. By December 1, one German soldier was writing home: "We are now at a distance of 30 kilometers from Moscow and can see some of the spires. Soon we will have surrounded Moscow, and then we'll be billeted in sumptuous winter quarters and I will send you presents which will make Aunt Minna green with envy."

And another German wrote home: "When you receive this letter the Russians will be defeated and we will be in Moscow parading in Red Square. . . ."

But then the cold and the defense took over, and the German offensive stopped. General Guderian, commander of the 2nd Panzer Army, ordered his forces to take up defensive positions.

"The offensive on Moscow has ended," Guderian wrote in his journal. "All the sacrifices and efforts of our brilliant troops have come to nothing. We have suffered a serious defeat."

It was December 5, 1941. The Germans could see the towers of the Kremlin, but they would never come any closer to them.

PART II
THE RETREAT BEGINS

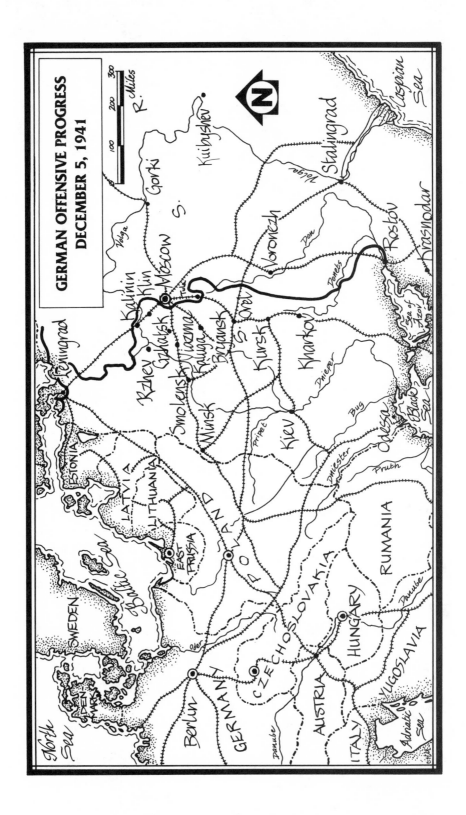

GERMAN OFFENSIVE PROGRESS
DECEMBER 5, 1941

7

Considering in retrospect what happened to prevent the Germans from taking Moscow and ending the war before winter as Hitler had planned, German historian Paul Carell summed up the Russian "Miracle of Moscow" of December 1941:

> Some of the German generals blamed it all on the weather. Some of them blamed it all on Hitler's miscalculations about the Red Army, a lack of judgment engendered by his visceral hatred of Communism. Suddenly out of nowhere on the Moscow front began to appear new Russian troops, healthy, well-fed, and highly trained troops from Siberia, where they had been keeping the Japanese at bay. They began to come in October, when Stalin's espionage network in Japan informed him that the Japanese had opted to strike south and attack Pearl Harbor, a fact he did not communicate to the Americans. Stalin had been holding the Siberian divisions for months, and only now released them and began bringing them west.
>
> These divisions with their splendid cold weather equipment and the superbly mounted cavalry from Turkestan played major roles in stopping the Germans at Moscow.

But the real reason for the German failure, said historian Carell, was:

> Too few soldiers, too few weapons, too little foresight on the part

of the German command, in particular a lack of antifreeze substances and the most basic winter clothing. The lack of antifreeze lubricants for the weapons was particularly serious. Would the rifle jam or wouldn't it? Would the machine gun work or would it jam when the Russians attacked? These were questions which racked the troops' nerves to the limit. Improvised expedients were all very well, while the troops were on the defensive, but to launch an attack or even an immediate counterattack with weapons functioning so unreliably was out of the question.

The fundamental error, which would not be realized at the top German level until Stalingrad, was that Hitler and his generals had badly underestimated their enemy and the Russian capability and willingness to endure enormous hardship and ceaseless fighting.

8

To win at Moscow the Germans would have had to have a fresh force of the same strength as that which had attacked on June 22.

To secure such a force, Hitler would have to rape the west. Five months of fighting had reduced his regiments to a third of their table of organization strength. The XL Panzer Corps's Reich Division and 10th Panzer Division lost 7,582 officers, NCOs, and men, or 40 percent of their strength.

The situation was suddenly impossible. Even if Hitler had chosen to bring in the new force, it would take him three months to transport them, for the German army was deeply mired in central Russia without adequate vehicles. By October 1941 the German situation in Russia was critical, but the high command did not realize it. By November there was no hope of victory. By December it became a question of averting a German disaster.

And what about the Luftwaffe, that prime weapon which had functioned so well in western Europe in the early days? At the outset of Operation Barbarossa, the Luftwaffe had performed splendidly. But as time wore on and panzers streamed ever deeper into Russia, the Luftwaffe bases became more and more remote from the front.

Because Hitler had stopped the drive on Moscow in midsummer against the advice of his generals, the Russians had been given time to ring the city with powerful antiaircraft batteries. The last Luftwaffe raid on Moscow was on the night of October 24, with only eight planes.

Why?

Because the whole Moscow region was alive with antiaircraft batteries. In the beginning of Operation Barbarossa, the Luftwaffe had performed as ably as it had in the Battle of Britain, so nearly won. In the early hours of the invasion Russian air power was smashed. But after Hitler had stopped his generals before Moscow, in the months since in the drive east, the Luftwaffe had suffered even more attrition than the ground forces. Now the Russians had brought in modern aircraft to replace the obsolete ones ruined in the first days, and the Soviet air force was twice as strong as the Luftwaffe on the Moscow Front.

Also, like the army generals, the German Luftwaffe leaders had erred. They had not provided for cold weather. The Russians had many airfields ringing Moscow with heated hangars. The Germans were using open airstrips, parking their planes on the strips and in revetments, exposed to the cold and unable to operate in subzero weather.

9

On the night of November 29 Marshal Zhukov advised Stalin that the Germans were "bled white" and the time had come to move.

The next morning he offered to the military commission a plan for a Western Front counteroffensive north and south of Moscow. He had been preparing for this all through the defensive operations since October. It was a part of the strategy evolved by the Russians at the beginning, after the shock of invasion had worn off: "Let the Germans wear themselves down, bring them to a halt, and then launch the counteroffensive. The objective was to end the German capability of attack, and give the Germans no chance to regroup and start a new offensive so close to Moscow."

The Russian countermove had come, nearly too little and too late. On December 1 the German 4th Army broke through the Russian line south of the Moscow-Smolensk highway. The 2nd Panzer Army made a hook to the west, and Field Marshal Bock told three of his generals that the Russians seemed about to break.

Then, on the afternoon of December 2, Bock told German Army Chief of Staff Halder that because of the cold and the stiffening Russian resistance, the hope of reaching Moscow was rapidly diminishing. It was true. The cold had come suddenly, too suddenly, and its implications were just being felt in the blasts of the Siberian wind.

On December 3 a blizzard was piling up snow all along the front, and Field Marshal Bock told General Jodl, the operations chief of OKW, that the troop strength of his central army group was almost at an end. He was going to continue the attack, he said, but only because his position was so exposed that to go on the defensive was more dangerous.

For two weeks the Germans had warning. The weather had grown colder and the temperature ranged between twenty degrees Fahrenheit and zero. On the morning of December 4 the thermometer stood at minus four. "Icy cold," Bock called it. It was going to get much, much worse.

Field Marshal Bock was concerned but not overly worried about his position. He did not think the Russians had enough troops and weapons to start a counteroffensive. He was still unaware of the approach of the Siberians.

The fact was that Stalin did have the troops. In addition to the Siberians, new units had been formed from the remnants of armies shattered in the summer. But until this moment Stalin had refused to commit them.

On December 4 the Military Commission (which meant Stalin) decided that the time had come. The Japanese were committed against the British, Dutch, and Americans, although the blow against Pearl Harbor had not yet fallen. The Russians knew that they had nothing to fear from Japan.

That night, in a telephone conversation, Stalin told Zhukov that the Kalinin Front would go to the offensive on the next day, and on December 6 the Southwest Front would attack.

On the night of December 4 the temperature on the Moscow Front dropped to twenty-five below zero, to the consternation of the Germans. Two months earlier, General Guderian, one of the most outspoken of the

German field commanders, had asked headquarters when he could expect to have winter uniforms for his troops. They were still fighting in their summer cottons. He had been sharply rebuffed—told to mind his own business. And, as now became bitterly apparent, nothing had been done in response to his request. That night one of Guderian's regiments suffered three hundred cases of frostbite. Next morning, tanks would not start, machine guns and artillery would not fire because their lubricants had congealed, and every army reported frostbite cases in numbers that were worrisome. In the paralyzing cold the Russians, who had winter uniforms, and whose weapons were adjusted for the cold, broke through the 9th Army line. General Georg-Hans Reinhardt, on the Volga River west of Kalinin, tried to launch a counterstrike, but his automatic weapons would not work and the cold affected his soldiers so badly that the attack had to be stopped before it had hardly begun.

General Guderian thought he could finally take Tula with his 2nd Panzer Army, but by midmorning he had changed his mind. His tanks kept breaking down, while the Russian tanks were operating very well. He now suggested a gradual withdrawal from the bulge east of Tula to the Don and Shat rivers.

Before noon on December 6 it was apparent to the Germans that a Russian counteroffensive had indeed begun. General Reinhardt told Field Marshal Bock that he would have to start pulling his 3rd Panzer Group back. That meant the 4th Panzer Group would also have to start pulling back, because it adjoined south of the 3rd Group.

On that day, December 6, at Germany army headquarters, Halder talked to Hitler about a general directive to cover the winter campaign. It was almost a new idea. They had been hoping for victory right up until this last moment. In October they had confidently talked about having the troops home for Christmas. In November they had realized that it was not going to happen, but they had refused to face the problem: overextension. They had ignored it and just now they were having to face it.

Halder told Hitler that German army strength was down 25 percent from the early days of the campaign.

Hitler snorted at this statement. Numbers meant nothing, he said. The Russians had lost ten times as many men as the Germans. If they had three times as many in the beginning, that still meant the Russians were worse off.

The Germans should hold, Hitler said. In the north they should be prepared to make contact with the Finns as soon as they had reinforcements. In the middle they had to hold. In the south they ought to be able to take Rostov and perhaps the whole Donets Basin.

This was Hitler talk, not a decision about the winter war. On December 7 the issue was brought to him again. The 3rd and 4th Panzer groups and the 2nd Panzer Army announced their withdrawal. Hitler frowned, but approved the move of the 3rd and 4th Panzer groups to "straighten their lines." He did not face the issue of the 2nd Panzer Army's withdrawal or the growingly serious situation of Army Group Center opposite Moscow.

On Sunday, December 7, Luftwaffe observation planes reported a continuing heavy rail traffic toward Moscow from the east. That meant more Russian reinforcements coming up.

On the ground the blizzard continued and the blowing snow cut visibility to a few yards. The roads were narrowed by snowdrifts. The roads running west were filled with German vehicles, heading back toward safety.

How far back?

No one knew.

The German front had begun to pull back from the Moscow-Volga canal.

The 3rd Panzer Group was having trouble even evacuating. Fifteen tanks and three big howitzers, half a dozen antiaircraft guns, and many trucks and cars had been abandoned to the storm. The vehicles would not start, and the weapons could not be towed. The grease and the oil were freezing even when the vehicles were running.

The 1st Panzer Division was stopped in its flight and ordered to fight a rearguard action to stop the Soviet thrust at Klin. The Russians were pressing, but slowly, with seven armies along Army Group Center's broad front, seven hundred miles from Tikhvin on the north to a point east of Kursk.

The main German reaction was shock.

Hour after hour on December 7, new Russian units entered the fray and broke radio silence. The messages were picked up by German radio monitors. Two dozen brigades and divisions were moving on Army Group Center. The Germans had been telling themselves that the Russians did not have new troops to throw into the battle and were moving soldiers from other areas. Bock still believed that.

But that day, the Army Group North spearhead that had been aiming to make contact with Army Group Center in the assault on Moscow found itself almost surrounded in the blizzard that raged in the area. The Russians had brought in twenty-seven trainloads of troops in three days. The Germans had been expecting to break through here, but now the Germans were outnumbered two to one.

Hitler promised help: a hundred tanks and twenty thousand troops within ten days. At Tikhvin, Field Marshal Wilhelm von Leeb could not wait. He had only five tanks operational and a few thousand half-frozen troops. That afternoon Leeb gave the order to evacuate Tikhvin.

All along the German line, generals were calling for help. The army columns strung along the roads, vehicles breaking down in the snow and cold, and the Russians coming nearer, slowly, but coming. Bock tried to get reinforcements to hold the Klin road junction that was vital to the German withdrawal. All he could scrape up was a single infantry battalion.

He was told that he could not have any significant replacements until mid-January, because they would have to come from the west, and the railroads east could not handle them for weeks.

He asked for some more divisions. Halder said he did not have any.

The commands began to break down. In order to salvage something, Bock put the 3rd Panzer Group under 4th Panzer Group command. The 3rd Panzer Group saw this as an abdication of responsibility, and morale plummeted. The command began to become confused, but the impetus was clear: the Germans were retreating with as much order as they could manage, but they were retreating fast.

Southwest of Moscow, Guderian was in deep trouble, trying to reduce the bulge, or salient, he had driven deep into the Russian lines. A few days before, it had seemed he was on the lip of victory. Now he was on the brink of defeat. His 2nd Panzer Army was suffering from all the troubles of the cold. The vehicles would not start and were being abandoned by the score. In two days one corps alone reported 1,500 frostbite cases, 350 of which required amputation, and that meant soldiers out of the fighting.

All up and down the front the German troubles multiplied. The German rail lines to the front clogged. The German locomotives could not hold their steam in the below-zero cold. But the Russian locomotives, which were built for the cold, had no trouble.

Guderian needed oil and fuel. He was not getting it despite promises to have it flown in. On December 9 Guderian told Bock that he was suffering a serious crisis of confidence in his army.

That day Bock told Halder by telephone that he needed reinforcement. Army Group Center could not stand off a determined Russian attack at any point along its whole front. He was already converting all his specialists, truck drivers, clerks, and cooks into infantry.

Halder said things would become better by the end of the month.

"We cannot wait until the end of the month," said Bock. "By then the army group will be *kaputt* [finished]."

"The German soldier does not go *kaputt*," said Halder.

Bock tried a new tack.

"I don't want to whine and complain," he said, "but we must have reserves."

"Your army group will certainly get whatever small reserves we can scrape together," said Halder.

And that ended the conversation.

No promises, no real hope of help for the front.

Bock gave orders to his generals to take the whole army group back sixty to ninety miles. This would bring them to the Rzhev-Gzhatsk-Orel-Kursk line. Then they would see what happened.

General Kleist pointed out that it would not help. The Russians could be attacking them on the new line within three days. The equipment losses they had already sustained and would continue to sustain in the retreat would weaken their army to the danger point.

Bock agreed. "I am at the point of sending the Fuehrer a personal telegram telling him that I am confronting decisions that go far beyond the military," he said.

He was obviously thinking of advocating a general retreat of the sort carried out by Napoléon after his failure to conquer Russia.

On December 10 the temperature suddenly dropped all along the front. The Russians attacked in the 2nd Army area down south. Half a dozen tanks attacked in freezing rain and drove a hole between two German infantry divisions. They were the 45th and the 95th divisions. A Soviet cavalry division galloped through the hole. The two German divisions were snowed in during the night, and the next morning their self-propelled guns would not move at all. They were literally bogged in snowdrifts all along their line. It did not make any difference that the vehicles were stuck; they had run out of fuel anyhow.

By December 11 the Russian cavalry had enlarged its hole, and more horsemen had come galloping through. They had driven a wedge fifty miles deep into the German line northwest toward Orel. A Russian infantry division now came through. Field Marshal Bock learned that the 2nd Army was about to be cut in two with an eighty-five-mile gap between the two parts, in the Orel-Kursk area.

While disaster was building, Hitler fidgeted at his headquarters. He issued a directive for the winter campaign that from a fighting soldier's point of view sounded like a fairy tale. He said because the weather had turned unseasonable, "larger offensive operations will be suspended."

Suspended? They had already stopped and the Germans were retreating.

There was not to be any retreat, said Hitler, except to prepared positions.

What did that mean?

The fairy-tale communiqué said Oberkommando des Heeres (the army high command) would start recalling the panzer and motorized divisions to Germany for refitting.

Recall to Germany? The divisions would be lucky if they could survive and get back to the rear areas, which at the moment seemed unlikely.

The Hitler directive caused the generals to wonder even more than before if their leaders knew what was happening at the front.

Guderian became so upset that Field Marshal Bock suggested he report personally to Hitler, which Guderian refused to do. Instead he asked "for the hundredth time," Bock said, if OKH and OKW really knew what was happening.

The significant point was that here in December 1941, for the first time in the entire war, the German military machine was proving incapable of dealing with a crisis. Always in the past there had been plenty of reserves, and sureness of command. The enemy might make a breakthrough—that was the nature of war—but within hours, or days, the resources would be summoned to the proper place to contain the enemy, and the crisis would end.

But it was not happening now.

PART III
HANDWRITING ON THE WALL: THE FIRST RUSSIAN OFFENSIVE

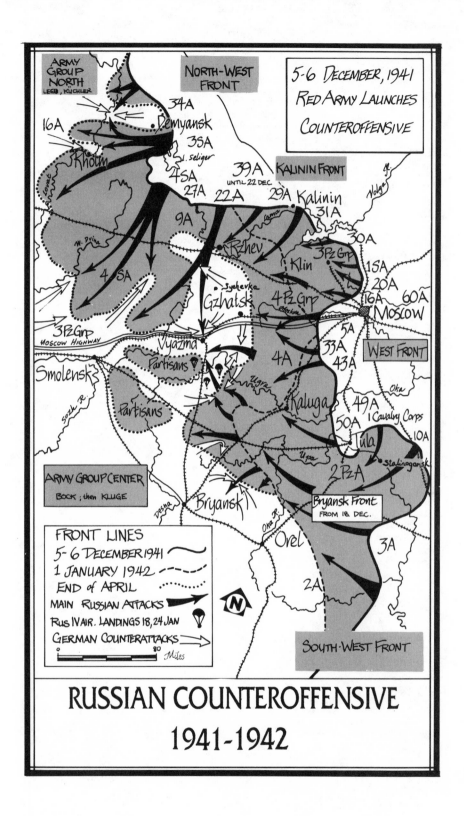

ARMY GROUP NORTH
LEEB, KUCHLER

NORTH-WEST FRONT

5-6 DECEMBER, 1941
RED ARMY LAUNCHES
COUNTEROFFENSIVE

34A

16A

Demyansk

Kholm

3SA

l. seliger

4SA

27A

39A
UNTIL 22 DEC.

22A

KALININ FRONT

29A Kalinin

31A

9A

Lama

30A

3 Pz Grp

15A

Rzhev

Klin

20A

16A

60A

Sychevka

4 Pz Grp

Moskva

MOSCOW

Gzhatsk

W. Dvina

4 SA

3 Pz Grp
MOSCOW HIGHWAY

Vyazma

Partisans

4A

5A

33A

WEST FRONT

Smolensk

Sozh R.

Partisans

Ugra

Kaluga

43A

49A

1 Cavalry Corps

50A

Tula

10A

ARMY GROUP CENTER
BOCK; then KLUGE

Ugra

2 Pz A

Stalinogorsk

Bryansk

Desna

Oka R.

Bryansk Front
FROM 18 DEC.

3A

Orel

2A

SOUTH-WEST FRONT

FRONT LINES
5-6 DECEMBER 1941
1 JANUARY 1942
END of APRIL
MAIN RUSSIAN ATTACKS
Rus IV AIR. LANDINGS 18, 24 JAN
GERMAN COUNTERATTACKS

0   80
Miles

N

RUSSIAN COUNTEROFFENSIVE
1941-1942

10

In the beginning of their first offensive, the Russians moved slowly and erratically. Marshal Zhukov finally ordered the Western Front armies to set up mobile groups with tanks, cavalry, and infantry to strike behind the enemy and not content themselves with trying to push him back frontally, which had been the Russian tactics in the first months of the war.

On December 10 the Russians cut the road out of Klin, which was the 3rd Panzer Group's only escape route to the west. The result was confusion. The road was under constant air attack by the Russians. One of the first signs of German panic was when they quit burying the bodies of their dead and left them as they lay. The service troops and other noncombatants were in full flight to the west, half-frozen and most of them without rations. The Germans were having supply problems and had been living off the land. Now it was common to see a soldier leading a calf on a rope or pulling a sled loaded with potatoes.

Some were heading across country when the road jammed and they did not want to wait for the traffic to clear. Traffic on the road inched forward, blocked hour after hour despite the day-and-night efforts of the traffic control troops.

General Guderian likened his 2nd Panzer Army to a whole series of baggage trains, moving slowly to the rear. It was no longer a fighting organization, and could not move to attack the Russian cavalry that harassed its flanks, because the panzers were out of fuel. Telephone lines collapsed in the ice and snow.

On the whole Army Center Front the usual disciplined action of a German army had come unzipped. Soviet partisans did their best to halt the advance. They blew up a bridge on the main line of retreat. At Vyazma they queered the switching signals on the rail line, causing two trains to crash head-on, thus blocking the tracks. They managed to sabotage a whole train of tank cars carrying motor fuel so that it reached 4th Panzer Group empty.

By December 12 General Halder was referring to the situation as "desperate" and the worst crisis of two wars. Hitler chose the moment to return to Berlin to declare war on the United States after the Japanese attack of December 7. The generals demanded some sign of attention from the high command, and finally on December 13 Field Marshal Brauchitsch appeared at Bock's headquarters, now at Smolensk. The way things were going, he was told, the 3rd and 4th Panzer groups would be destroyed in ten days. If they were going to save the troops, they would have to extricate them and sacrifice the tanks and other stalled equipment. This was the substance of Bock's conversation that day with Brauchitsch. Should the Army Group stop and fight, which might well mean its total destruction? Or should it withdraw with the loss of much of its equipment?

Brauchitsch was noncommittal, but he went off to confer with Kluge and Guderian, and learn their stories. General Rudolf Schmundt, Hitler's aide, arrived in Smolensk representing the Fuehrer. Brauchitsch came back from the front to recommend the withdrawal be continued, and they got Hitler's apparent approval by telephone to Berlin.

On the night of December 14 the temperature dropped to thirty-three below. Next morning, Field Marshal Leeb told Hitler the time had come to withdraw from Tikhvin. Hitler could not make up his mind to approve and stalled. Hitler returned to Wolfsschanze, his Eastern Front headquarters, in Rastenburg, East Prussia, December 16. He approved Leeb's decision to withdraw. It was at this point, the German generals noted, that Hitler decided to take full authority for decisions into his own hands. Brauchitsch was now out of the decision-making process.

Thus were set into motion the processes that would lead to the German disaster at Stalingrad, more than a year before the actual disaster occurred.

On the morning of December 18, Hitler's orders reached Army Group Center. They were astounding:

"Commanding generals, commanders and officers are to intervene in person to compel the troops to fanatical resistance in their positions without regard to flanks or the rear." Such a policy, he said, was the only way to give him time to bring up the reinforcements from Germany that he had ordered.

With this order, Hitler completed a process he had begun to consider at the time of the march into the Rhineland six years earlier when his generals had funked and wanted to turn back. He now had complete authority in his own hands.

Brauchitsch resigned. Marshal Bock was asked to go on "sick leave." Halder was reduced to the status of errand boy. When General Guderian took an airplane to Hitler's headquarters on the morning of December 20, his 2nd Panzer Army was already in flight on the ground, and so were the other armies. The 4th Panzer Group was destroying its trucks and weapons for lack of gasoline. They were down to a quarter of normal. Nearly all Hitler's generals responded with General Guderian.

"I will take these orders and file them," he said. "I will not pass them on even under threat of court-martial."

But at headquarters the interview with Hitler was stormy and brief. Hitler ordered him to hold his position exactly where he stood. The same order to hold at all costs was circulated through the armies.

11

All this German generalship maneuvering came just as the first phase of the Soviet offensive was coming to an end. By December 16 the Russians had eliminated German salients aimed at Moscow, and most of the Russian objectives had been reached: Stalinogorsk, Klin, and Kalinin. A half dozen Siberian and Ural divisions were on their way to the front, as General Zhukov issued his second-phase directive. He wanted the rest of the winter spent in driving the German Army Group Center back 150 miles to the point they had occupied in October. But Stalin had greater aims, no less than to surround and destroy Army Group Center.

By this time the Germans had managed to bring winter clothing as far as the railheads, but it still had not reached the troops, because the armies did not have the transportation to deliver them. Not a third of the available clothing had been issued by the end of the year. The Germans were improvising. Russian civilians found their winter furs and felt boots being requisitioned by the Germans. On a local basis this requisitioning relieved some units here and there.

The disparity in weapons was now becoming apparent as well. The 2nd Panzer Army had only 70 tanks in operation and 168 under repair. Since June it had been given 970 tanks. The Russian T-34 tank had proved to be the master of the German tanks, and the most effective German weapon against them was the field artillery. But the Russians did not yet have enough of the powerful tanks to keep going long.

Still, they had enough force on Christmas Day to make General Guderian continue his retreat in defiance of the orders of Hitler. That day Guderian asked to be relieved of command and was, and was transferred to the reserve. He left the Eastern Front and was replaced in command of the 2nd Panzer Army by General Rudolf Schmidt.

All along the line the Germans were nearly exhausted after weeks of fighting and now fighting the cold as well. The commanding general of the German 6th Infantry Division said his men were physically and psychologically finished. "Today," he said on Christmas Day, "I saw men whose boots were frozen to their frozen feet. These men would rather let themselves be beaten to death than to attack in this condition."

The commander of the 26th Infantry Division said of one regiment: "It can no longer be considered a regiment. It has only two hundred men. The Russians have cut its communications. Its radios are frozen and its machine guns are frozen; and the machine-gun crews are dead alongside their weapons."

It was basically the same all along the German line. Army Group Center was disintegrating. Field Marshal Kluge, who had taken over from the totally dispirited Bock as commander of Army Group Center, tried to get permission for the armies to withdraw to safety. Hitler refused. Kluge said that his troops were mentally and physically exhausted.

"If that is true," said Hitler, "then it is the end of the German army," and hung up the telephone on the field marshal.

On the night of December 31 Kluge again talked to Hitler, asking permission to withdraw two of his armies, which were threatened with disintegration.

Kluge: I request freedom of action. You must believe that I will do what is right. Otherwise I cannot function. We do not only want what is best for Germany, we want what is best for you.

Hitler: Fine. How long can you hold the new line?

Kluge: That I cannot say.

Hitler: Enemy pressure will also force you out of the new line. . . .

Kluge: We are under compulsion. One can turn and twist as much as he pleases. We must get out of this situation.

Hitler then said he would have to consult with Keitel and Jodl and Halder. Later that night he spoke to Kluge again. There would be no major withdrawals, he said. Too many weapons and too much equipment would be lost.

Kluge said he had already given orders to his generals to withdraw.

Hitler replied that it was impossible to initiate a major movement without the approval of the supreme command. The troops must stop right where they were.

So that night Kluge sent orders to his generals countermanding all the earlier ones. Only local movements would be allowed, and all reserves were to be sent to the front immediately. The troops of Army Group Center were ordered to hold the line everywhere.

This grim news reached the Eastern Front in the early minutes of the new year. To make the orders more palatable, Hitler tried a ploy he was to repeat at Stalingrad: he elevated the 3rd and 4th groups to army status, although the physical strength of each was more like that of a corps.

Hitler gave a New Year's proclamation to Germany's people which was carried in the *Volkischer Beobachter*, the Nazi Party newspaper. He spoke of the victories of 1941, and promised more for 1942, and he lamented the series of events that had forced war on him, Adolf Hitler, a man of peace. Actually Hitler was a very worried man. His generals had gone as far as they could go in refusing to accept his authority without disputing it. What would the next step be?

In order to force his will on the generals, Hitler addressed them by letter. The Soviet high command was finished, he said, and was using the last of its resources to exploit the icy winter and thus defeat the Germans. If the Germans stood fast on the Eastern Front, the final victory in Russia would come in the summer of 1942.

For that reason, all the units were to hold, even if they appeared to be surrounded. Gaps in the line would be filled up by new divisions that would be coming from Germany and the west. Trucks and supplies were already on the way, he said.

"To hold every village, not give way a step, and fight to the last bullet and grenade is the order of the hour."

If a single locality could not be held, it was to be put to the torch, to tell the world that the courageous troops of Germany had done their duty.

The truth of the matter was that help was a long way away. The army had the authority to mobilize a half million reserves by the end of April, but this was January. Possibly four divisions could be produced from the Replacement Army by the end of the month. After that, the reserves would have to come out of the industrial force, and these men would have to be trained. This would take several months.

The army high command did not at that moment know where it would find the weapons to equip the new divisions. The current production of artillery, machine guns, and mortars was not enough to cover the recent losses on the Eastern Front. The army was scouring its resources for trucks, buses, and other vehicles, and the search was going on as far away as France. And once these vehicles were driven east, they would need repairs.

12

Hitler's order to the men of the Eastern Front to hold at all costs came at the time that Stalin was pressing his generals to carry out the second phase of the Soviet first winter offensive, to surround and wipe out Army Group Center.

The first moves had been made in the last five days of December, when the Russians had sent two armies into the gap between the German 4th and 2nd armies. At the same time, up north, the Russian 39th Army was driving south from Novoye toward Rzhev, and pointed like a gun at the flank of the German 9th Army. In the south Zhukov's 10th and 50th armies were moving to get behind the Germans. But the southernmost Russian armies, the 3rd and the 13th, were exhausted from their earlier fighting and unable to take the initiative.

What were the Russians now to do?

On the night of January 5 the Russian Military Commission assembled to discuss Stalin's idea of a general offensive against the Germans.

"The Germans are in disarray," he said, "as a result of their defeat at

Moscow. They are badly fitted out for the winter. This is a most favorable moment for the transition to a general offensive."

Stalin's plan called for the destruction of the German forces in the Leningrad region, west of Moscow, and in the south, all at once. The main blow would be launched against Kluge's Army Group Center. This would be done by the Northwest Front, the Kalinin Front, and the Western and Bryansk fronts, which would encircle and destroy the Germans in the Rzhev-Vyasma-Smolensk area. The Leningrad Front, the Northwest Front, and the Baltic Fleet would relieve Leningrad and destroy German Army Group North. The Southwest and Southern fronts would destroy Army Group South and liberate the Don Basin, the Caucasus, and Crimea.

From the standpoint of the objective observer, there were a few problems with this concept. First, the Russians did not have the resources to carry out an offensive on the scale Stalin envisaged. It was too great, too massive, too unwieldy.

General Zhukov said just this in response to Stalin's request for comments. In Leningrad and the south, he said, the Germans were very strong, and unless Stalin could produce enormous numbers of artillery pieces, such moves would never succeed. The German weak point was on the Central Front, where Army Group Center had not recovered from the blows in the Moscow fighting. They had to build up reserves and tank units and reinforce the forces with men and equipment. He favored reinforcing the Western Front and mounting a powerful offensive there.

The Zhukov view was endorsed enthusiastically by the men responsible for the production and delivery of the weapons needed at the front. There simply were not enough guns and tanks and planes to send to all three major fronts.

"We must grind the Germans down, so that they cannot attack in the spring," said Nikolai A. Vosnesenskii. He was the head of the military procurement effort. Marshal Timoshenko supported the Zhukov view. Two members of the committee, Malenkov and Beria, supported Stalin.

But it was all window dressing. Stalin had already decided on the general offensive, and the orders had already been issued to the field commander. Zhukov wondered why he had been consulted, since his advice was ignored. The reason must have been that Stalin had miscalculated. It was not the first time that the dictator had allowed his desire to overcome his judgment in this war. Once again Russians would pay for his error with their blood.

Within forty-eight hours after the meeting, the orders were in hand.

Zhukov was told to encircle the German Central Front army from the south, while the Kalinin Front did so from the north, and it was to be completed by January 11.

Stalin said nothing about the difficulties he was forcing on his commanders. The temperature had dropped to thirty to forty degrees below zero, and snowfalls obliterated the roads. The Russian soldiers were struggling to move food supplies and ammunition, both in short supply. The Soviet dumps contained only a day's supply of food and no reserves of fuel. Several of the armies on the Kalinin and Western fronts did not have ammunition for their artillery. The shock troops at the front had virtually no food. General Yeremenko, their commander, was hoping to put together enough food to give his men one good meal on the night before the offensive began.

13

The German Army Group Center at that moment consisted of the 9th Army, the new 3rd Panzer and 4th Panzer armies on the north, the 4th Army in the center, and the 2nd Panzer Army and 2nd Army on the south. Stalin's ambitious plan was to encircle all of them.

In the center, the Kalinin Front and the Western Front concentrated to encircle Vyazma on the Moscow-Smolensk road, 125 miles west of Moscow and 90 miles east of Smolensk. The railroads fanning out from this place carried almost all the supplies to the German armies.

Stalin talked about encirclement, but Zhukov and the commander of the Kalinin Front actually used brute force and frontal attack as their main tactic.

The Germans held the villages, and the Russians attacked them with tanks and artillery and then with infantry. For an attack, the Russians first sent in "tramplers." These were unarmed men who went ahead of the infantry and vehicles to spring the land mines and paid with their lives. As each attack progressed, the snow was covered with the bodies of the tramplers. This disdain for human sacrifice was a central factor in the Russian system and rendered inoperative the best defense plans of the

Germans. How effective is a minefield against a tank army that is preceded by hundreds of walking men, who blow the mines so that the tanks may pass?

The Germans had the advantage of the shelter of the villages. When the Russians attacked and a village was falling, the Germans burned all the *izbas*, or cottages. The ground was frozen solid, and so the Russians would have no shelter at all.

In the second week of January the Russians were attacking all along the front, and the German armies were virtually separated into four groups, each of them nearly surrounded. On the night of January 9 a blizzard came down on Army Group Center's headquarters. Neither side could move. The war was suspended for twenty-four hours. The respite cheered Hitler, who pointed out how easy it was to hold the line.

"Every day of continued resistance," he telegraphed the field commander, "is decisive. It provides the possibility of bringing reinforcements into action to buttress the front. Therefore the break-ins must be eliminated."

In fact, the "steadfast" doctrine had little to do with the reality of the situation in Army Group Center just then. On January 12 the Russians bombed the railroads, harrying the German supply lines. The next day the Russians pressed forward, and the Germans retreated again. Staff officers were retreating to Vyazma. The railroad yards at Sychevka were the scene of a pitched battle and no more trains got through. Hitler kept talking about "closing the gaps," but the Russians kept opening the gaps with more troops and more armor. Finally, on January 14, Hitler had to order the general retreat to the Koenigsberg Line (K-line), which ran from Rzhev to Gzhatsk to Orel to Kursk. Hitler considered this to be a great concession. "This is the first time in this war that I have issued an order for a major withdrawal."

It went completely against his grain, and he determined that he would not permit it again, a decision and a mind-set that would control the progress of the Battle of Stalingrad a few months later.

Hitler's generals breathed sighs of relief. By yielding, Hitler had let them save their armies.

The Russian offensive moved, from north to south. In the north, Field Marshal Leeb's Army Group North was ordered to stand fast. Leeb asked to be allowed to retreat or to be relieved. He was relieved of command forthwith. Field Marshal Georg von Kuechler took over. The Russian armies surrounded the Germans, but did not have the strength to exploit their advantage. So the war in the north settled down to slow motion at the end of January. The Russians encircled about 100,000 German troops at Demyansk, but the Germans held and reinforced this "fortress" by air. Leningrad continued to be cut off, and the people there were in desperate condition.

The situation on the Eastern Front was a cause for concern in all Germany that winter. Field Marshal Walther von Reinchenau, the commander of Army Group South, suffered a stroke. Rundstedt and Brauchitsch were gone. So were Guderian and Hoepner, and Field Marshal Strauss. All but Reichenau had left in policy disputes with Hitler. Hitler asked Field Marshal Bock to come back from Germany and take Army Group South, and he did.

When Bock got to Poltava, the headquarters, he discovered that the Russian Southwest and Southern fronts were attacking. The scene was a German salient on the Don River called the Izyum Bulge. The north face of the bulge was protected by General Friedrich von Paulus and his 6th Army. They held in spite of repeated Russian attack, and the bulge was saved.

But it was in the center that the Russians really threatened. By mid-January the 4th Army was struggling desperately to survive, with Hitler scolding them every time they retired a foot. On January 19 General Ludwig Kuebler, commander of the 4th Army, quit, and he was replaced by Colonel General Gothard Heinrici. The morale of the army hit an all-time low. The soldiers could not understand the orders. One day they were told to hold at all costs. The next day they were retreating.

The fighting was desperate in knee-deep snow and temperatures that dropped to forty below. Frostbite and exhaustion claimed as many casualties on both sides as did bullets. On several occasions Russian soldiers who were captured fell dead from exhaustion before they could be interrogated.

Slowly the 4th Army retreated to the Koenigsberg Line, fighting every day to close the gaps the Russians opened in their lines. They saved many of their guns by bringing them on sledges, over the snow, drawn by horses. Many of the horses had been requisitioned from the Russian peasantry, leaving them with no means of carrying out the spring planting. It was a harsh war, with no quarter even considered, but those were costly horses. By February 1942 the German situation maps showed

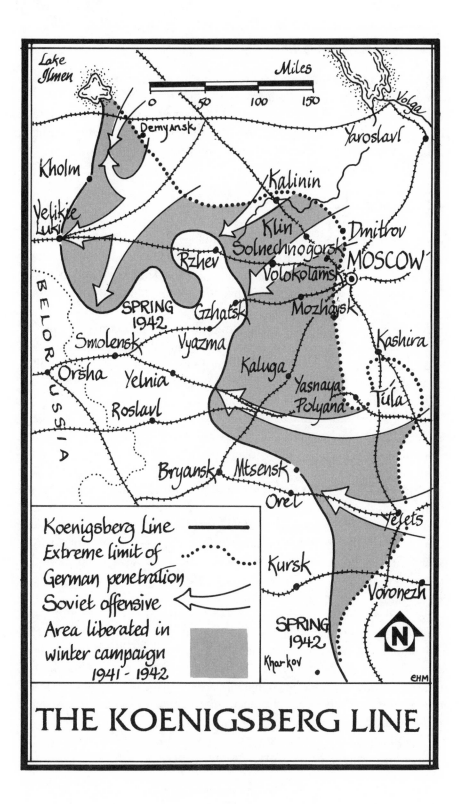

THE KOENIGSBERG LINE

the positions of their own and the Russian armies. And behind all their own armies, the space was dotted with red question marks and the word *Partisanen*—partisans. The German occupation policies everywhere had given the Soviet army a new arm, the partisan arm, which was now being broadened to harry the enemy wherever he might go.

Zhukov and the Kalinin Front were moving steadily to encircle Army Group Center at Vyazma. They very nearly did so, but there were not enough men for the task and the Germans managed to hold. By February 12 Field Marshal Kluge estimated that for the first time in two months the situation of Army Group Center was under control. Hitler observed that he now had accomplished his first objective, the elimination of the danger of panic for the Germans.

Victory had seemed nearly in the hands of the Russian armies trying to close in on Army Group Center. But as the official Russian war history noted, the situation was changing: "The situation of the Soviet troops in the western direction became decidedly worse. Weakened by extensive battles they lost their offensive capabilities."

Stalin had asked too much.

The Germans had stopped at the K-line and regrouped. The 129th and 133rd Russian armies were cut to pieces. The 39th Army and several other units were in trouble.

In spite of this, Stalin's desire for victory was such that he ignored his troubles and the condition of his armies. Attack was the order of the day.

On February 16 he ordered Zhukov to mobilize all the strength of the Kalinin and Western fronts to achieve "the final destruction of Army Group Center." Zhukov was to smash the enemy, drive to Vyazma and beyond on March 5, and on his left other Russian forces were to "liquidate" the enemy in the Bryansk area.

To do this Zhukov needed reserve troops and he got some, but the quality was steadily declining. No more Siberian or Urals divisions were available. These new troops were retreads, leftovers from the broken mass armies of the year before, and hastily enlisted factory workers and farm boys. And now time and the change of seasons was to play another major role. It was nearly time for the beginning of the *rasoutitsa*, the heavy spring rains that turned the land into a sea of mud.

The spring thaw worked from the top downward, first turning the snow and ice into water over the frozen ground. After that the topsoil melted centimeter by centimeter, creating a layer of slippery mud over the still frozen subsoil. Day by day the subsoil loosened and more mud was created. For about six weeks the water had nowhere to go until the thaw was complete, and the mud became so pervasive that only the high-wheeled Russian peasant carts could get through it.

As they waited for the thaw, both sides were so nearly exhausted that they could not carry out the grandiose plans of their leaders. Hitler wanted the 4th Army to stage a counterattack. The army did not have the strength. Stalin wanted his victory. His troops could not give it to him.

By March 25 the thawing process was under way. The daytime temperatures rose above freezing and the snow and ice began to melt.

But then in the Vyazma area a late winter storm buried the German army in snow for several days.

General Zhukov was given new orders by Stalin: to carry on the offensive for another thirty days and drive the Germans back to a line halfway between Vyazma and Smolensk. But Zhukov did not have the strength to do it, and his 33rd Army was trapped by the Germans after putting out too deep a salient. Only a handful of the troops escaped, and the army commander, General M. G. Yefremov, committed suicide.

In the last snatches of winter the Germans and Russians sparred along the entire front from the far north to the south, without being able to make any definitive progress either way. German forces were under siege in several places, but were being resupplied by air and were holding out as Hitler had ordered them to do. It was difficult for the Germans, as in the situation at Kholm and Demyansk in the north. At Kholm thirty-five-hundred German troops were surrounded for several weeks. The Luftwaffe undertook to supply these forces by air, but after a month the Germans had lost forty-six planes in this attempt. On February 25 they sent ten more Ju-52s to Kholm and four of them were shot down. After that they supplied the town by glider.

Hitler did nothing but make promises to the Kholm garrison. A relief force led by General Horst von Uckermann got to a point within sight of the city, but was bogged down in the snow. Hitler promised to get them into action again, but could not do it. His response to the problem was to write an order of the day honoring the Kholm garrison, thus substituting rhetoric for reinforcements. It was a process he would repeat at Stalingrad.

At Demyansk the German II Corps, which was surrounded, needed three hundred tons of supplies a day and this required a sustained airlift.

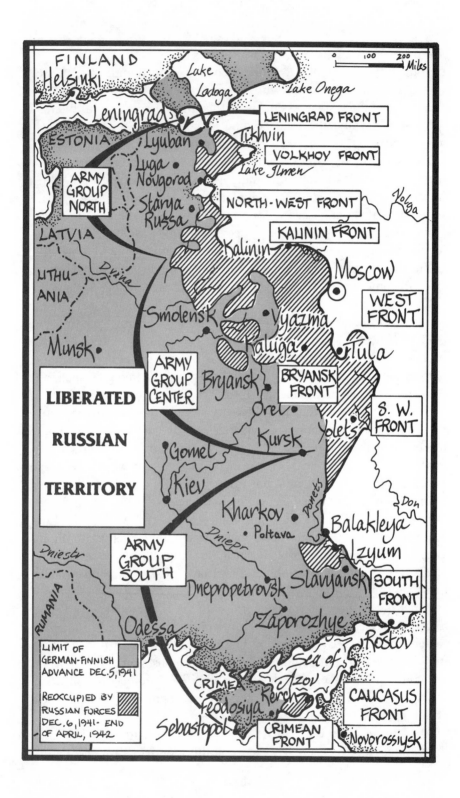

(It was the first sustained airlift in aviation history.) To carry it out, the Luftwaffe had to assign half its transport planes to the task. The Ju-52s flew in groups of twenty to forty, with fighter cover. The deliveries fell short of the supplies needed, but they kept the German troops going and gave the Luftwaffe and Hitler confidence in its ability to carry out sustained airlift, a matter that would become of supreme importance in the Battle of Stalingrad.

The sparring continued until April, when the spring thaw turned the land into a sea of mud and stopped virtually all military activity. In May the Soviets opened a drive on Kharkov, and the Germans responded with a counteroffensive.

Hitler had proved his point. By forcing the German armies to stand fast he had saved millions of marks' worth of equipment, and the reinforcements that were coming in the spring would make the German armies strong enough to move again.

14

The war of 1942 was not the same war that it had been the previous year. German strength would never again be that of June 1941.

The element of surprise had been lost. The battle of war production was being won by the Russians. Still, the Germans had regained strength over the winter, and Hitler now had hope of completing the conquest of Russia before the snow fell again. On May 17 the Germans began to move against the Izyum Bulge, using two panzer divisions of General Paulus's 6th Army. On May 28 the battle ended with the surrounding and capture of 240,000 Russian prisoners, 1,200 tanks, and 2,600 artillery pieces.

This seemed like the old days, but the reason for the German victory was that Stalin had overextended himself in his attempt to turn a limited victory of the winter into a general offensive when he did not have the resources to sustain it.

As was Stalin's habit, he blamed his generals for the defeat on the Donetz, and they clamped their mouths shut. It was obvious to the

Russians that the Germans would now go on the offensive, and they had to convert very quickly to a new defensive strategy.

Marshal Timoshenko, the commander of the Soviet forces in the south, expected a drive this summer against the south to get oil. But instead of concentrating their reserves in the south, the Russians concentrated them in the center, on the Kalinin-Tula-Tambov-Borisoglebsk-Stalingrad line. In early summer this seemed to be a mistake.

A little later it would turn out to be great good fortune for the Russians, as Hitler changed his plans.

PART IV
THE RUSSIANS ARE FINISHED: HITLER'S BIG PLANS

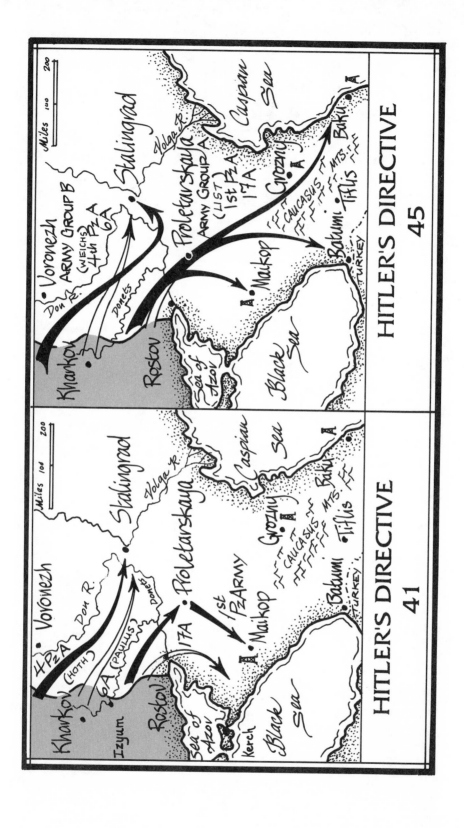

HITLER'S DIRECTIVE 45

HITLER'S DIRECTIVE 41

15

In the spring of 1942 the Germans debated the future course of the campaign in Russia. Many of the generals said a resumption of the offensive was impossible. They should consolidate and strengthen their positions to hold what they had gained, said Halder. They should withdraw to the Polish frontier, said Rundstedt as had Leeb. But by the time of decision, Rundstedt was gone, and the other generals were intimidated by Hitler's assumption of total power over the armies in the east.

General Guenthen Blumentritt, who was deputy chief of the general staff at the time, said Hitler was guided by three factors in his decision on war policy.

First, he hoped to win in 1942. He did not believe the Russians could increase the strength of their armies. He would not listen to evidence that they were growing stronger. General Halder quoted intelligence sources that said more than six hundred tanks a month were coming out of the Russian factories. Hitler slammed his fist on the table. "Impossible," he said.

As always, he did not believe what he did not want to believe.

Second, Hitler did not know what else to do but attack. He would not listen to the idea of withdrawing from the Russian adventure.

Third, Munitions Minister Albert Speer and economic czar Goering urged him to continue the attacks because they needed the oil from the Caucasus and the grain from the Ukraine to continue the war.

This was the thinking that controlled Hitler's decisions that spring.

The Germans did not have the strength in 1942 to do what they had done in 1941: launch a great offensive on three broad fronts. After the defeat on the Moscow Front the previous year Hitler hesitated to try there again. He chose to strike south for the Caucasus oil fields, although that move would extend his flank past the main body of the Red Army. That was the decision that was made. The only other offensive was to be in the Baltic to take Leningrad and link up with Germany's Finnish allies. Army Group Center would remain on the defensive.

Army Group A was created for the advance to the Caucasus, and Army Group South was reduced in strength to create it. But when the scheme of strategy was worked out in April, there was some very fuzzy understanding by the generals as to what the real objectives were. Hitler wanted to smash the Russians by breaking the power of their army in the south, capturing the seat of the Russian economy, and then taking the option of wheeling up behind Moscow or down to the Baku oil fields. But his generals had far less ambitious hopes, and they disregarded the last part of the plan. The result was that OKW, the supreme command of the armed forces, had one plan, and OKH, the command of the army, had another.

OKH by April had a plan that envisaged concentration of operations around Stalingrad. Was the place to be captured? Not necessarily, said the army. It was to be exposed to heavy fire so that it lost its importance as a center of war industry and communications. It was a central point in the occupation of the Donetz Basin and the land inside the large bend of the Don River.

To Hitler, Stalingrad was important for more reasons than as a way station. Better than his generals, he recognized the emotional as well as military significance of that city, Stalin's own city and his industrial pride and joy. Hitler would use Stalingrad as a fulcrum, while the main armies wheeled south to occupy the Caucasus. Then, having given the Red Army a major defeat in the south, the Germans would move large forces north along the Volga River and cut the communications of the Russian armies defending Moscow, while sending probes to the Urals.

THE CITY OF STALIN

In those early months of 1942 Stalingrad was very much on Hitler's mind, although he had not yet been able to determine exactly the place it would occupy in his war policy. In Hitler's preoccupation with Stalin as the supreme dictator, he had mentioned several times the importance of the Germans taking the city of Stalin, partly for its propaganda value as Stalin's namesake, partly because of its importance as the industrial center of the Don basin and the Volga. But there was more to it than that. The symbolism of Stalingrad was always high in Hitler's mind, although to his generals it was just a place on the map. As the winter turned to spring, urged by his various advisors to various courses of action, Hitler's mind kept coming back to Stalingrad.

Hitler did not communicate his ambitious plan to Halder and the army high command, so the army thought in terms of Stalingrad and not the area south of the Don River.

The result was that as the campaign opened that spring, the army thought Stalingrad was the objective and that the forces in the Caucasus would have only a blocking role, while Hitler thought the block would be established at Stalingrad and the major forces would move north or south, depending on the situation that developed.

When the name of Stalingrad had first come up at the Orsha Conference in November 1941 (where it was decided to take the obvious risk and press on toward Moscow), General Paulus, who would be the central figure in the Battle of Stalingrad, was General Halder's deputy. Halder at that time had said that in 1942 they would thrust south to Stalingrad, but for the purpose of occupying the Maikop-Grozny area, which meant the Caucasus oil fields.

To Field Marshal Kleist, who would later command Army Group A:

> The capture of Stalingrad was subsidiary to the main aim. It was only of importance as a convenient place, in the bottleneck between the Don and the Volga, where we could block an attack by Russian forces coming from the East. At the start Stalingrad was no more than a name on a map to us.

The reorganization of the German forces in the south brought creation of two—not one—new army groups. Army Group B was created under General Maximilian von Weichs. It comprised the 2nd Army, the 4th Panzer Army, and the 6th Army, which Paulus commanded that spring. Field Marshal Wilhelm List was given Army Group A, which included the 1st Panzer Army under Kleist and the 17th Infantry Army.

Hitler, going over the head of Halder, spoke to Kleist about his plans, but only vaguely. Kleist and his panzer army, said the Fuehrer, were to be the instruments whereby Germany would be assured of its oil supplies in perpetuity, and the mobility of the Russian army would be eliminated. It was all going to happen in the Caucasus. So Kleist went into the campaign with no concern at all about Stalingrad, because he had no conception of what was really on Hitler's mind.

On paper the German armies on the Eastern Front in the spring of 1942 were just as strong as in 1941, and if the Romanians, Hungarians, and Italians are included, the number of divisions was greater. The number of panzer divisions had been raised from nineteen to twenty-five.

GERMAN STRENGTH

In the summer of 1942 the German strength in Soviet Russia was 6.2 million men, including 810,000 Axis troops, 3,230 tanks and self-propelled guns, 56,000 guns and mortars, and 3,400 aircraft. The Germans were superior to the Russians in manpower, artillery, and mortars. The Russians had a slight numerical superiority in tanks, but the Germans had superiority in quality.

But in quality and morale the army of the east was already declining. The moral fiber of Germans on the Eastern Front was suffering severely. As everyone knew, the war on the Eastern Front was a different kind of war. Once the troops passed into the occupied territory, they entered a land where the old morality meant nothing. Here Naziism at its most savage was in total control. One young officer, who had just arrived from Germany, was ordered to shoot 350 civilians. The order said they were partisans, but a look at them belied it. There were too many women and children in the group.

The civilians were herded into a big barn. The young officer hesitated and was reminded by a superior that the penalty for disobedience was death. He stalled for ten minutes and then carried out the order with machine-gun fire. He was so shaken by the experience that he vowed to get out of the east as quickly as possible and never to return. Later he was wounded and survived to do so.

But he was one of the lucky ones. The German soldiers in the east knew of the mass murders, deportation, deliberate starvation of prisoners, the burning alive of schoolchildren in their schools, the use of patients in hospitals for target practice. The soldiers could stay sane only by taking on a veneer of indifference. But the horror of it had already seeped back to Germany, and the words "Eastern Front" had acquired a sinister significance. When a soldier told folks back home that he was going to the Eastern Front, their eyes glazed and their attitude acquired a forced gaiety. It was as if the soldier had just announced that he had a fatal disease. The men of the Eastern Front were lionized in the press as heroes, but somehow the people knew that what was going on in the east was inhuman and deadly far beyond the horrors of war.

16

As the opposing armies licked their wounds and prepared to reenter the deadly combat that spring, their intelligence officers assessed each other's strengths and weaknesses.

SOVIET WEAPONRY

One of the great shocks to Hitler and his generals was the discovery after the battle of Moscow that the Russians were ahead of them in weaponry. The T-34 tank was superior to anything the Germans had in 1942, and when they introduced the Panther and Tiger tanks in 1943, the Russians had already gone on to the KV1 tank, which was again superior.

It was not just a question of design and power but also a question of

((continued next page)

(*continued from preceding page*)
production. The Russians were producing thousands of tanks by 1943, and their production continued to climb as the German production faltered.

The Germans did have an effective weapon against the tanks, a hollow-core explosive shell that could knock out the crew of a whole tank if fired from an 88mm gun. But these were in short supply.

The Russians also had the *katyusha*—known as Stalin's Organs—multiple rocket launchers which could put up a barrage from thirty-six barrels carried on the back of a truck. The Germans copied the *katyusha* and introduced it in 1943 in North Africa as the *nebelwerfer*. They also supplemented their own very effective 88mm guns with the Russian 76mm antitank guns captured in the early days of the Stalin suicidal army attacks.

The German infantry was going into action with the same weapons used the previous summer. The difference was in the number of submachine guns in the infantry divisions, greatly increased, and the addition of a full-strength battalion of 88mm guns to the panzer divisions. The motorcycle battalions were abandoned, and those troops equipped with half-track personnel carriers. These infantrymen were now called *Panzergrenadier*, and their firepower and mobility would become famous.

The German tanks had been improved with bigger guns, up from 37mm in the PKwIII tank to 50mm. A fourth company was added to each tank battalion, but there was no other change in weaponry. The Germans had lost three thousand tanks, and only thirty-two-hundred had been produced in 1941. The compensation was that the North and Central Army groups had been reduced in tank strength, and many of these tanks had been moved south.

As for the Russians, Hitler's skepticism about Halder's claims for Soviet tank production proved right. Russian tank factories at Kharkov and Orel had been captured by the Germans. The KV factory in Leningrad could not get its tanks out of the Leningrad enclave. The factories in the Urals were only beginning to produce in quantity. One of the most important tank factories was at Stalingrad, the old tractor works.

In the terrible defeats of the mass armies in 1941, the Russians had lost twenty thousand tanks. Several thousand tanks had come from Britain and

America, but some of them had been captured on their train flatcars by the Germans, and many of the others were obsolete by the time they arrived. In the spring the Russians had twenty new tank brigades, and more troops from Siberia, freed by the drive of the Japanese into Southeast Asia and the Pacific. The Russian army had about thirty rebuilt rifle divisions to throw into battle and half a million half-trained reservists. Stalin was sure, however, that his forces were in better array than those of his enemy. Even the local defeats of Russian forces in the battles of February and March had not convinced him that the German army was springing back.

The Russians knew what the Germans planned—movement in the south—and Stalin decided to counter it. The first spring offensive, then, was launched in the Crimea on April 9, on the Kerch Peninsula. The Russians attacked Field Marshal Erich von Manstein's army, not knowing it had been reinforced by the 22nd Panzer Division and one other division and by General Wolfram von Richthofen's 4th Air Fleet. The Russians were not strong enough to prevail, and in a few days Manstein had cleared the Kerch Peninsula and was ready to assault Sevastopol. The Russian army lost 100,000 prisoners and 200 tanks without achieving anything at all.

SOVIET STRENGTH

Defection was a serious problem in the Red Army, particularly in the first year of the war, and the Soviets countered it with their own form of military terrorism. In May 1942 the SMERSH (Death to Spies) organization was established under Lavrenti Beria, the chief of internal security, to deal specifically with military deserters. SMERSH was given enormous power to deal with those suspected of disloyalty and their families, including that of execution without trial. A new guidance on penal battalions was also published. By 1942 each Russian front commander had ten to fifteen penal battalions at his disposal. The battalions were headed by staffs of ordinary soldiers and officers. Discipline was enforced by a guard company. Staff and guards were highly paid and got special pension benefits for this unpleasant and sometimes dangerous work. The penal battalions were only employed in offensives and counteroffensives and were not allowed weapons until they
(*continued next page*)

(*continued from preceding page*)
entered the line. Then they were backed by guards and machine gunners who forced them forward to lead the attacks. They often attacked through minefields as "tramplers," whose bodies by the score marked the passage of the Red Army through a field. In the assault on the "Cauldron" at Stalingrad sixteen penal battalions were concentrated in the 21st Soviet Army area and twenty-three in the 65th Army area on the Don Front.

Official Soviet army casualties during the war were listed as 20 million but were actually much higher, including the penal battalions, whose statistics were not kept. Gorbachev gave another figure, 27 million, in May of 1991. In most Soviet attacks, several penal battalions were completely wiped out.

The second Russian spring offensive was launched against the Germans on the Volkhov River by General Andrei Vlasov with some fresh Siberian troops. But the Germans fought doggedly. They sealed off the Russian salient in a pocket and captured Vlasov and his staff. This offensive was a total failure also.

The third Soviet offensive was launched by Marshal Timoshenko against Kharkov, on May 12. They ran into General Paulus with his fourteen fresh divisions of the 6th Army. The Russian northern force drove Paulus back to the Belgorod-Kharkov rail line, but was not strong enough to go farther. The offensive stalled in north and south, and Timoshenko asked permission to slow it down, but Stalin responded that Kharkov must be captured.

Meanwhile the Germans were planning their summer offensive. In April Field Marshal Bock prepared the first draft of the directive for the summer, urged by General Halder. It was to be called Operation Blau. It would involve additional troops and a change in the command setup of Army Group South.

Operation Blau would be divided into two sections. For Blau I, Army Group South had the 2nd Army, 4th Panzer Army, Hungarian 2nd Army, and 6th Army. The point of thrust would be Voronezh, and after taking that place the army would move south forty miles along the Don to Korotoyak, where Blau II would begin in the middle of July.

Blau II involved the 1st Panzer Army's strike east of Kharkov along the north side of the Donets River, with the 4th Army going south along the

Don. In the process they would meet the 6th Army. The three armies would divide the large pocket into several smaller ones, and the Italian 8th Army would help out. Blau II would be completed in the second week of August and would put the Germans on a line from Boguchar on the Don to the confluence of the Derkula and the Donets, 180 miles west of Stalingrad. At this point Army Group South would be split. Army Group A would take over the 1st and 4th Panzer armies. The 11th and 17th armies were to take Rostov and occupy the eastern Donets Basin. The two panzer armies would then clear the lower Don and develop the thrust of Stalingrad.

What was left of Army Group South would be called Army Group B. It would include the 6th Army and the 2nd Army and the allied armies. It would cover the rear of Army Group A as it headed down into the Caucasus.

On May 18 Kleist unleashed an offensive here against the Russians at Izyum, and it began to gain ground. Timoshenko asked permission to withdraw, and again it was refused by Stalin. On May 19 General Paulus began to move toward Kleist, and on May 23 the two German forces met and had the noose around the Timoshenko forces. Less than a quarter of two Russian armies escaped the trap, and they lost all their equipment. Moscow admitted 75,000 casualties, and Berlin claimed 240,000 prisoners. Like so many of the statistics that came out of this war on the Eastern Front, you could take your choice or believe neither.

So all the Russian spring offensives were a total failure, and they reduced the Russian forces significantly. The Russians had given Timoshenko most of their tanks, and these were lost. Now the Russian forces in the field had about two hundred tanks, giving the Germans a better than ten-to-one advantage.

17

The Germans were nearly ready for the opening of Operation Blau. Early in June the last plans were made. The objective would be not only to capture territory but to destroy the Russian armies once and for all. Hitler talked confidently of victory this year.

A key element in Blau I was the XXXX Panzer Corps under General

Hans Stumme. He would take over the armor of Paulus's 6th Army in the drive from Voronezh, and with the 4th Panzer Army to the south he would create a small tight pocket, trapping the Russian troops there. Those troops would be cleaned out by the Hungarian 2nd Army and the infantry of the 6th Army while the panzers went on and did the same again farther south and east.

The success, of course, depended on speed and secrecy. Hitler was very emphatic about the need for the tightest of security, and he impressed it on his field marshals. If the Russians ever got wind of the plan, it would be like giving them a weapon.

As the June days grew hotter and the time grew nearer for the launching of Operation Blau, General Stumme waited at his headquarters on the edge of Kharkov. He was comfortably quartered in a villa that had belonged to the commissar of heavy industry for the Kharkov region. It was good living, which pleased General Stumme, because he liked good living. He was a brilliant officer, called "Fireball" by his officers, though not in front of him, partly because of his red face (high blood pressure) and partly because of his enormous energy. He was a small man, with the pugnacity of small men, and he wore a monocle, which was another indication of temperament. He was idolized by his soldiers because he knew their problems and tried to solve them, standing against higher headquarters from time to time on their behalf. In the field he was successful because of his quick reactions and the total loyalty of his officers and men.

As the general waited for action again, he indulged himself and his staff in good food and good drink.

"War is bad enough," he told his officers. "Why eat badly as well? No, gentlemen, not me."

On June 19 the general was giving a dinner party. The guests included the three divisional commanders of his corps and the corps artillery officer. Several members of the general's staff were also present.

It was a wonderful meal, of the sort a conquering general can put together in enemy territory where the people are starving. The main course was roast venison. The general's intelligence officer, Lieutenant Colonel Franz, had shot a roebuck while on a reconnaissance trip in the countryside. They had caviar and Crimean champagne, discovered by the mess officer in a Kharkov warehouse. They talked about the future. The generals expressed their gratitude to General Stumme for delivering to them two days earlier a précis of the complex operations which they would be undertaking in a few days. Earlier they had been informed verbally, because of Hitler's crazy insistence on supersecurity, and they had pleaded for something in writing that they could digest. Stumme had considered the matter. It was strictly against orders to put anything about Operation Blau in writing, but then, what the high command wanted, and what was possible in an operation setting, were often opposed. Panzer leaders needed all the information they could get, and they needed a clear understanding of what was expected of them. Stumme had acceded to his commanders' request and provided them with a half-page outline of the problem. The message was marked "For the eyes of divisional commanders only," and it covered only the first phase of Operation Blau. The corps chief of staff had supervised the top-secret distribution by reliable couriers.

This evening the officers were talking about the remarkable exploit of General von Mackensen of III Panzer Corps, who had just opened a breach in the enemy lines for the 6th Army's jump-off in Operation Blau. Mackensen had attacked a Russian force in the north of Kharkov and east of the Donets, netting 23,000 prisoners and giving the 6th Army a point of departure to cross the river by eliminating what would have been the opposition.

Lieutenant Colonel Hesse, the operations officer, was illustrating with the silverware just what Mackensen had done.

Then came a telephone call for Hesse from the duty officer of the 23rd Panzer Division.

When he got on the telephone, Hesse learned that Major Reichel, the division chief of operations, was missing. He had taken off in a Fieseler Storch reconnaissance plane to fly to XVII Army Corps and check the division's deployment area. He had not returned. He had with him his map board and the file with the typed note about dispositions for Operation Blau I.

When General Stumme was informed, the flap began, at the divisional and corps levels. All divisions and regiments were requested to find out whether any incidents had occurred, and above all to find out what had happened to the Storch.

The next morning a reinforced company of the 336th Infantry found the Storch in a small valley. It was empty. There were no traces of fire. The gasoline tank had a hole in it. The aircraft had run out of fuel and landed.

A search of the area disclosed two fresh graves thirty yards from the aircraft. The graves were opened and one soldier said he thought he recognized the body of the major but it had been so disfigured that he was not sure.

No one could be sure if the major was dead or alive, or what had been disclosed to the Russians.

The incident was reported to army headquarters at once. General Paulus, who was an old friend of General Stumme's, had no recourse but to report to higher authority.

Hitler was not at eastern headquarters, but Field Marshal Keitel advocated the most severe sort of punishment for the officers involved in this breach of security.

General Stumme was relieved, and so were several members of his staff and the commander of the 23rd Panzer Division. They were tried for violation of security by a special court headed by Goering. Stumme was sentenced to five years imprisonment and the commander of the 23rd Division to two years. Goering interceded with Hitler, however, and the sentences were remitted and both men went to Africa, Stumme to be chief of staff of the Afrika Korps.

But the problem persisted. Did the Russians know about Operation Blau?

The answer was yes, but . . .

On June 20 Marshal Timoshenko telephoned to Stalin to tell him that he had papers captured from a German officer whose plane had crashed behind the Russian lines. The officer had been killed when he would not surrender. The papers showed German plans for an offensive.

Stalin was deeply suspicious of the report. His conspiratorial mind told him that this was a plant and so he refused to believe it. It was, Stalin told Colonel General Fillipp Golikov, commander of the Bryansk Front, "a big trumped-up piece of work by the intelligence people."

At Fuehrer headquarters the question was: What shall we do with the Blau plan now that we suspect the Russians might be onto it?

Field Marshal Bock and General Paulus of 6th Army were against doing anything at all to alter the plan. The offensive was about to begin, which meant there was not much the Soviets could do in time anyhow. General Mackensen had mounted his "trailblazing" operations to put the 6th and 4th Panzer armies into favorable positions for the start of Operation Blau. To interfere now would be to jeopardize the whole. It was all going to start moving on June 28. So it was decided to go ahead according to the plan.

The Germans were quite right. Nothing was done by the Russian high command to use the advantage.

GERMAN OFFENSIVE

JULY, 1942

The Russians now knew that the offensive of the German armor, controlled by Generals Kleist and Paulus, was going to move south.

On June 28, 1942, three German armies attacked the Russians on both sides of Kursk, and the 11th Panzer Division moved toward Voronezh, the key rail center on the Don River. Two days later the southern half of the army group attacked below Kharkov and the 1st Panzer Army crossed the Donets River. The Germans were driving toward the Don pocket. The Russian 40th Army was cut to pieces. The Russian 13th Army moved north, which widened the opening for the Germans. The Russian 21st and 28th armies retreated as fast as they could. General Paulus's panzers reached the Don on both sides of Voronezh on July 5.

At this point it would have been very easy for the Germans to capture Stalingrad, which was virtually undefended by the Russians, occupied as they were with Voronezh and the south. During the second week of July the fighting was at Voronezh and south of the Donets. In the broad corridor of land that separated the parallel courses of the Don and the Donets—over one hundred miles across—there was very little indication of the Red Army.

Hitler was very pleasantly surprised.

"The Russian is finished," he told Halder.

"I must admit it looks like it," Halder said.

And so the aims of the German army were once more changed in midstream by their leader. The original plan had been for General Hoth's panzer army of eleven divisions to have led Paulus's 6th Army to Stalingrad, where Paulus would establish the block to prevent a Russian attack, and then Hoth would go into reserve.

Now OKW said that Hoth would swing southeast and leave Stalingrad alone to Paulus's 6th Army. This would be easy if Army Group A stood still. But the world was not standing still and neither was Army Group A.

Stalin had at first refused to believe that the Germans were turning south and planned to pivot on Stalingrad, but by July 12 even he was convinced. The Southwest Front had been ripped apart, and the Southern Front was threatened by the German drive.

By July 13 Hitler seemed on the verge of his greatest victory in the east, but he was concerned that his armies were not taking as many prisoners as he had hoped. The prisoner count was his best indication of his destruction of the Russian armies, and that is what he now wanted. Only eighty-eight thousand Russian prisoners had been taken in the Blau Operation. Hitler was annoyed. He fired Field Marshal Bock, apparently because he did not want to share the glory of the victory with anyone, and he refused to let the general staff be mentioned in articles about his victories. All this was an indication of how rapidly Hitler's xenophobia was growing.

On the night of July 13 Army Group A and Army Group B were ordered to continue operations on the lower Don. There was no mention of Stalingrad. The Russians were to be pursued and cut up in the south. A day later Hitler shifted his headquarters from East Prussia to Vinnitsa in the western Ukraine in a compound named Werewolf.

The Russians were now alive to the German intentions to cut up their armies as well as take territory, and in a sense they were ahead of the German thinking. Confused by Hitler's rapid changes of mind, the Germans had not placed much importance on Stalingrad, seeing it simply as a hinge on which they would move their operations south. But the Russians saw Stalingrad as the central position in the whole German drive.

On July 14 a state of war was declared in the Stalingrad area. The Defense Committee decided that no matter where the Germans were headed at the moment, their real objective was to envelope Moscow from the east. Stalin decided that the defense would be anchored at Stalingrad.

Stalin set up the Stalingrad Front. That decision, early made, was a stroke of genius which rescued Stalin from the mass of error in which he had mired the winter and spring Russian offensives.

He ordered Timoshenko to command the Stalingrad Front and Nikita Khrushchev as commissar. The front was assigned three armies, the 62nd, 63rd, and 64th. They were sprawled all over central Russia as far back as Tula. The problem was to get them to Stalingrad fast.

As for the Germans, in the changing of the plans, Hitler believed he could bring the Russian armies to a final confrontation by heading south. Army Group A was detached from Army Group B and sent south to take the Caucasus.

Army Group B was now to attack Stalingrad, smash the enemy, take the town, and cut off the isthmus between the Don and the Volga.

Two panzer armies were sent to cross the Don. As General Kleist later observed: "The 4th Army could have taken Stalingrad without a fight at the end of July, but it was diverted to help me cross the Don. I did not need its aid and it simply got in the way. . . ."

When the German armies got across the Don, the orders were changed again. One German division was to be sent southeast, and the rest of the 4th Panzer Army was to move north and take Stalingrad on its unprotected southern side.

Paulus, meanwhile, was now ordered to march down the Don corridor on Stalingrad.

Russian resistance to the 6th Army's movement was at first negligible, but the 6th Army got badly strung out on the two-hundred-mile march. Meanwhile the trains were bringing new Russian units from the east as fast as the rails would carry them. A race was on, between Russian defenders and the German attackers, to reach the city of Stalingrad.

General Vasili Chuikov was at that time the commander of the Reserve Army at Tula, four infantry divisions, two motorized divisions, and two armored brigades. They were ordered to Stalingrad, to use 7 different railroad stations, and then to make a forced march of 125 miles to reach the city. Chuikov himself was sent south, to restore some sense of order to the battered armies of Timoshenko, which had been so thoroughly mauled around Voronezh.

When Chuikov reached Stalingrad, he came across two divisional staffs who were traveling in five trucks filled to overflowing with cans of fuel. He asked where they were going and where the Germans were, and they could not give him a sensible reply. They had obviously lost control and faith. As Chuikov could see, his first task was to restore the morale of his fighting men.

On the steppe he met the staffs of two divisions who claimed to be looking for the headquarters of the 9th Army. They were in three cars, also loaded with petrol tins. He asked them, "Where are the Germans? Where are our units? Where are you?" They could not answer the questions.

He found the same slackness at the 21st Army, which was assigned to the right flank at Stalingrad. He was distressed at the lackadaisical attitude of General V. N. Gordov, who seemed to have lost his will to fight. Then, to his horror, Gordov was appointed commander of the 64th Army and Chuikov was to be his deputy. Because he was a defeatist, Gordov ordered only part of the army inside the Don bend and kept the reserves on the east side of the river. Chuikov was critical of the decision. Gordov did not listen. General Yeremenko and Khrushchev arrived and Gordov was sent to Moscow, but there he emerged again as commander of the Stalingrad Front. Chuikov was acting commander of the 64th Army. The

Russian 62nd Army, under General A. L. Lopatin, was ordered to stand and fight on the Chir River.

The other German thrust was proceeding down the Don across the Donets, and headed toward Rostov. General Paulus's 6th Army had turned its attention north toward the Don and the Chir. On July 17 two of Paulus's divisions entered Bobovskaya on the upper Chir.

Hitler was bemused with "small, tight encirclements," and he ordered one on the lower Don. His generals protested that to throw more troops into the area would be to cause confusion, but he would not listen. He did, however, order the 6th Army to move in the northeastern quarter of the Don bend and make it difficult for the enemy to build a defense west of the Volga.

Now rain began, heavy rain that paralyzed the German armies seeking to encircle Rostov. As Hitler fidgeted in the rain, he changed the orders one more time. Stalingrad assumed a new immediacy. Paulus was to take the 6th Army to Stalingrad and capture it by a high-speed assault, for which he was to have reinforcements.

On July 20 the Germans were closing on Rostov, but when they got there, the Russians were gone. The whole campaign had been a failure in the matter of prisoners.

On July 25 General Paulus made an attempt to capture Stalingrad on the run. He had been marching for two weeks and his troops were tired, but he saw that the resistance in the last few days' approach had been minimal, so he did not wait, but fed his troops into battle. At the same time, the Russians were arriving from the east to defend the city, and doing the same.

The 62nd Army was on the line and the 64th Army was also in the Don bend. The 57th Army was being re-formed as well as several other armies that were being used as cadres for the new 1st and 4th Tank armies. East of the Don, the Russian population of Stalingrad was at work building four concentric defense lines around the city. The effort was supported by the Russian 8th Air Army, which was assigned to the Stalingrad Front. On July 23 General Gordov replaced Marshal Timoshenko as commander of the Stalingrad Front. That same day General Paulus submitted to OKH his plan to take the city. He would sweep to the Don on both sides of the Kalach River and then drive a wedge of armor across the last thirty miles.

For several days the 6th Army had been overrunning the defenses of the 62nd and 64th Soviet armies without knowing it.

Fighting really developed on July 24. The Soviets held at Serafimovich and at Kremenskaya. The XIV Panzer Corps ran out of gas and had to stop northeast of Kalach. On July 25, while the Germans were still waiting for fuel, sixty Russian tanks cut the road behind, and two hundred Russian tanks attacked the 3rd and 60th Motorized divisions. The Germans were not dismayed, but they were concerned. "For the moment a certain crisis had developed," said the chief of the German XIV, LI, and XXIV Panzer corps, which were shoulder-to-shoulder on the way to Stalingrad. But the Russians were still holding a forty-mile-wide, 20-mile-deep bridgehead from Kalach to Nizhne Chirskaya.

The struggle for Stalingrad was joined, although the Germans still did not recognize the significance of the battle to come. Here would be decided the fate of Hitler's whole drive east. The Russians had accepted the challenge he did not know he had laid down so openly. They were now to commit their whole strength to Stalingrad. If the Germans triumphed, then the plains beyond the Volga would be open, and Moscow and the Urals would be theirs. The Red Star would be replaced by the Swastika and the eastern empire would be won. The fate of half a world was hanging in the balance as the Battle of Stalingrad began.

PART V
INTO THE BREACH . . .

GERMAN ADVANCE
EARLY AUGUST, 1942

18

Hitler's directive No. 45 completely changed the German strategy of the war. Sensing that the Russian armies were defeated, he increased his demands. No longer would it be enough to drive into the northern Caucasus. No longer would it be enough to use the Stalingrad area as a hinge. Stalingrad must be captured as well as the Caucasus. Both objectives must be achieved simultaneously. The 4th Panzer Army, which had been sent south and had cluttered up Kleist's 1st Panzer Army operating area, was now told to make a left turn, head back up, and attack Stalingrad from the south.

The Russians sensed that Stalingrad was the key to their defense. The very name "Stalin's city" was indicative of its importance in the Soviet scheme of life. It was the center of industry in the whole region, stretching twenty-five miles along the west bank of the Volga. Its population of six hundred thousand people were mostly factory workers in three huge complexes: the Red October steel plant, the Stalingrad tractor factory, and the Barrikady ordnance factory.

Stalingrad before the war was a beautiful city, if one admired the gingerbread architecture of which Stalin was so fond. It was a city of parks and trees and grassland, with open spaces running down to the Volga— here almost a mile wide and dotted with attractive islands. The west bank of the river was steep, with many caves jutting into its sides, and inside the city the landscape was hill and dale. One of the hills, the Mamayev

Kurgan, was 335 feet high and commanded a fine view of the center of the city. There was no bridge across the Volga, but there were important rail lines on both sides and ferries. After the fall of Rostov to the Germans, Stalingrad was the most important port on the river in Russian hands. It would not be given up without a fight.

When Rostov was under attack in mid-July, Stalin had suddenly become aware of the danger to Stalingrad and, as noted, had put the city on a war footing on July 19. The next day, Alexie S. Chuyanov, the city defense chairman, reported about the measures he would adopt. These included converting an industrial city of more than half a million people to a fortress. All that had been done so far was to improve the antiaircraft defenses.

At this point 180,000 civilians were rushed out to build defenses. They dug trenches and tank traps and built fire points. Specialists from the 5th Pioneer Army and the 28th Military Construction Administration came in to help. The Defense Committee organized eight "annihilation battalions" involving eleven-thousand men who were enjoined to fight off German parachutists. Industrial goods were moved to the east bank of the Volga, along with stores and livestock. Anything transportable that was not needed for military defense was moved away, and some of the women and children were evacuated from the city. Streets were blocked with barricades, and men and women labored by the river to build the defenses.

On July 21 Stalin appointed General Gordov commander of the Stalingrad Front in one of his typical precipitate actions.

Two days later the German assault on Stalingrad began.

German Army Group B had been split into four subgroups for the attack on Stalingrad.

The northern group consisted of two panzer, two motorized, and four infantry divisions. It was to attack on July 23 from the Golovsky-Perelazovsky area, to capture the bridge over the Don River at Kalach.

The central force consisted of one panzer and two infantry divisions. It was to attack on July 25 from the Oblivskaya-Verkhne-Aksenovsky area, also toward Kalach.

General Paulus's 6th Army was to come from the west and clear away the Russian forces deployed west of the Don. Thus the road to the Volga would be open.

GERMAN ADVANCE · JULY 1942

The southern group, which consisted of one armored division, one motorized division, and four infantry divisions, was to cross the Don at Tsimlyanskay on July 21. It would advance on Stalingrad from the south.

The commander of Army Group B, General Weichs, had a force of thirty divisions and twelve hundred aircraft, outnumbering the Russian forces in the Don bend by two to one. For all practical purposes, too, the Germans had air superiority, and most of the Russian units that would have to face the Germans were newly formed.

On July 23 five German divisions attacked the right wing of the Russian 62nd Army north of Manoylin. Other troops attacked the Russian 64th Army on the Tsimla River.

From a German account, this is how the attack went:

It was evening. Dusk was falling when the sergeant responsible for this one section waved his infantrymen to him. They listened intently as he told them what they were to do. He had a large map of the district, on which he showed them the points they would take. Theirs was a shock unit. They would be in the absolute front of the line.

They stood and stared at each other for a long time. Now they knew. They were going into a full-scale attack. A sense of foreboding settled on the men. Soon, they knew, some of them would be dead. Some of them would be killed. They all knew it, and yet none of them could imagine his own death. He could imagine himself burying his comrades. But he could not think of himself lying mortally wounded. That was something that happened to other people, but never to oneself.

The night came, a soft summer night with a feeling of coolness after the hot day on the Russian steppe. They went down into their shelters. In the depths of one, someone was playing a harmonica, and his friends were singing. Then came the sound of gunfire. The music stopped. Everybody jumped, but then all quieted down once again.

A corporal came up. The first Russian line was only four hundred meters away from them, he said.

"Not so bad," said an old veteran. "At least we can sleep. At Smolensk the Popov's holes were less than a grenade's throw from ours."

By dawn they had reached the no-man's-land. The soldier records:

A dozen flares lit up the air over their hill, and Russian fusillades of fire shook them. Grenades were falling all around them.

"Dig," shouted one soldier.

"Nobody move!" shouted the old soldier. If they moved they would draw attention and then they might all be killed. In their shock, the others obeyed him.

A flare burst overhead, and they wondered they were not yet killed. Just beyond them lay the bodies of the Russian and their grenadier, and then six foxholes that marked a forward Russian position. The Russians had not seen them.

The old soldier told them to play dead. If the Russians thought they were dead, they would not waste grenades on them.

A grenade exploded on the other side of the hill and the old soldier's number two machine gunner groaned. He was hit. The old soldier told him to shut up; the boy heard and gritted his teeth, but stayed quiet.

In the light of the flares they could see the Russians coming, as they crawled out of their holes and across the land ahead. The Russians came as far as the barbed wire, then they looked around and turned and went back.

The old soldier laughed. The Russians were just as scared as they were. Somebody had told them to go out and look around and they had gone out and looked around.

The German squad breathed again.

The sergeant decided to move out of this position.

Then somewhere out there a German must have pulled a wire attached to a string of mines. Everything began to come apart, in the shaking of explosions. For a moment they thought all those German soldiers had been blown to pieces. Then men began jumping up and rushing through the tangles of barbed wire. The squad opened fire with the two machine guns. The 7.7mm cartridges were devoured by the guns, and they spat fire at the Russians. Behind came the roar of the German infantry. The Russians were attempting a defense, but from every side German soldiers were pouring through the barbed wire, breaking over the trenches. Ahead and to the right the artillery was bombarding a town. Spirals of smoke rolled along the ground from the fires the shells had started.

Then came the rumble of tanks, and in a few seconds they were dodging as the panzers came through. Some were stopped by mines. One tank went by the squad's hillock, crossed the trench that was now overflowing with Russian bodies, and plunged on. A second tank followed and a third plunged through the bloody paste of the trench. More tanks came pouring out of the woods behind them, crushing the saplings and the grass. They headed straight for the infantrymen, who had to get out of the way. Any wounded who could not move just had bad luck.

A tank came by so close it nearly hit the hill. One of the soldiers of the squad lay there, watching the treads inches from his nose.

One soldier remembered it:

I retain nothing from those terrible minutes except indistinct memories which flash into my mind with sudden brutality, like apparitions, among bursts and scenes and visions that are scarcely imaginable. It is difficult even to try to remember moments during which nothing is considered, foreseen, or understood, when there is nothing under a steel helmet but an astonishingly empty head and a pair of eyes which translate nothing more than would the eyes of an animal facing mortal danger. There is nothing but the rhythm of explosions, more or less distant, more or less violent, and the cries of madmen, to be classified later, according to the outcome of the battle, as the cries of heroes or of murderers. And there are the cries of the wounded, or the agonizingly dying, shrieking as they stare at a part of their body reduced to pulp, the cries of men touched by the shock of battle before everybody else, who run in any and every direction howling like banshees. There are the tragic unbelievable visions, which carry from one moment of nausea to another: guts splattered across the rubble and sprayed from one dying man onto another, tightly riveted machines ripped like the belly of a cow which has just been sliced open, flaming and groaning, trees broken into tiny fragments, gaping windows pouring out torrents of billowing dust, delivering into oblivion all that remains of a comfortable parlor. And then there are the cries of officers and noncoms, trying to shout across the cataclysm to regroup their sections and companies. That is how we took part in the German advance, being called through the noise and dust, following clouds churned by our tanks to the northern outskirts. All resistance was overwhelmed and once again everything was either German or dead, and a sea of Russian soldiers had drawn back into the limitless confines of their country.

After three days of fighting, XIV Panzer Corps broke through the defense of the 62nd Russian Army and advanced to Klamensky on the Don, outflanking the 62nd Army from the north. The Russian 1st and 4th Tank armies tried to intervene, but these armies were less than a week old, they were still only partly equipped and commanded by infantry officers who were inexperienced in tank warfare, and their attacks were complete failures.

Hitler now intervened again in a way that would have its effects on the Battle of Stalingrad. On July 23 he transferred Manstein's five divisions from the Crimea to the Leningrad Front, assuming that the Russians were almost beaten. At the same time he transferred two experienced panzer divisions, the *Liebstandarte* and *Grossdeutschland*, to France, to face an illusory Allied invasion.

Hitler's optimism that the Russians were nearly through continued.

The XIV Panzer Corps drove a wedge between the Russian 62nd and 64th armies as it headed for Kalach along the west bank of the Don. On August 1 the Russians sent the 57th Army to the Don and the 51st Army south of the Volga bend. This action gave the front a perimeter of nearly 450 miles. Stalin decided to establish a new command.

General Hoth's 4th Army, ordered to attack Stalingrad from the south, turned north on August 1. Two days later it had reached Kotelnikovo and the Aksai River, sixty miles southeast of Stalingrad. This move speeded Stalin up and he gave the command to General Chuikov, or so he indicated at the moment. On the way south Chuikov found two divisions of the 51st Army wandering across the steppes, not quite sure where they were going. He commandeered them and put them behind the Aksai River, and put a brigade of marines behind. Chuikov learned that the 208th Infantry Division from Siberia was detraining somewhere, but no one was quite sure where. He found them. They had been attacked by air and the survivors scattered. They were thoroughly disorganized, and the division commander wanted to resign. While Chuikov was trying to round up the troops, there was another Luftwaffe attack, and his radio was put out of action. Finally he improvised a force and reorganized the defense along the Aksai River.

While Chuikov was doing all this, in Moscow Stalin was meddling with command again. On August 1 he called General Yeremenko, one of his most effective commanders, who had been wounded in the defense of Moscow as commander of the 4th Shock Army. Yeremenko said he was ready to return to duty, and Stalin gave him command of the Southeast Front.

Four days afterward there were two major commands, Stalingrad Front and Southeast Front, and the headquarters of both, by Stalin fiat, were at Stalingrad.

On August 6 General Chuikov's improvised defense was attacked by the German and Romanian infantry. Chuikov's troops held the line.

To the northwest, General Paulus's 6th Army was waiting at the end of July for fuel and ammunition after its drive. By August 4 Paulus received enough supply to go ahead for one day's march, about thirty miles. He was eager to get going and ordered the attack to begin on the Kalach bridgehead on August 8. Hitler, now anticipating an enormous harvest of prisoners in the Don pocket, asked him to start the attack a day earlier.

In the bend of the Don the Russian forces were in trouble. The 62nd Army had lost most of its eight infantry divisions, which had fought their way out of the German pocket maze, but at the cost of leaving most of their weapons behind. But after its failures the 1st Tank Army had been disbanded and the 62nd Army got its equipment.

On the morning of August 7, the XIV and XXV Panzer corps smashed into the Kalach bridgehead. By late afternoon they had put the Russian 62nd Army in a pocket. For the next four days, together with infantry, they attacked and they captured Russian prisoners.

The road from Kalach to Stalingrad seemed to be the logical route, but it had problems for the Germans. It was crossed by steep gullies that would force tanks to make long detours and could be used by the Russians for deep defense. So General Paulus decided to take another route. He would send his two panzer corps north to the northeast corner of the Don bend, to establish bridgeheads for the advance to Stalingrad.

The loss of Kalach spurred the Russians to even greater activity. More rifle divisions and more tank corps were summoned to Stalingrad. Stalin changed his mind again about command and gave General Yeremenko command of both the Stalingrad and Southeast fronts. Stalin would not back down from a pigheaded decision, so Yeremenko had to operate with two commands, two deputy commanders, two chiefs of staff, and two staffs. It seemed hardly the way to win battles.

In August the Germans were closing in. General Hoth had come up from the south to a point forty miles south of Stalingrad. General Paulus began an attack, and in two days his panzers cleared the entire loop of the Don and had moved to about sixty miles north of the city. But here his tanks ran into marshy ground. The advance stalled. From Stalingrad, Yeremenko rushed the 1st Guards Army up to establish a twenty-mile-long bridgehead that ran from Kremenskaya to Sirotinskaya.

On the morning of August 21 Paulus's LI Corps attacked east across the Don, taking the Russians by surprise. The Germans soon had a bridgehead three miles long and five miles wide. By the next morning the German engineers had put up twenty-two bridges, and the panzers of V Panzer Corps were crossing the river.

So the Germans planned the last act. They would capture Stalingrad. At his headquarters, Hitler was ecstatic. His dream was just about to come true. After this it would be simply a question of rolling up the enemy on the way to Moscow. All else would fall into place. The Russians were finished!

PART VI

"YOU WILL CAPTURE STALINGRAD BY AUGUST 25 . . ."

—ADOLF HITLER

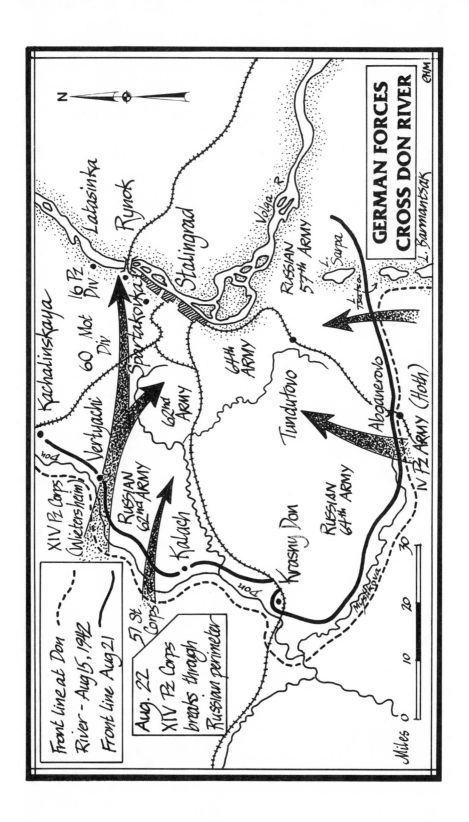

GERMAN FORCES CROSS DON RIVER

L. Barmantsak

Volga R.

Volga

Rynok

Latasinka

Stalingrad

Spartakovka

16 Pz Div.

60 Mot Div.

Kachalinskaya

Vertyachi

Don

XIV Pz Corps (Wietersheim)

RUSSIAN 62nd ARMY

62nd ARMY

64th ARMY

RUSSIAN 57th ARMY

L. Sarpa

L. Tsatsa

Tundutovo

Abganerovo

Kalach

Krasny Don

Don

RUSSIAN 64th ARMY

Myshkova

IV PZ ARMY (Hoth)

51 St Corps

Aug. 22
XIV Pz Corps breaks through Russian perimeter

Front line at Don River – Aug 15, 1942
Front line Aug 21

Miles 0   10   20   30

N

19

On the morning of August 4, 1942, General Yeremenko arrived at Stalingrad. As his aircraft came in and circled to land, he looked down on the city, sitting like a long worm on the west bank of the Volga. Stalingrad. Sixteen miles of factories and defense effort for the Soviet Union, its factories still belching smoke even as the enemy approached the gate.

The general was met by a car sent from headquarters by his political commissar, Lieutenant General Nikita Khrushchev. After greetings, Yeremenko settled in to work in the command post, an underground installation near the western shore of the Volga, in a deep canyon called Tsaritsa Gorge. The bunker had two entries, one at the bottom of the gorge and the other at the top, leading into Pushkinskaya Street. Inside, the bunker was protected by heavy doors and staggered reinforced partitions.

Yeremenko's first task was to learn what he had to work with. His appointment had been as head of the Southeast Front, which adjoined the Stalingrad Front. The command was divided between the two fronts. It was one of those impossible situations that Stalin kept creating by insisting on acting on his own intuition rather than on the advice of his generals. The Stalingrad Front had been established first and was commanded this week by General Gordov. That front ran from the town of Kalach, forty miles to the west in the Don River basin, to this command post. The new front ran south of that line.

Yeremenko looked at the map to the west. It was farm country, which had been harvested of wheat in the past few weeks and sent east in thousands of freight cars, even though German planes had machine-gunned the harvesters as they worked. And from the farms most of the livestock had been put across the river to safety, as well as thousands of tractors, threshing machines, and combines manufactured at the Stalingrad tractor plant.

His first task was to slow the Germans down. There was little manpower, but Yeremenko managed to assemble a force of tanks, antitank guns, and *katyusha* rocket launchers, which was dispatched to Abganerovo to fight off General Hoth's 4th German Panzer Army. A handful of rocket launchers, a handful of antitank guns, and fifty-nine tanks were supposed to fight off the 4th Panzer Army. Miraculously they enjoyed some success. Hoth was slowed down between Abganerovo and the Sarpa Lakes. The Russians found that the Germans were very sluggish. They did not put their tanks into operation without infantry and air support. They were cautious and indecisive, the Russians noted, and the German infantry showed no resolution in its attacks.

There was reason for this attitude, and it showed in the letters home of the German soldiers. The Germans were suffering from a surge of overconfidence.

"The company commander says that the Russian troops are completely broken," said one letter. "To reach the Volga and take Stalingrad is not so difficult for us. Victory is not far away."

"Our company is tearing ahead," wrote another German soldier. "Today I wrote Else 'We shall soon see each other. All of us feel that the end, Victory, is near.'"

In this atmosphere who wanted to get killed unnecessarily? No one. So the company commanders relaxed and the soldiers relaxed, and the drive slacked off, until the army commanders suddenly cracked down with disciplinary measures.

Yeremenko recognized that Kalach, directly west of Stalingrad on the Don, was the key to the city. He ordered the 20th Brigade to hold there or destroy the big Don River bridge.

So much for the moment, but almost immediately there were other troubles. With the news that the Germans were coming, the people of Stalingrad panicked, and the city had to be put under martial law.

Then, on August 7, General Paulus's XIV Panzer Corps broke through the 62nd Army of the Stalingrad Front, immediately to Yeremenko's right, when General Lopatin tried a counterattack with three divisions. The Russians were surrounded on three sides. The 62nd Army head-quarters panicked and deserted the troops to rush back to the safety of Stalingrad. Part of the army managed to escape only with heavy losses. Paulus had scored a great victory, taking fifty-seven thousand prisoners and one thousand tanks. The only bright note for the Russians was that the German advance stopped on the right bank of the Don. The situation was critical. Yeremenko could get no cooperation from Gordov. He reported this to the Military Commission in Moscow. Obviously the Military Commission convinced Stalin that this situation was in error, for on August 13 Yeremenko learned that he had this top-heavy command with both fronts and two deputies.

On August 15 the Germans attacked to take the Don River bridge at Kalach. The 20th Motorized Brigade engineers blew the bridge. A little more time was gained.

Hitler was growing restless. Paulus's victory over the 62nd Army only whetted his appetite. He wanted Stalingrad and he wanted it in a hurry. On August 19 Paulus issued orders for the capture of the city. The attack was to begin August 23, led by the XVI Panzer and the 3rd and 60th Motorized divisions commanded by Lieutenant General Hans Hube. They would make a path across the corridor from the Don to the Volga. When they reached the northern suburbs of Spartakovka, Rynok, and Latashinka, they would then move south into the city. Forces behind them would mop up and widen the corridor. The 4th Panzer Army would come up from the south after the 6th Army had sealed it off on the north. The LI Corps would head east from Kalach to Stalingrad at the junction between the Russian 62nd and 64th armies.

The Germans on the Stalingrad Front were of two minds about the Russians. In the order of attack, Paulus speculated. On the one hand, he said, the Russians were expected to defend the Stalingrad area stubbornly. On the other hand, "It is possible that the destructive blows of recent weeks have deprived the Russians of the strength for a decisive resistance."

There was evidence to support each point of view. In the outskirts of Stalingrad citizens had put up crude signs on the trees: Death to the Invader. But in Stalingrad on the night before the German attack, the garrison commander disappeared, fled to the east, leaving his command in utter confusion. Military vehicles got lost and accidents began to pile up on the roads. Garrison troops began to make their way across the river to escape.

There was only one way to find out whether or not the Russians would fight, and at 4:30 on the morning of August 23 General Richthofen's 4th Luftflotte opened the attack with a thousand tons of bombs laid down ahead of the panzers and on the north side of Stalingrad. The Russian destruction of the bridge at Kalach had no more than discommoded the Germans. The engineers had built several bridges across the Don farther downriver, and on this morning of August 23 they screeched and rumbled beneath the weight of the panzers crossing.

Stalingrad was sleeping as the German columns toward the city headed up the road from Kalach. In the Dsherzhinsky Tractor Works, which was the formal name of the Stalingrad tractor factory, production was on a twenty-four-hour basis as it had been for months, and sixty T-34 tanks were being put together that night. At five o'clock in the morning someone rushed in with news of an enemy breakthrough at Kalach. The production line clanked to a halt.

The supervisors called a meeting to organize defenses of the factory.

At the Tsaritsa Gorge command posts, General Yeremenko was awakened by a duty officer. The Germans had broken through and the panzers were on their way, he was told. He began routing out his staff officers while he waited for his breakfast.

A few hundred yards away at Red Square the public loudspeakers warned the people of air raids, but since there had not been any air raids recently, no one paid much attention. The Stalingrad Soviet had decided not to tell the public about the tank attack that was developing. It might cause a panic.

So work in the city began as usual. Women workers dropped their small children at the public nurseries and went to work as they did every weekday. Anyone who had listened to the air raid warnings seriously in the morning was quickly disabused. No raids came. The sun rose in the sky, bright and hot. It was just another summer's day in Stalingrad.

But in the command post the noise and excitement increased by the hour as units reported in. Officers and soldiers passed in and out of the bunker. General Yeremenko was anchored to the telephone, taking call after call. The commander of the 8th Air Force reported a battle at Rossoshka, with two columns of tanks followed by trucks and infantry moving along the road. That was just twenty-five miles northwest of Stalingrad.

Yeremenko ordered the air force to put up all the aircraft of the Stalingrad Front that would go into the air. They were to strike at the columns of motorized infantry and the tanks. He also telephoned the commander of the air forces of the Southeast Front and ordered him to strike Hube's tank column.

The commander of the antiaircraft defenses called and reported he could hear German tanks through his sound detectors at Bolshaya Rossoshka. The general told him to be ready to turn his antiaircraft guns against the tanks.

Commissar Khrushchev telephoned. What was the general doing to stop the enemy?

Yeremenko was juggling his handful of troops, trying to put enough in the northwest to slow down the Germans and trying to keep enough in the suburbs to stop them when they arrived.

He called Colonel A. A. Sarayev, commander of the 10th Division of troops of the NKVD. These were internal security troops and they had no heavy weapons, but they were the only troops Yeremenko had and they would have to undertake the defense of the thirty-one-mile perimeter.

At eight o'clock Yeremenko called headquarters of the 62nd Army. It soon became clear that the Germans were heading at high speed straight for the city.

Engineers arrived at the bunker to announce proudly that they had just completed a pontoon bridge across the Volga, linking Stalingrad with the eastern shore. Yeremenko thanked them for doing the job and then told them to destroy the bridge.

Their eyes goggled. "Destroy the bridge?"

"Destroy the bridge," he repeated. "It must not fall into enemy hands."

The officers went away.

Commissar Khrushchev arrived and reported that the party organizations and workers units were prepared to join the defense and wanted assignments.

A general called in from the west, to announce that a big warehouse had been burned down by the enemy. Yeremenko shut him up and told him to stop gossiping and get down to business. The general in charge of communications called in a panic to announce that the Germans had shot up a trainload of ammunition, food, and reinforcements.

"The enemy tanks are moving on Stalingrad," he shrilled. "What are we going to do?"

"Your duty," said Yeremenko. "Stop panicking."

Yeremenko's staff officers arrived, and he ordered them to put together the remnants of two tank corps and block the German advance.

Colonel Sarayev of the NKVD came in.

"The German tanks are ten miles from Stalingrad and moving fast toward the northern part of the city," said Yeremenko.

"I know," said Sarayev.

"What have you done?"

"I have told the two regiments on the north and northwest to be ready for battle."

Yeremenko instructed him to also send the reserve regiment in the Minima suburb to the Barrikady factory.

Lieutenant General Golikov, Yeremenko's deputy for the Southeast Front, reported that the 4th Panzer Army had begun attacking from the south at 7 A.M. and by noon had captured the railroad station at Tinguta, the seventy-four-kilometer marker. The 38th Rifle Division was half-surrounded. But elsewhere the Germans had been beaten. The general was preparing a counterattack on Tinguta. Yeremenko approved, and he issued a few more orders.

Lunch was brought in, but there was no time to eat. The deputy chief of staff in Moscow wanted to know how things were going. While Yeremenko was on the telephone General Lopatin of the 62nd Army called.

He had bad news. The German tanks and infantry with strong air support had wiped out a regiment of his 87th Rifle Division and the right flank of the 35th Guards Rifle Division, north of Rossoshka Malaya.

From every area came reports of the battle. The NKVD was fighting tanks and motorized infantry east of Orlovka.

The stream of military calls was interrupted by Minister Vyacheslav Malyshev of the State Defense Committee calling from the tractor factory.

"From the factory we can see fighting going on north of the city," the minister said. "Antiaircraft gunners are fighting tanks. Several shells have already fallen in the factory area. The enemy tanks are advancing on Rynok. We have prepared the most important targets for blowing up."

"Don't blow anything up yet," said Yeremenko. "Defend the factory at whatever cost. Get the workers' detachment ready for battle and keep the enemy out of the factory. Help is on its way."

The minister was at the tank training center with Major General Feklenko. He had two thousand men and thirty tanks, and they would defend the factory. Yeremenko appointed Feklenko sector commander and told him to organize the defense of the factory; two brigades—one tank, one rifle—were on their way.

On the river the steamers moved back and forth.

In the factories the factory defense committees organized the workers to fight. Those who knew how to use a gun were given white armbands, rifles, and bandoliers of ammunition and moved to the riverbank. Evacuation committees began organizing the family women and children to move across the Volga.

CITIZEN SOLDIERS

After General Richthofen's 4th Air Fleet had demolished the city of Stalingrad, Political Commissar Khrushchev feared the Red Army would collapse. He organized five thousand members of the Red October Metallurgical Works to fight beside the troops of the 62nd Army. Five thousand rifles were rounded up, and the men were split into brigades. The whole operation was supervised by the NKVD, which had been keeping a sharp eye on the factory workers for years.

This was a Soviet factory, not a western one, and most of the workers were single men who lived in barracks. Their daily lives were not so very different from those of the Russian soldier, even before the war. Most of them had been assigned to this factory and would stay there during their workaday lives. The factory had its "garden city" about which the government had made much, but the wooden houses and quiet little gardens represented a minority of the workers, the privileged few.

As for the others, the NKVD prison in the center of town was a grim reminder of what happened to those who did not follow instructions. In this desperate hour the prisoners were turned out to fight for their freedom, under the eyes of the NKVD companies.

The air raid sirens continued sporadically, and the loudspeakers warned of impending doom. But nothing happened that afternoon. In the factories the hubbub of production was succeeded by the hubbub of preparation, but in the city at large, most people did not sense that anything unusual was happening.

Late in the afternoon came a call more frantic than the others, and this time the antiaircraft guns around the city began firing.

As the aircraft came to Stalingrad, General Hube's tanks began to attack southwest at Rynok. They were met by mortar and antiaircraft fire and then by tank destroyer battalions with antitank rifles. The fighting centered around Sukhaya Mechetka creek half a mile north of the tractor factory. After several hours Hube's tanks retired. They were low on fuel and tomorrow was another day. As they left, the defenders of the factory were being reinforced.

The ground fighting had ceased for the day when the planes came to Stalingrad; six hundred Stuka dive bombers and Ju-88 bombers came in neat V-formations, as if they were showing off. They unloaded their bombs above the city, mostly in the residential districts. In a few minutes the whole city seemed to be blazing. The white wooden houses of the workers began to flare up and the fires spread, block after block. The city water department building collapsed. The telephone building collapsed, too, and civil telephone service stopped suddenly. The plant of *Stalingrad Pravda*, the local newspaper, was bombed. Factories and public offices were bombed and destroyed.

The bombing reached its peak at seven o'clock in the evening. By that time the City Soviet's offices had been destroyed and the government was operating from a network of cellars. The decision was made to continue to publish *Stalingrad Pravda*. When it was discovered that the plant was wrecked, a car was summoned to take the material to the tractor factory, which had a printing press. That night a special issue of *Pravda* would be printed there. As the car moved, it passed the blazing oil tanks on the banks of the Volga and the slopes of Mamayev Hill, the viewpoint of the city, which were covered with still shapes, bodies. The editor of *Pravda* did not know it yet, but the German air attack that had come as a total surprise had killed forty thousand citizens of Stalingrad. Nearly every wooden building in the city was burned, including acres of workers' housing in the suburbs. The flames made it possible to read a newspaper forty miles away. It was a raid in the traditions of Rotterdam, Warsaw, Belgrade, and Kiev, a raid to kill people and sow terror.

NIGHT RAIDS

Night raids against Stalingrad were started at the same time as the day raids. A characteristic feature was that the raids were carried out chiefly on moonlit nights. As a rule, the airplanes came from the direction of the moon toward the center of the fires started in the daytime. They came singly or in small groups, spaced in time and altitude. The majority of the raids took place at altitudes from twenty-five hundred to five thousand meters.

The searchlights had to operate on moonlit nights and oftentimes with broken cloudiness, making it possible for the airplanes to escape behind clouds. Operation in the area of the town itself was particularly difficult. The haze from the dust raised by the bombing, and the thick smoke of fires hanging sometimes in a continuous curtain over the town often made it impossible for the searchlights to operate. Taking this into account, the enemy frequently approached the town after the release of bombs, covering themselves with a belt of smoke stretching toward the town, in this way avoiding illumination by searchlights.

Soviet General Staff Study,
Battle for Stalingrad

In twelve hours the panzers moved thirty-six miles and reached the Volga north of the city and advance units reached the suburb of Rynok, where the tramcars were still running. When they had encountered resistance at the Barrikady factory in Rynok, and silenced it with the guns of their tanks, they looked over the carnage of the battle scene. They saw pieces of bodies covered with bits of calico and lace. They had been fighting women, the women workers of the factory. Some of the tankers vomited.

A RUSSIAN WOMAN SOLDIER REMEMBERS

No one had an easy time at the front. That was especially true for us Russian girls.

From the outset girls enlisted even when they had to forge their birth dates from age 17 to 19. But soon we were being called up too. Most of us thought the war was something heroically romantic and the very first brush with reality had a sobering effect.

(continued next page)

(*continued from preceding page*)

Yes, it was difficult everywhere. The badly wounded were so helpless they had to be cared for. The wards were crowded. The air was heavy with scents that were anything but perfume. The younger men who were recovering courted the nurses insistently. There was no threatening them with the front line—that was where they were all headed anyway. What was a girl to say to a soldier who was going to battle tomorrow, whose chance of returning was very slim and who, on top of everything else, was so attractive—see you after the war?

It is easy to talk about it today. At that time, death stood ready and waiting behind each and every one of us. Besides, life will go its own way, even if there's a war on. Marriages were solemnized. Regimental orders pronounced couples man and wife and changed the wife's name to that of her husband. Abortions, banned in the country in those days, were permitted at field hospitals. Those who wished to have their babies were demobbed, provided with an allowance and sent home. Many of us remained single all our lives. The happiness of front line love was short lived.

There had been virtually no resistance to General Paulus's march. The morrow should bring the culmination of the Fuehrer's current dream. Stalingrad would be theirs.

That was what the Germans said. But the Russians were ready to dispute them. That night of August 23, the Military Commission sent General Yeremenko a message:

You have enough strength to annihilate the enemy. Combine the aviation of both fronts and use it to smash the enemy. Set up armored trains and station them on the Stalingrad belt railroad. Use smoke to deceive the enemy. Keep after the enemy not only in the daytime but also at night. Above all do not give way to panic, do not let the enemy scare you, and keep faith in your own strength.

There was no question about it, the Russians were going to fight for Stalingrad.

PART VII
THE DESTRUCTION OF A CITY

20

STALINGRAD MUST DIE!

Hitler's preoccupation with Stalingrad had now become intense. After the 4th Panzer Army reached the banks of the Volga on August 23 he kept pressing General Paulus to hurry up and capture Stalingrad. Goering showed up for the situation meetings and announced that his Luftwaffe's air reconnaissance to the north of Stalingrad had not uncovered any Soviet troop concentrations worth bothering about. So what was the delay all about? Hitler could not understand.

The more he thought about Stalingrad, the more determined he became to make an example of the city, and that had been carried out admirably. Just as soon as Paulus captured Stalingrad the female population was to be deported to become slave laborers and whores for the Germans, and the male population was to be exterminated.

The fires started by the German bombers burned all night. The bombing had destroyed the water mains, and the fire fighters were nearly helpless. All they could do was rescue people and try to pull down burning buildings to keep the fires from spreading.

Dar Gova, the southern section of Stalingrad down by the Volga, was a nest of workers' houses, white bungalows surrounded by picket fences and flower gardens. By morning this pleasant workers' community had become a wasteland of ash and charred wood. The nearby sugar plant was in ruins. Only a huge grain elevator still stood.

North of the elevator the Tsaritsa Gorge marked the line of the city center. Here were a hundred blocks of stores, office buildings, and apartments, bounded on the east by the Volga and the ferry landing and an avenue along the Volga shore. Farther north this was cut by another deep ravine, the Krutoy Gully. On the western side of the Krutoy Gully lay another residential district, which had also been destroyed by flame.

In the center of the city the railroad station was partially destroyed, and east of it the office buildings occupied by the city and party authorities had been wrecked. *Pravda*'s building on Red Square was in ruins, and so was the post office on the east side of the square. On the northeast corner stood the ruins of Univermag department store. Its most useful part now was the huge warehouse beneath the store.

North of Red Square some of the white-brick apartment buildings still stood on the wide boulevards, many of them now rutted and pocked with bomb craters and shell holes. Most of the concrete and brick buildings, even those still standing, had been gutted by the flames. Here and there a tall smokestack rose over the rubble that had been a factory.

Some of the oil storage tanks along the Volga had been set aflame, and they had spewed their fiery contents down into the water, to set fire to the docks and jetties. Most of the boats and ships pulled up at the docks had been bombed out, sunk, or burned.

That night Luftwaffe General Richthofen told his officers that they had made the equivalent of two thousand bomber sorties on Stalingrad. He was eminently satisfied with the destruction he had wrought. This should help bring the Russians to their knees.

As one German soldier wrote home: "The whole city is on fire; on the Fuehrer's orders our Luftwaffe has sent it up on flames. That's what the Russians need, to stop them resisting. . . ."

Late that night, August 23, General Yeremenko prepared the daily situation report which must be sent to Moscow before midnight. It told how Germans had pierced the Russian defenses on the left flank in the Vertyachi-Peskovada area, and how in the Latashinka sector they had gotten to the Volga. The front was thus cut in two. The German units that had entered the northern suburbs of Stalingrad had been halted, but the tractor factory was under fire and the two rail lines linking Stalingrad with the north and northwest and river communications were all in

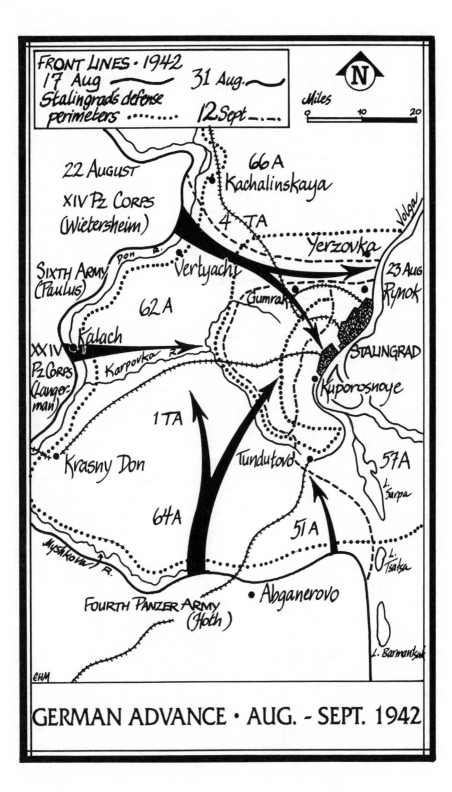

FRONT LINES · 1942
17 Aug ———— 31 Aug ∿
Stalingrad's defense
perimeters ········ 12 Sept —·—·

N

Miles
0   10   20

22 AUGUST
XIV PZ CORPS
(Wietersheim)

66 A
Kachalinskaya

4 TA

Volga

Yerzovka

23 AUG
Rynok

SIXTH ARMY
(Paulus)

Don R.

Vertyachi

62 A

Gumrak

STALINGRAD

XXIV
PZ CORPS
(Langer-
man)

Kalach

Karpovka R.

Kuporosnoye

1 TA

Krasny Don

Tundutovo

57 A
L. Sarpa

64 A

51 A

L. Tsatsa

Mishkova R.

FOURTH PANZER ARMY
(Hoth)

· Abganerovo

L. Barmantsak

EHM

GERMAN ADVANCE · AUG. - SEPT. 1942

danger. The bombing of the city had hurt grievously and impeded military operations. All the officials of the area, including Commissar Khrushchev, signed the report. Then Yeremenko telephoned Stalin in Moscow. He told the dictator honestly that the situation was very bad and that some of the party and civil officials wanted to blow up the factories and transfer everything movable across the Volga. He and Commissar Khrushchev opposed the idea.

Stalin was furious and cursing. He was also adamant:

Evacuation and destruction of plants would be interpreted as a decision to surrender Stalingrad. He said the State Defense Committee forbade it. That meant Stalin forbade it. The defense must be organized to stop the Germans.

"Not a step back" now became the watchword of Stalingrad.

That night Stalin ordered General Alexander Vasilevsky from Moscow to fly to Stalingrad and assess the situation and give General Gordov a hand in rescuing the 64th Army.

On August 24 at 4:30 in the morning Group Drumpen of the 16th Panzer Division launched an attack against Spartakovka, the northern-most industrial suburb of Stalingrad. The attack began with bombing by the Stukas, and then the tanks, grenadiers, artillery, and engineers moved forward. The infantry was absent, because in the forty-mile run of August 23 the 16th Panzer Division had outrun the 3rd and 30th Motorized divisions. The 3rd Motorized Division was twelve miles back and the 60th was twenty-two miles behind the panzers. All three units were little islands in a sea of Russian hatred.

General Hube, seeing his danger out in front, ordered his troops into a "hedgehog," a circular pattern with the division's heavy artillery in the center, covering all angles.

Still, the advance on the twenty-third had been so rapid, and the Russians so stunned, that the Germans expected an easy victory. Instead, they ran into a rocklike defense in the northern outskirts of the city where the NKVD men had organized the defense. On the grounds of the tractor factory, General Feklenko's troops fought. At Tinguta, General Golikov's tanks stopped the German advance.

The suburb, they found, was heavily fortified, and every building was a barricade. A dominating hill known to the Germans as "the big mushroom" bristled with pillboxes, machine-gun nests, and mortars.

Rifle battalions and workers militia from the factories and elements of the 62nd Army were here. They had their orders from Stalin: "Not a step back."

By noon it was apparent to the Germans that with the forces available they could not take Spartakovka. The Russians launched a counterstroke and had two of General Hube's combat groups on the defensive.

Those T-34 tanks from the tank factory, some of them still unpainted and without gunsights, attacked straight from the assembly lines. Some of them penetrated the German lines as far as the command post of the 64th Panzer Grenadier Regiment. The one success of the Germans this morning was the capture by the Panzer Jaegers of one ferry landing on the Volga, the one that linked the city with the railroad to Kazakhstan. They then prevented the Russians from receiving reinforcements across the river from that part of the east bank.

But by day's end the position of the 16th Panzer Division was perilous. The Soviets were holding the approaches to the northern part of the city and were bringing in troops from Voronezh. The success of the German effort depended on holding and strengthening that slender corridor across the land from Kalach to the Volga. In this day's fighting the Germans had actually been forced back more than a mile.

The 3rd Motorized Division had left the Don bridgehead at the same time as 16th Panzer Division on the morning of August 23, but had been sidetracked, first by taking a covering position in the Kuzmichi area, and then by the capture of a Russian supply column, which yielded jeeps and tractors and trucks. While they were assembling the loot they were attacked, first by a section of Russian tanks and then by the 35th Russian Rifle Division, reinforced by tanks, which was driving south to counter the Germans.

The Soviet 35th Rifle Division moved south in the rear of the 3rd Motorized Infantry Division and overran the rear sections of the XIV Panzer Corps and forced its way between the bridgehead formed by the Germans and the Tartar Ditch, and stopped the German infantry from closing the gap and reaching Stalingrad. As a result the German communications were cut, and the 16th Panzers were out on a lonely limb. The 3rd Motorized Division did manage to link up with the 16th Panzer Division, but now it had to be a defensive linkup over eighteen miles extending from the Volga to the Tartar Ditch. The Russians were attacking from all sides. Supplies could reach the Volga only by air or by panzer convoy along the narrow corridor.

On August 24 the Russian 62nd Army withdrew slowly along the Karpovka River and the rail line. General Hoth had forced the 64th Army back to Tundutovo, but it was holding.

At his command post General Paulus read the situation reports of his three divisions. There was no more talk in the command post about "lightning victory." Now the problem was to preserve these three units, each of them perilously open to attack. Paulus needed reinforcements and supplies. He called on the Luftwaffe to begin dropping ammunition and food to the 16th Panzers.

On August 25 the Regional Communist Party Committee of Stalingrad proclaimed a state of siege of the city:

> Comrades and citizens of Stalingrad!
>   We shall never surrender the city of our birth to the depredations of the German invader. Each single one of us must apply himself to the task of defending our beloved town, our homes, and our families. Let us barricade every street; transform every district, every block, every house, into an impregnable fortress.

The 6th German Army now tried to break into Stalingrad from the west. A group of tanks advanced toward the central section of the city. They were halted by an improvised combat group of tanks and infantry under the command of General Kovalenko. This group relieved the 87th Rifle Division at Bolshaya Rossoshka. They held for two days against a force of seventy German tanks, which had surrounded them, and they destroyed twenty-seven of the tanks. Their principal weapon was the Molotov cocktail.

General Yeremenko's aim was to force the Germans to abandon their corridor through the Don pocket to the Volga.

The Russians made several attacks, but their problem was that they did not have the strength to carry them through. The fighting was more or less a standoff, with neither side able to make substantial gains.

The city was still burning from the fires started by the Luftwaffe bombing. The downtown district was a pile of rubble. The NKVD prison had been emptied; there were more important matters than punishment of the citizens. The insane asylum had been opened, and the crazed wandered about the ruins not knowing where to go or what to do. The military and civil authorities had to worry about civilians, getting them across the Volga and to safety now that the main ferry landing was threatened by the Germans.

On August 25 Colonel Semyon Gorokhov appeared with a brigade of six thousand men, straight from the east. He was assigned to the tractor factory defense. More troops, marines from the far east and factory workers, were put on a line along the Mokraya Mechetka River, a mile above the tractor factory.

The Germans came back in the air and tried to stampede the population, bombing the embankment that was now jammed with women and children waiting for ferries to take them to the east side of the river. The Stukas bombed the rescue vessels, too, sinking several of them. The Volga was full of bodies that afternoon.

During the next three days, there was no change in the fighting for the city. To the west the roads were jammed with retreating soldiers and peasants from the collective farms, heading east with what they could carry. The ferry stages were crowded with refugees waiting to go across. General Chuikov made a trip to the east side of the river and described the scene:

> From time to time a German shell would burst in the river, but this indiscriminate shelling was not troublesome. From a distance we could see that the pier was crowded with people. As we drew closer many wounded were being carried out of the trenches, bomb craters, and shelters. There were also many people with bundles and suitcases who had been hiding from German bombs and shells.
>
> When they saw the ferry arriving they rushed to the pier with the one idea of getting away to the other side of the river, away from their wrecked houses, away from the city that had become a hell. Their eyes were grim and there were trickles of tears running through the dust and soot on their grimy faces. The children, suffering from thirst and hunger, were not crying but simply whining and stretching out their little arms to the water of the Volga.

On August 29 General Hoth launched a new drive of the 4th Panzer Army from Abganerovo. The attack went very well and penetrated both the 64th and 62nd Russian armies. The Russian 126th Division panicked. The 208th Division surrendered en masse. Thousands of troops were captured without a fight.

There seemed to be a good opportunity for the Germans to encircle the 64th and 62nd armies, if General Paulus would attack from the north as Hoth came from the south. But Paulus was too much worried about the perilous position of his army, strung out as it was, and he would not move. When the Russian pressure was relieved on September 2, Paulus sent his tanks to make contact with Hoth's, but it was too late by the time they arrived. The encirclement was perfect, but there was no one inside the trap. The Russians had withdrawn in the nick of time.

But the Germans were now pressing hard on the city from all directions. The morale of the Russian armies was extremely low, and some commanders took draconian measures to stop desertions and surrenders, shooting down their own soldiers accused of cowardice in the face of the enemy. One regimental commander lined up his troops and walked down the line shooting every tenth man of the first one hundred in the regiment. The pile of bodies was meant to be a warning to the others to stand fast.

On September 2 the Germans undertook another bombing and bombardment of Stalingrad. The city was now one massive smoking ruin, and the fires could be seen for miles. Worst was the fact that the ferries, the only way of bringing food and supplies and reinforcements across the river, were under constant German bombing and bombardment. Only by moving supplies at night were the Russians able to keep going, and somehow they did.

The 62nd Army attacked General Hoth's 4th Panzer Division to keep it from linking up with Paulus, but the attack failed. The 64th and 62nd armies retreated slowly, steadily toward Stalingrad. General Paulus was trying to keep his flank from the west protected, and General Yeremenko was trying to bring in troops from the east and north.

In Moscow on August 26 the State Defense Committee had appointed General Zhukov as Stalin's deputy commander of the Soviet forces. The next day Zhukov was called to the Kremlin and briefed by Stalin on the situation at Stalingrad. At the time of that meeting General Vasilevsky and Commissar Malenkov, who was Stalin's eyes and ears, and Minister Malyshev were in Stalingrad. Zhukov was to go to Stalingrad within the next twenty-four hours.

Stalin went over his plans with Zhukov. He was sending new armies to Stalingrad. Zhukov then went to the new Stalingrad Front headquarters at Malaya Ivanovka. Yeremenko had moved here from the center of Stalingrad, because his defenses had been cut in two. The Stalingrad Front stretched from north of the Paulus breach from Babka on the Don to Yerzovka on the Volga. The Southeast Front contained the city and the southern area behind it. Yeremenko had moved to this new headquarters, twenty-five miles to the north, near Ivanovka. General Gordov, Yeremenko's deputy for this front, was not there, but they were briefed by two of his operators. Zhukov was not well impressed with their recognition of the situation. When he met Gordov, he was better impressed with the grasp of the problem, but the future looked anything but good. The three armies that Stalin was sending were not the best, and they were badly equipped.

Stalin sent an urgent message to Zhukov:

> The situation in Stalingrad is getting worse. The enemy is 3 versts [two miles] from Stalingrad. They can take Stalingrad today or tomorrow, unless the northern group of troops gives help urgently. Get the commanders of the troops of the north and northwest Stalingrad Front to attack the enemy without delay and get to the relief of Stalingraders. No delay can be tolerated. Delay at this moment is equivalent to a crime. Throw in all aircraft to help Stalingrad. In Stalingrad itself there is very little aviation left. Report at once on all measures taken.
>
> Stalin

Zhukov telephoned Moscow. Stalin upbraided him over the telephone, but Zhukov said his people were not ready to attack and all he could do was launch all the air strikes possible until they were. Stalin listened, which was rare for him.

On September 5, under Stalin's urging, Zhukov supervised an attack by the 24th Army. It failed, but Stalin was pleased because the attack had drawn German attention away from Stalingrad for a moment.

The Russian emphasis shifted to air counterattack, and all available aircraft were moved to the Stalingrad Front from the east.

ZHUKOV

It took a while for General Zhukov to get to know Stalin and for Stalin to appreciate his finest general. Zhukov had come to Moscow out of the Siberian steppe where he had decisively routed the Japanese army in two major encounters in 1938 on the Mongolian-Manchukuo border.

The Japanese had been testing the water to decide whether to strike north against Russia to secure the natural resources they needed to carry on the China war, or to strike south against British Malaya and the Dutch East Indies. When the Kwantung Army attacked the first time, Zhukov sent them reeling back with a loss of ten thousand men before Emperor Hirohito. The Kwantung Army took the bit in its teeth and tried again, this time at Nomonhan. A whole Japanese division, reinforced with planes and tanks and special troops, hit the Mongolian cavalry. Zhukov lost no time in rushing up his first-class Siberian divisions, backed by tanks and aircraft.

In a month the Japanese division was wiped out and the Japanese lost most of their tanks and planes. They admitted to a loss of twenty-five thousand men, but the figure was actually much higher. The Russian tanks and planes were so far superior to those of the Japanese that the Tokyo generals decided they must rebuild their army before they would be ready to attack the Russians, and made the decision to strike south.

But even though the actions against Japan brought Zhukov to Moscow as deputy chief of the Russian general staff, he did not have Stalin's confidence any more than any of the generals. Stalin operated on the policy of divide and rule. For every Zhukov he had a Budenny, who was still studying the tactics of World War I.

After the Germans began their three-pronged drive, and the danger to Leningrad seemed worst, Stalin sent Zhukov to stop the Germans before Moscow, and Zhukov did.

When that had been done, Zhukov argued for a new Soviet offensive in the winter and spring of 1942 against Army Group Center, which was in confusion. But Stalin was obsessed with winning the war on all fronts at once and issued orders for a general offensive. A strategy meeting was called in the general staff and Zhukov and Marshal Vasilevsky argued for a single strong offensive. At the end of the

(continued next page)

(*continued from preceding page*)
meeting Stalin decreed that they should conduct a general offensive.

"You were wasting your time," Marshal Boris Shaposhnikov told Zhukov at the end of the meeting. "Stalin had already made up his mind before you spoke, and the orders had already been issued."

"Then why did he ask me for my opinion?" Zhukov asked.

That's how Stalin was, said Marshal Shaposhnikov.

But Zhukov soon learned how to deal with Stalin. The secret was to make Stalin believe that the opinion being given him was Stalin's own idea. Ultimately this ploy, plus a series of successes, brought Stalin to accept Zhukov's opinions, and he was able to speak up and argue with Stalin as could no other general.

One day after the initial successes of the Stalingrad campaign, Stalin was again talking about a general offensive.

Curtly, Zhukov said it would not be wise.

After the meeting, General Rokossovsky, who had been jailed by Stalin during the purges, expressed surprise that Zhukov spoke up. "You should not irritate him," he warned.

Zhukov laughed. "He has to be told the truth," he said.

South of Stalingrad General Hoth's 4th Panzer Army began a drive that the general hoped would take them into Stalingrad, but as they approached the hilly suburban towns of Krasnoyarmeysk and Kupersnoye, the Russians began to dig in, and a new sort of war was begun. The panzers were stalled in the narrow streets of the towns, and the Russians sniped at them and picked off the tanks with Molotov cocktails. The German artillery came into use in point-blank street fighting. The Germans began to take the sort of casualties that the Russians had been taking for months. Company commanders and platoon leaders were shot down one by one. This was an entirely new sort of war to the Germans, although they did not recognize that it would be the mark of the whole Stalingrad campaign. The Germans did not change their ways. They continued to use the tactics of size and force that had so far brought their victories. In other words, they refused to recognize the change and refused to learn street-fighting techniques.

At the moment, outside the city streets, it did not seem so important. On September 9 the 4th Panzer Army reached the hills above the Volga at Kuporosnoye.

In Stalingrad the defenses were manned by the 62nd and 64th armies, or what was left of them. The 112th Rifle Division had only 150 men left. The 187th had 180 men, and the 390th had 300 men. The 99th Tank Brigade consisted of 180 men with sixty tanks. This was all the armor left of the 62nd Army. Stalingrad was now divided into three sectors, north, central, and southern. About 40,000 men and one hundred tanks held the central sector.

In command of the army came General Vasili Ivanovich Chuikov to replace General Lopatin. Zhukov had flown to Moscow to confer with Stalin and they had planned the defenses, including this change.

The Germans had advanced and cut off the 62nd Army, which was isolated in a horseshoe, with one tip at Rynok on the Volga and the other at Kuporosnoye, twenty miles downstream. The Germans had complete air superiority, and most of the antiaircraft guns had been moved to the east bank of the Volga.

Morale was so low in Stalingrad that several of General Chuikov's staff officers claimed illness and deserted across the Volga. Chuikov went to work. He gave pep talks to raise morale. The War Council of the Stalingrad Front issued a new directive: "The enemy must be smashed at Stalingrad."

This directive did help morale. The shattered remnants of the 62nd Army got ready to fight again.

A RUSSIAN SOLDIER REMEMBERS

The northwestern perimeter of the city is the scene of savage encounters and every street and every house has been turned into a battlefield. There is hand-to-hand fighting in the suburbs. The first floor of a building is often occupied by Germans while the Red Army continues to hold the second and third floors. Floorboards are yanked up and gaps made in ceilings and walls. There is fighting in apartments and corridors.

We drew back to Stalingrad not because it was easier to defend. Our troops know what Stalingrad and the Volga mean to the country. Especially Stalingrad. But we are hard pressed. Although the Germans are suffering appalling losses, our casualties are heavy, too. We are also sustaining considerable losses in manpower and weapons. On top of

(*continued next page*)

(continued from preceding page)

everything else, this theatre of war is a difficult one. Communications are bad, and the contours of the land are not an asset. In spite of these difficulties not a single one of the men fighting for Stalingrad has entertained the idea of surrendering the city, of withdrawing. We want victory. Today we think of it with still greater intensity than we did two or even three weeks ago.

> —Russian soldier's statement in
> September 1942, from Vladimir
> Karpov's *Russia at War*

On September 12 General Paulus flew to Vinnitsa, the new Fuehrer headquarters in the Ukraine, and discussed his concerns. He wanted some more of the allied armies to shore up the left flank of the 6th Army along the Don River. Hitler promised to look into the matter. Hitler was depressed about the way matters were going in the Caucasus, where the Germans were bogged down. He brightened when Paulus said he expected to have possession of Stalingrad in a few days.

On September 13 the Russian 62nd Army's bridgehead averaged about five miles. The important points were Rynok on the north (the site of the first German breakthrough), Spartakovka, called the Garden City, the Stalingrad tractor plant, the Barrikady plant, and the Barrikady housing area. Then on the riverbank to the south lay the Red October plant and its housing district. Then came Mamayev Hill, the high point of the city. This was the borderline between industrial Stalingrad and the business and residential districts of the south, with two railroad stations, the Univermag department store, and many other buildings that would soon become famous in the story of the struggle for Stalingrad.

21

When General Chuikov became commander of the 62nd Army, he told Khrushchev that he intended to lead the army in valiant fighting. "We shall either hold the city or die there," he said. Then he began considering ways to avoid the latter contingency.

Chuikov had noted some of the propensities of the German Wehrmacht that seemed to him to indicate points of weakness. One was the German infantry and tank delay in attacking until they had air support from the Luftwaffe. This was the standard *Blitzkrieg* tactic which had begun in Poland. Just as long as the Germans had air superiority the tactic had worked very well. Another perceived weakness of the Wehrmacht was the dependence of the infantry on tanks. The panzers must attack before the infantry would move. The third weakness was the tendency of the Germans to avoid close combat. Chuikov had noticed that the soldiers began fighting their weapons usually when they were still out of effective range of the enemy.

General Chuikov told himself that the way to fight the Germans was to force the infantry to fight in close combat and to take steps to avoid attack by air and tanks.

"Every German soldier must be made to feel that he is living under the muzzle of a Russian gun," Chuikov said.

One of Chuikov's first tasks was to discover where the headquarters of his own 62nd Army was actually located. Nobody seemed to know. Yeremenko thought it was in the bunker in the Tsaritsa Gorge, but it was not. The general wandered about the city, looking at the ineffectual street barricades, and finally found an officer who could direct him to the command post, which was at the foot of the Mamayev Hill. He scrambled up the hill to a dugout, where he found General Nikolai Krylov, his chief of staff. Krylov was on the telephone shouting at the commander of an armored formation who had withdrawn to the bank of the Volga without orders, deserting a hilltop, thus putting his headquarters behind that of the 62nd Army. The armor commander was brought in, given a few hours to put his command post back where it ought to be, and threatened that otherwise he would be given the treatment for traitors, which was to shoot them out of hand.

General Golikov, the deputy front commander, arrived at the command post, and Chuikov asked him for several extra divisions. He was facing perhaps fourteen reinforced German divisions supported by one thousand planes of the 4th Luftflotte. He had three armored brigades, with only one tank among the three, and several infantry divisions, each equal in strength to a regular battalion. He had an infantry division which had no heavy weapons. He had two infantry brigades near full strength. His 8th Air Force was hardly to be counted against the German air superiority. He had the continued presence of General Lopatin, former commander of the army, who was so completely dispirited that he was infecting the staff. (That day two senior officers disappeared across the river, convinced by Lopatin that fighting was no use.)

Rousing messages from Yeremenko and Khrushchev did something to restore morale, but what really helped was the news that reinforcements were on the way: ten divisions, two armored corps, and eight armored brigades. The 62nd Army would receive ten thousand men and one thousand tons of supply within the next three days.

That night General Chuikov and General Krylov stayed up late planning an attack to secure the landing stages, which were within the range of German guns. But when morning came, General Chuikov was awakened by the thunder of guns and bombers. A German offensive, starting with bombs from the Luftwaffe and an artillery barrage, had forestalled him. The Germans had attacked first. The German LI Army Corps had launched a two-pronged attack against central Stalingrad, with two panzer divisions, one motorized division, and three infantry divisions. By afternoon they had overrun the machine tractor station and its housing area and the airfield, and had nearly reached the bank of the Volga.

The main objective of the Germans was three-hundred-foot Mamayev Hill, the site of the 62nd Army command post, and the key point in central Stalingrad. The Germans hoped here to break through to the Volga.

The constant bombing and shelling of the hill disrupted the Russian communications, so under fire they moved the command post from the hill to the Tsaritsa Gorge command post. Chuikov had no food that day. His lunch was being cooked in a hut on the side of the hill when the hut was wrecked by a German bomb. The cook then tried to get dinner from a field kitchen, but the field kitchen was also destroyed by a bomb. The cook and the waitress then gave up, and the generals went hungry.

The German offensive gained ground that day largely because the Luftwaffe came over in groups of fifty and sixty planes and bombed the Russians nonstop as they tried to counterattack. By noon the Germans had brought into action tanks and motorized infantry. The main blow was aimed at the central railroad station, and although the Russians caused heavy losses, the Germans kept coming. Whole columns of tanks and motorized infantry were breaking into the center of the city. The Germans seemed to believe the battle was then won, and they began drinking and singing to celebrate. Drunken soldiers were lurching along the streets in the city center. The front line was only half a mile from the command post in the gully. Chuikov's last reserve of nineteen tanks was on the outskirts of the city. He ordered a battalion, nine tanks, to come to the command post. When they arrived, he assembled officers and men and sent a task force from the railroad station to the landing stage. The Russian snipers watched the enemy at play and shot them down. Hundreds of Germans were killed, but German troops kept flooding into the center of Stalingrad. The illusion of victory persisted because the Germans could see the Volga. The fighting came to within eight hundred yards of the command post. That night Chuikov ordered the rest of his reserve of nineteen tanks, to stop the Germans from breaking through to the Volga.

On the second day of this German offensive, September 14, the promised division, the Rodimtsev Division, began to arrive on the east side of the Volga. General Chuikov decided to leave the artillery on the east bank and bring only troops and antitank guns across the river.

But first they had to get across, and while they were coming, the 62nd Army, or what was left of it, had to fight to hold central Stalingrad.

Chuikov called in Colonel Sarayev of the NKVD. He sent him to organize his men into squads of ten and twenty in the strategic buildings. These "storm groups" were the Chuikov answer to the Wehrmacht fighting technique. He created a series of minifortresses in the city, commanding street intersections. Nazi panzers were funneled into approach roads where the artillery across the river had them zeroed. When the tanks bogged down, the storm groups then dealt with the German infantry. By fighting at extremely close range the storm groups eliminated the threat of the Luftwaffe. The planes could not come in without endangering their own troops.

Two regiments of the new division were assigned to clear the Germans from Mamayev Hill in the south to the Tsaritsa River in the north. The third regiment was to occupy Mamayev Hill and dig in. That night they crossed the river in launches and any other craft they could lay their hands on. They landed in the darkness and scrambled up the incline. They got lost and stumbled over rubble and wreckage, but they managed to form a defense line on the edge of Mamayev Hill. On September 15 the fighting for the hill began again, and the central railway station changed hands several times. By the end of the day, the hill was a no-man's-land, but on the morning of September 16 the Russians recaptured it. But that was not to be the end of that struggle. The combat over the hill continued almost uninterruptedly until the end of the Battle of Stalingrad.

That night the battle raged only five hundred yards from General Chuikov's bunker. Just before dusk the tank commander arrived to report that his last tank had just been put out of action. The fighting began to subside. Chuikov took stock. The Germans had advanced to occupy many buildings in the center of the city. Again they had reached the central railway station, but it kept changing hands. It was vicious street fighting now everywhere in central Stalingrad.

The Guardsmen of General A. I. Rodimtsev's division were fighting elements of the 22nd Panzer Division and the 71st and 295th infantries. Most of the fighting was on Mamayev Hill, and it looked as though the position would be lost, so Chuikov brought over the last regiment of the division and posted it on the hill to be ready to fight at dawn.

The German attack on the city caught a number of civilians still in their houses. The Germans slaughtered some and let others go. It all depended on the mood of the soldiers; they had a license from Hitler to kill anyone at all.

On September 16, Luftwaffe General Richthofen wrote in his diary that the "mopping up" in Stalingrad was going very slowly in spite of the fact that the Russians were very weak there. "The truth is that our own troops are both few in numbers and listless in spirit, and the High Command already has its eyes turned toward Astrakhan."

On September 16 the Guardsmen of Rodimtsev's division were so beset by three German divisions that even the coming of the last regiment, the 42nd, seemed a questionable gesture, but the troops assailed the summit of Mamayev Hill and captured it. The losses were very heavy: when the first platoon got to the top of the hill, only six men were left of the thirty who had started. The Germans were as badly off. One sergeant of the 71st Division complained to the division intelligence officer that there were only nine men left of his entire company. The others were dead on the slopes of the hill.

One German soldier described this war:

I know in my bones what our watchword "courage" means—from days and nights of resigned desperation, and from the insurmountable fear which one continues to accept even though one's brain has ceased to function normally. I know that one can call on all the saints in heaven for help without believing in any God, and it is this that I must describe, even though it means plunging back into a nightmare for nights at a time, for that is the substance of my task to reanimate with all the intensity I can summon, those distant cries from the slaughter-house.

Too many people learn about war with no inconvenience to themselves. They are about Verdun or Stalingrad without comprehension, sitting in a comfortable armchair, their feet beside the fire, preparing to go about their business the next day, as usual. One should really read such accounts under compulsion, in discomfort, considering oneself fortunate not to be describing the events in a letter home, writing from a hole in the mud. One should read about war in the worst circumstances, when everything is going badly, remembering that the torments of peace are trivial, and not worth any white hairs. Nothing is really serious in the tranquility of peace. Only an idiot could be disturbed by a question of salary. One should read about war standing up, late at night, when one is tired, as I am writing about it now at dawn, while my asthma attack wears off. Those who read about Verdun and Stalingrad and expound theories later to friends over a cup of coffee, haven't understood anything. Those who can read such accounts with a silent smile, smile as they walk, and feel lucky to be alive. . . .

THE RUSSIANS' CONTEMPT FOR DEATH

The Germans poured on the lead. A bitter joke in circulation from Stalingrad times told of a soldier going into battle carrying 150

(continued next page)

(*continued from preceding page*)
cartridges; when he was carried to the field hospital he had 151—he
hadn't even had a chance to fire his gun.

Contempt of death was also written about and acclaimed as valor.
But by 1942 there was too much of this contempt going around and the
distance to victory was as great as ever. Sometimes the going gets so
hard that death seems a welcome deliverance. These are no empty
words.

Gradually they stopped writing about this contempt of death. The
mission of the soldier was not to die with dashing defiance, but to kill
the enemy.

—A Russian soldier

22

The fighting at Stalingrad settled on the central railroad station. On the
morning of September 17 the Russian defenders came under heavy attack
from a force of Germans with automatic rifles, supported by twenty tanks.
The Russians were driven out, recaptured the station, were driven out
again. The station changed hands four times that day, but at the end of
the day the Russians had it again. The whole area was strewn with
burned-out tanks and hundreds of bodies of men of both sides.

That night the Tsaritsa bunker became untenable because German
artillery fire was too intense. General Chuikov moved his headquarters
command post then, circuitously, by road to Ferry 62 and then by
armored launch back across the Volga. In the process, they lingered and
nearly missed the last ferry just after sunrise. Chuikov had to run for it,
barely got on board, and instructed the helmsman to come back to the
east bank for the rest of the staff. When he counted noses, he discovered
that several of his senior staff members were missing. They had
evaporated into the crowds on the east bank, so downcast about the
prospects of victory that they deserted.

Chuikov's new command post was on the Volga bank, underneath some oil tanks. They used some half-sunk barges and dug trenches for shelter. The engineers set to work to build dugouts. Now, instead of in the center of the city, the command post was located eleven miles from the fighting.

In the center of the city the fighting went on day after day. Since September 14 about fifty Russians had been holding the big grain elevator, south of the Tsaritsa Gorge. On the night of September 17 they were reinforced by a platoon of marines. The fighting was merciless. The Germans came up in a tank with a white flag and called on the Russians to surrender. The Russians refused, and told the Germans to leave their tank where it was. When the Germans tried to jump into the tank, the Russians blew it up.

On September 18 the swarm of Luftwaffe planes that was forever above Stalingrad suddenly disappeared. They had been drawn off to German forces fighting against an attack mounted by Zhukov to the northwest to relieve the pressure on Stalingrad. The 1st Guards Army launched this attack at 5:30 on the morning of September 18 after a preliminary artillery bombardment.

The Russians gained three thousand yards, but were then stopped by a German infantry counterattack. That day Zhukov ordered General Chuikov to launch a counterattack in northern Stalingrad to clear the enemy away and link up with the northwest armies. But by afternoon, Chuikov knew that the Russian attack in the north had failed. He did not need messages. The Luftwaffe planes suddenly reappeared over Stalingrad, as suddenly as they had left.

On September 19 Chuikov staged an attack northward as ordered, to join another attack by the forces in the northwest. Chuikov's troops made some progress, but the northwest attack failed again. On September 20 the Luftwaffe set about one task: to blow the main railroad station to pieces.

"After the bombing—and an artillery bombardment—the station buildings were on fire. The walls burst apart, the iron buckled, but the men went on fighting."

A major strongpoint on the northern edge of the city was the big grain elevator. For three days the Germans had pounded the elevator with artillery, setting the grain on fire. Here is a Russian account of the fighting:

> In the elevator the grain was burning. The water in the machine guns evaporated, the wounded were thirsty but there was no water near.

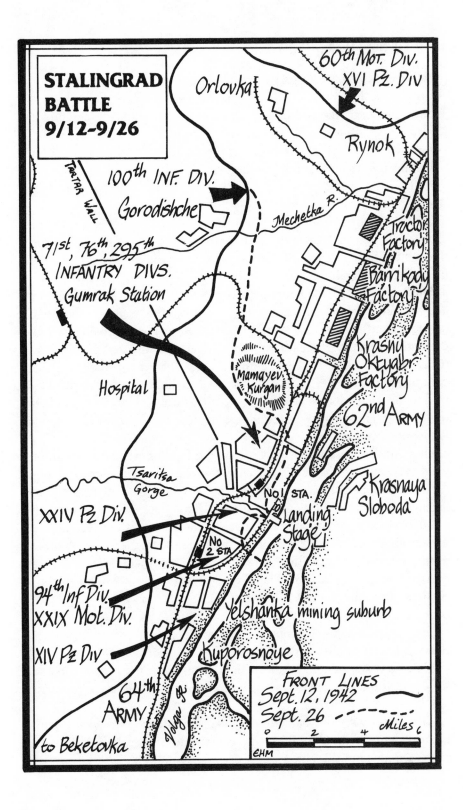

STALINGRAD
BATTLE
9/12–9/26

Orlovka

60th Mot. Div.
XVI Pz. Div

Rynok

TARTAR WALL

100th INF. DIV.
Gorodishche

Mechetka R.

Tractor Factory

71st, 76th, 295th
INFANTRY DIVS.
Gumrak Station

Barrikady Factory

Krasny Oktyabr Factory

Mamayev Kurgan

62nd ARMY

Hospital

Tsaritsa Gorge

No 1 STA.

Krasnaya Sloboda

XXIV Pz Div.

Landing Stage

No 2 STA.

94th Inf Div.
XXIX Mot. Div.

Yelshanka mining suburb

XIV Pz Div

Kuporosnoye

64th ARMY

Volga R.

FRONT LINES
Sept. 12, 1942
Sept. 26

to Beketovka

0 2 4 Miles 6

EHM

This was how we defended ourselves twenty-four hours a day for three days. Heat, smoke, thirst, our lips were cracked. During the day many of us climbed up to the highest points in the elevator and from there fired on the Germans. At night we came down and formed a defensive ring around the building. Our radio equipment had been knocked out the first day and we had no contact with our units.

The German infantry broke through and started up the stairs of the elevator. The Russians drove them back in hand-to-hand fighting. But on the night of September 20 the Germans captured the elevator and put out the fires in the grain.

On September 21 the fighting moved to Red Square, to a nail factory and the Univermag department store, which was the headquarters of one of the Guards 42nd Regiment's 1st Battalion. The German artillery concentrated on the department store. German infantry invaded the store, and in hand-to-hand fighting every officer in the battalion command post was killed. The rest of the battalion pulled back, yard by yard to the Volga. Its last position was a three-story building on the corner of Krasnopiterskaya and Komsomolskaya streets, which forty men defended for five nights.

Here from a Russian account is how the fighting went: "At a narrow window in the semi-basement we set up the heavy machine gun, with our emergency supply of ammunition—the last belt of cartridges I had decided to use at the most critical moment. Two groups, six in each, went up to the third floor and the attic. Their job was to break down walls and to prepare lumps of stone and beams to throw at the Germans. A place for the seriously wounded was set aside in the basement. . . ."

After five days the basement held twenty-eight seriously wounded men. Only twelve men were still able to fight. The only food was a few pounds of scorched grain. There was no water.

The German attacks stopped, but they kept up the fire from their heavy-caliber machine guns.

"The Germans attacked again. I ran upstairs with my men and could see their thin, blackened and strained faces, the bandages on their hands."

The nurse with the battalion, Lyuba Nestertenko, was dying with blood flowing from a wound in the chest. She tried to help bind up a man's wound, but she failed.

The German attack was beaten off. In the silence that gathered they could hear the fighting on Mamayev Hill and in the factory area.

"How could we help the men defending the city?" the commander of the battalion asked himself. "How could we divert from over there even a part of the enemy forces, which had stopped attacking our building?"

They decided to infuriate the Germans by raising a red flag over the building in defiance. But they had no red material. One soldier who was severely wounded took off his bloody undershirt, wiped his wound with it to get more blood, and handed it to the officer.

The Germans shouted through a megaphone: "Russians, surrender. You'll die just the same."

The red flag went up over the building.

"Bark, you dogs. We've still got a long time to live," shouted a Russian soldier.

They beat off the next attack with stones, firing occasionally and using up the last of their grenades. Suddenly from behind a wall appeared a tank. They had no antitank gun and only one antitank rifle with three rounds. The officer handed the rifle to an antitank man and sent him out through the back to fire at the tank point-blank, but before he could get into position he was captured by German tommy gunners. What the antitank man told the Germans nobody knew, but an hour later they began to attack again precisely at the point where the heavy machine gun was located.

The Germans believed the Russians were out of ammunition and they came bravely forth, standing up and shouting and marching down in a column. The column came up to attack, advancing along the line of fire of the heavy machine gun:

"I put the last belt in the heavy machine gun at the semibasement window and sent the whole of the 250 bullets into the yelling, dirty gray, Nazi mob. I was wounded in the hand but did not let go of the machine gun. Heaps of bodies littered the ground. The Germans still alive ran for cover in panic. An hour later they led our antitank soldier onto a heap of ruins and shot him in front of our eyes, for having shown them the way to my machine gun."

There were no further attacks, but the Germans turned the artillery on the building and a torrent of shells fell on it.

"Again we heard the ominous sound of tanks. From behind a neighboring block stocky German tanks began to crawl out. This clearly was the end. The Guardsmen said goodbye to one another. With a dagger my orderly scratched on a brick wall: 'Rodimtsev's guardsmen fought and died for their country here.'"

The tanks pushed the walls of the building down. That night six Guardsmen, all wounded, got out of the building. They staggered toward the Volga. They ran into a patrol and were lighted by German flares and discovered. But the silent knifing of a German guard got them away unmolested. They encountered another patrol, and another German was knifed silently. They crossed the railroad line, went through a minefield, and reached the Volga, where they built a raft of pieces of wood from the wreckage of a building. They went into the Volga, where they drifted for several days until they were rescued—six men of a battalion.

General Chuikov wrote later:

> By this time, we had nothing left with which to counterattack. General Rodimtsev's 13th Division had been bled white. It had entered the fray from the moment it had crossed the Volga, and had borne the brunt of the heaviest German blows. They had to abandon several blocks of houses inside central Stalingrad, but this could not be described as a withdrawal or a retreat. There was nobody left to retreat. Rodimtsev's Guardsmen stood firm to the last extremity, and only the heavily wounded crawled away. From what those wounded told us, it transpired that the Nazis, having captured the station, continued to suffer heavy losses. Our soldiers, having been cut off from the main force of the division, had entrenched themselves in various buildings around the station, or under railway carriages— usually in groups of two or three men—and from there they continued to harass the Germans night and day.

A WAR BALLAD

The most popular song of the Russian troops in Stalingrad was written by war correspondent Alexei Surkov during the battle of Moscow. It was criticized by the authorities as negative, but the soldiers continued to sing it.

> In our dugout a log fire's aflame
> Weeping resin, it sputters and sighs
> The accordian's tender refrain
> Sings of you and your smile and your eyes.

(*continued next page*)

(*continued from preceding page*)
We are now light years apart
And divided by snow covered steppes
Though the road to your side is so hard
To death's door it's four easy steps.

Marshal Goering was confident of quick victory and sent a message to General Richthofen to report to him immediately as soon as it happened.

"That won't be for quite a long time," Richthofen wrote in his diary.

Others in Berlin waited impatiently for the victory, which had now assumed major status all over Germany. Several newspapers printed premature reports with big headlines announcing the fall of Stalingrad. At General Paulus's headquarters a group of German war correspondents bedeviled the general every day with the question: when? when? when? He found it hard to keep giving them a tired smile.

At Fuehrer headquarters in Vinnitsa, Hitler had gone into a sulk because affairs were going badly in the Caucasus and Stalingrad refused to fall. For ten days he had not spoken more than a few words to his staff generals. He ate his meals alone, pored over the situation maps, and spoke only to his dog. The tension grew steadily.

At Stalingrad the whole thirty miles of the straggling city had now become the front, running from the Sukhaya Mechetka River on the north to Krasnoarmeisk in the south. At no point was the fighting more than three miles from the Volga, and in some places it was only a mile. On the river the traffic was under constant shell fire from the German artillery. The steamer *Borodino*, loaded with wounded, was sunk and hundreds drowned. The steamer *Joseph Stalin* was sunk, and a thousand women and children perished.

In the center of the city every one of these September days was a day of death.

The Russians had great difficulty in reinforcing the city center. As one Russian put it:

There were times when these reinforcements were really pathetic. They'd bring across the river—with great difficulty—say twenty new soldiers, either old chaps of fifty or fifty-five or youngsters of eighteen or nineteen. They would stand there on the shore, shivering with cold and fear. They'd be given warm clothing and then taken to the front line. By the time these newcomers reached this line, five or ten out of twenty had already been killed by German shells, for with those German flares over the Volga and our front lines, there was never complete darkness. But the peculiar thing about these chaps was that those among them who reached the front line very quickly became wonderfully hardened soldiers. *Real frontoviks.*

By September 21 the Germans had cleared the bed of the Tsaritsa River, which split Stalingrad, and spread out over the center of the city. The lie of the streets, running east-west, favored the German attack from the west to the east aiming at the Volga. German guns could pour fire down the streets from one end to the other. German troops set up fire points and roadblocks at the western end and then fought their way to the other end. The tanks moved up, the Russians let them come, and then the infantry moved and the Russians began to fire. The tanks used their heavy guns to destroy whole buildings from close range. The job of German tank crews was very difficult. Russians with grenades and antitank rifles could cripple the tanks in the narrow streets by getting a hit in the engine grille or the thin armor of the rear deck.

Stalingrad now had the appearance of a great pile of wreckage, huge mounds of rubble in the city blocks, with single walls half-shattered, with doors hanging askew, sometimes parts of flooring still attached, the doors blowing in the wind, opening and closing for ghosts, surrounded by heaps of bodies and parts of bodies. The city center had begun to stink: the hot wind picked up the smell of the decaying corpses and thrust it into every cranny.

The Russians had changed their military tactics here, using small, heavily armed storm groups to carry out lightning attacks on buildings and strongpoints. General Chuikov said:

> City fighting is a special kind of fighting. The buildings in a city act like breakwaters. They broke up the advancing enemy formations and made their forces go along the streets. The troops defending the city learned to allow German tanks to come right on top of them—under the guns of the antitank artillery and antitank rifle-men; in this way they invariably cut off the infantry from the tanks and destroyed the enemy's organized battle formation.

By September 24 the Germans occupied most of the center of the city and the central steamship pier, which created new difficulty for the Russians in the matter of reinforcing and supplying their troops on the west bank of the Volga. But the Russian artillery and the *katyusha* rocket launchers on the east bank fired away day and night, and the artillery had a great deal to do with the ability of the Russians to hold on.

As the writer Konstantin Simonov put it:

> We could certainly not have held Stalingrad had we not been supported by artillery and katyushas on the other bank all the time. I can hardly describe the soldiers' love for them. And as time went on, there were more and more of them, and we could feel it. It was hard to imagine at the time that there was such a concentration of guns firing their shells at the Germans, morning, noon, and night, over our heads.

At Vinnitsa on September 24 Adolf Hitler fired the army chief of staff, General Halder. Next day, General Paulus celebrated a sort of victory in Stalingrad, when a Swastika flag was raised over the Univermag department store, which symbolized the center of the city.

General Paulus knew that the battle was far from ended, but Germany waited and Hitler demanded signs of success. So the flag went up even as the Russians continued to fight for Mamayev Hill, and their embattled little fortresses.

PART VIII
THE FIGHT FOR THE FACTORIES

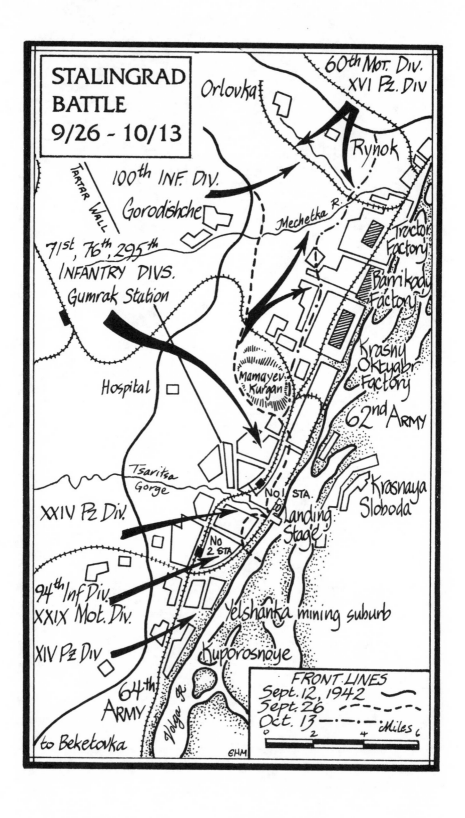

STALINGRAD
BATTLE
9/26 - 10/13

60th Mot. Div.
XVI Pz. Div

Orlovka

Rynok

TARTAR WALL

100th INF. DIV.
Gorodishche

Mechetka R.

Tractor Factory

71st, 76th, 295th
INFANTRY DIVS.
Gumrak Station

Barrikady Factory

Krasny Oktyabr Factory

Hospital

Mamayev Kurgan

62nd Army

Tsaritsa Gorge

No 1 Sta.

Krasnaya Sloboda

XXIV Pz Div.

Landing Stage

No 2 Sta.

94th Inf Div.
XXIX Mot. Div.

Yelshanka mining suburb

XIV Pz Div

Kuporosnoye

64th Army

FRONT LINES
Sept. 12, 1942
Sept. 26
Oct. 13

Volga R.

to Beketovka

0   2   4   Miles   6

EHM

23

All during this period of intensive fighting in the streets of Stalingrad, General Zhukov had been nurturing the idea of a Russian counteroffensive to bring disaster to the Germans.

He was well aware of the difficulties.

"As for the Soviet troops," he said, "they had suffered such heavy casualties in the fierce fighting on the approaches to Stalingrad, and were to suffer more within the city itself, that they were unable to defeat the enemy with existing forces." But . . .

"We knew that von Paulus's Sixth Field Army and Hoth's Fourth Tank Army, two of the Wehrmacht's most effective striking forces, had been so weakened in the gruelling fighting for Stalingrad that they would be unable to complete the capture of the city."

So at the end of September the Russians could see temporary stalemate, but only temporary. By November, Zhukov knew, supreme headquarters would have at its disposal strong new mechanized forces equipped with the T-34 tanks. In addition, the new breed of Russian field commanders had shucked off all the old fears and concerns left over from Stalin's 1930s purge of the Red Army, and had learned how to fight Germans. The command structure of the Red Army in the fall of 1942 was nothing like it had been in the early months of mass armies and mass defeats.

Zuhkov and Vasilevsky had mentioned this to Stalin at the Kremlin on

September 13. Stalin had not then been ready to consider so advanced a plan. But at the end of the month Stalin had again summoned General Zhukov to Moscow. At that point several important decisions had been made. First, the disposition of forces was going to be changed. The Stalingrad Front would be changed to be called the Don Front, and the Southeast Front would be called the Stalingrad Front. General Gordov, who would listen to no one, was dismissed as commander of the Don Front, and General Konstantin Konstantinovich Rokossovsky would take over. By mid-November the Russians would be strong enough to undertake a major offensive. They would have eleven armies, several mechanized, cavalry, and tank corps, 13,500 guns and mortars, 1,100 antiaircraft guns, 115 detachments of rocket artillery (*katyusha*), 900 tanks, and 1,115 aircraft for the offensive, and they would destroy the German forces at Stalingrad. In the meantime, the forces that existed would have to make more sacrifices to hold in the north of the city in the factory section, so six reconstituted divisions were ordered across the Volga to reinforce the 62nd Army. Reinforce was hardly the word, for very little remained of that army at the end of September, except its headquarters.

What was essential, and in this Commissar Khrushchev was all-important, was that the Russian troops fighting for Stalingrad keep the Germans pinned there until the offensive could be launched.

In this, the Russians' greatest ally was Adolf Hitler. During the month of September, General Halder and others had tried to persuade Hitler to halt the offensive for the winter, draw back and regroup, gathering strength for the coming year. Hitler would not listen. He would not retreat one step from the Volga. On this issue Halder was dismissed, and Hitler continued to press General Paulus to achieve a victory at Stalingrad. Hitler returned to Germany, where he opened the great Winter Relief Campaign a the Sportspalast. He spoke about his objectives:

> We had three objectives: (1) To take away the last great Russian wheat territory. (2) To take away the last district of coking coal. (3) To approach the oil district, paralyze it, and at least cut it off. Our offensive then went on to the enemy's greatest transport artery, the Volga and Stalingrad. You may rest assured that once there, no one will push us out of that spot.

Lieutenant General Vasilii Chuikov (center), commander of the 62nd Army during the fighting for Stalingrad.

Marshal Zhukov.

The battlefield in Stalingrad, 1942.

Street fighting in Stalingrad, 1942.

Street fighting in Stalingrad, November 1942.

Stalingrad, September 1942.

Street fighting in Stalingrad, 1942.

Stalin followed by Marshal Zhukov.

A German POW after Stalingrad's fall.

Women soldiers serving at the front.

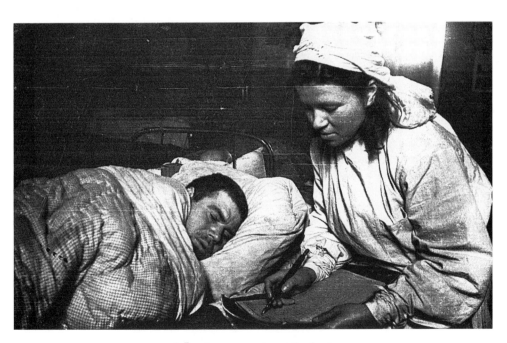

A Russian nun serving at the front.

Sergeant Yakov Pavlov, Hero of the Soviet Union, together with a group of Soviet soldiers, for 58 days staunchly repulsed the German attacks in a dilapidated house in Stalingrad. The small group, defending one house, destroyed more German soldiers than were lost during the occupation of Paris, November 1942.

Victory at Stalingrad.

Workers begin the rebuilding of Stalingrad.

Stalingrad. On January 31, 1943, more than 90,000 German soldiers, including 2,500 officers and 24 generals, were taken prisoner, which meant an end to the encircled army group. Field Marshal Paulus, commander of the 6th German Army, taken prisoner by Soviet troops, on his way to the headquarters of the 64th Army.

Field Marshal Keitel, representative of the German Supreme Command signs the instrument of Germany's unconditional surrender on May 8, 1945.

The Wehrmacht at Stalingrad.

24

As of September 27, nine-tenths of Stalingrad was in German hands. The Russians coming across the Volga were now being sent to the factory section. As they came, three slogans were seared into them by propagandists:

Every man a fortress!

There's no ground left behind the Volga!

Fight or die!

Generally morale was high, but where it was not, the NKVD troops were there to capture any who tried to desert and shoot them on the spot. The foothold in Stalingrad must be held at all costs.

General Paulus just then was contemplating the cost of Stalingrad to his 6th Army. In the six weeks since the army had begun moving from the Don River, he had 7,700 soldiers killed and 31,000 wounded. Ten percent of his army had been lost, and now the worst battle was yet to come, the struggle for the industrial district. Paulus was running short of both men and ammunition. He sent a message to the headquarters of Army Group B asking for more reinforcements. Paulus's quartermaster was worried, too, but for a different reason. The 6th Army required 650 tons of supply a day to survive, and all of it came over the single railroad track to the railhead at Chir.

In the structural changes that accompanied the dismissal of General Halder, General Schmundt, Hitler's military aide, emerged as chief of personnel of the German army. He and General Paulus had become confidants, and he told Paulus that if he pleased the Fuehrer with his conduct of the Stalingrad campaign, which he had done to date, then he might well get the job currently held by General Jodl as chief of staff of Oberkommandowehrmacht. This information tended to make Paulus more than usually responsive to Hitler's whims.

General Chuikov continued to bring in troops to the Skudri ferry crossing that handled the area from Rynok down to the tractor works. The troops came at night by every available craft, most of them to Crossing 62, behind the Red October factory and the Barrikady plant. This area was located under overhanging palisades from the high bank of the Volga.

Every night the soldiers came, and every night the Germans on

Mamayev Hill spotted the boats and ordered the German artillery to fire on them. On their boats the soldiers were in the hands of Communist Party agitators, who gave them pamphlets on street fighting and guarded the rails of the vessels to keep the troops from jumping overboard. For there was reason to jump overboard on many of these craft. German artillery zeroed in on the vessels and poured a rain of shells at them. When men were hit and died, others tried to leap. They were restrained, and if they succeeded they were shot in the water by the political officers.

By this means one hundred thousand new troops had been brought to Stalingrad by the first of October, but they were killed so steadily that General Chuikov still had only fifty-three thousand troops left. The 62nd Army had lost more than eighty thousand men in the past month.

Chuikov was reinforced, but quietly. While he was to get ten divisions to fight the Battle of Stalingrad, twenty-seven divisions were being brought in assembly areas behind the Stalingrad Front. A new army group called the Southwest Front was established secretly, and Lieutenant General Nikolai F. Vatutin was given command.

A handful of Russian soldiers held out in little enclaves in the center of the city. A lieutenant of the 42nd Regiment named Zabolotnov took over a building on Solmechnaya Street and set up a small fortress there. He was killed, but his men hung on in Zabolotnov's house. A sergeant named Pavlov and three other men captured a damaged building, killed the Germans hiding inside, and set up another little fortress, 250 yards from the bank of the Volga. The building had a large field of fire, and the Russians inside held out against tanks and infantry. They were not really all Russians but a microcosm of the immense land called the Soviet Union. Some were Russians, some were Ukrainians, some Georgians, some were from Uzbekistan and some from Kazakhstan. Here in Stalingrad they were united in their hatred of the Germans and their determination that the Swastika should not fly over the city.

The key to the defense of the central city was the steep Volga bank and its weathered sandstone gorges. On the east side of the river were the hospitals, the supply dumps, the assembly points for the soldiers, and above all the artillery, out of reach of the Germans. On the west side of the river were the sewers, now empty, which flowed into the river. Now, disused, they became passageways for the counterattacks of the Russian storm groups. As night fell, squads of attackers, half a dozen men, heavily armed, would set out along one of these sewers. They would lift a manhole cover and out would come a machine gun to go into position.

Then they would wait for a German column, spray the rear of the advancing German formation with gunfire, and before the Germans could react, the manhole cover would go back into place, and the attackers would have disappeared.

The Germans never accommodated themselves to this style of warfare. They continued to use traditional methods of attack, battering at buildings with tanks and artillery, making frontal assaults that were always costly and sometimes disastrous.

German General Doerr had this to say about the fighting:

> The time for conducting large-scale operations was gone forever; from the wide expanses of steppe land, the war moved to the jagged gullies of the Volga hills with their copses and ravines, into the factory area of Stalingrad, spread out over uneven, pitted, rugged country, covered with iron, concrete and stone buildings. The mile, as a measure of distance, was replaced by the yard. G.H.Q.'s map was the map of the city.
>
> For every house, workshop, water tower, railway embankment, wall, celler and every pile of ruins, a bitter battle was waged, without equal even in the first world war with its vast expenditure of munitions. The distance between the enemy's army and ours was as small as it could possibly be. Despite the concentrated aircraft and artillery, it was impossible to break out of the area of close fighting. The Russians surpassed the Germans in their use of the terrain and in camouflage, and were more experienced in barricade warfare for individual buildings. . . .

By the end of September when the fighting moved to the factory area, the Germans were losing their spirit for the conflict, as is shown in the entries of one diarist for the period of the battle so far:

Sept. 1: "Are the Russians really going to fight on the very bank of the Volga? It is madness. . . ."
Sept. 8: "Insane stubbornness. . . ."
Sept. 11: "Fanatics"
Sept. 13: "Wild beasts"
Sept. 16: "Barbarism . . . not men but devils."
Sept. 26: "Barbarians . . . they use gangster methods."

Here, on Mamayev Hill, and in a few other spots, the Russian soldiers held out, but the real action had now moved north. On October 2 the Germans shifted the focus of their artillery to the factory district. The shelling found the oil storage tanks, which almost everyone had believed were empty. But they were not empty and they blew up and sent waves of orange flame down into the river. General Chuikov's new command post was in the shadow of the oil tanks, and when the flames came down, they isolated his command. The telephone wires all burned away, the dugouts were filled with smoke. But Chuikov and most of his staff survived and moved up the shoreline closer to the factory complex.

25

Before attacking the factory complex, at the first of October, General Paulus insisted on eliminating the Russian salient around the town of Orlovka, three miles west of the tractor works. The Orlovka salient jutted out north about five miles and was a mile wide at the neck. The Germans surrounded it with the XVI Panzer Division, the 60th Motorized Infantry Division, and the 100th and the 389th Infantry divisions. These troops were all guarding the northern flank of the 6th Army against a breakthrough by General Yeremenko to relieve Stalingrad. The 60th Motorized Division was given the task. On September 30 the Germans attacked, into the teeth of a Russian air raid. That night their officer counted noses. A company of 120 men had gone out, and only 30 returned. But with several such sacrifices, the salient was eliminated. General Chuikov saw that the Germans were determined to take the salient, and he did not want to waste troops fighting for it, so that night he moved the defenders out. His intelligence told him that the Germans were concentrating tanks and infantry in the gullies around the Red October factory and in preparation for an attack upon the tractor plant and the Barrikady factory. He decided to make a counterattack and move his infantry into position. That night the Russian 39th Guards Infantry Division began crossing the Volga from the east bank.

The next day, however, the Germans drove a deep wedge into the Russian line, and for a time it seemed they would break through into the

Red October factory. A German pincers met on the Orlovka salient, cutting off a battalion of Russian infantry. The battalion had only two hundred rounds of ammunition per rifle and two days' food supply. But they held out for five days, and on the seventh of October, 120 survivors got back to the Russian lines, leaving 380 dead and wounded on the field.

General Smikhotvorov's division, one of those reconstituted units that had been sent into action, suffered horribly in these days. It lost three regimental commanders and three battalion commanders on the first day. After less than a week in action it was reduced to two thousand men. But to help out now came the 308th Infantry, made up mostly of Siberians.

The Germans now turned to some new tactics to try to press into the factories. They dressed a battalion of troops in Red Army uniforms and sent them down one gully toward the Volga. The Russians discovered the nature of the unit and wiped it out to the last man. But the Germans were getting closer to the Red October factory. There the men of the 13th Guards Division held solidly in the first days of October.

On October 3 the Germans prepared to attack the Red October factory with three German infantry divisions and two panzer divisions on a three-mile front. That night another Russian division began to come to the rescue. But the way it came was an indication of the Russian troubles. The troops came that first night without their antitank guns, because there were not enough boats, and without their headquarters or their medium tanks. They were rushed directly into the line at the tractor factory.

General Paulus meanwhile had been bombarding Army Group B with requests for reinforcements, and so Hitler sent him the 29th Motorized Division and the XIV Panzer Division from Hoth's 4th Panzer Army plus individual replacements from the Ukraine. The replacements did not last long in these hellish conditions. In one sector six replacements came to the 9th Flank Division one night. They were cautioned to keep their heads down, but one by one they satisfied their curiosity by gazing across at the Russian positions. Next morning four of the six replacements were dead.

On October 4 the Germans began the attack on the tractor factory with elements of the XV Panzer, 60th Motorized, and 389th Infantry divisions. The Russian reinforcements made all the difference and the German advance was stopped. The pressure was on General Paulus. Hitler had now demanded the capture of Stalingrad by October 15. The 37th Guards Division was driven back, but they contested every foot of ground. At the end of the day the Germans had gained one block of flats in the factory housing development. That evening the *katyusha* rockets scored a great success, wiping out a German battalion with one salvo. For the day, Paulus's losses were four battalions for one block of flats. The attack was suspended.

On October 13 the Russians counterattacked, but gained only two hundred yards in one sector and three hundred yards in another. That was all.

On October 14 Paulus sent five divisions against the tractor factory and the Barrikady factory. This was billed as "the final offensive." The Luftwaffe sent all available planes into the air to fly three thousand sorties that day.

General Chuikov recalled:

> They bombed and stormed our troops without a moment's respite. The German guns and mortars showered on us shells and bombs from morning until night. It was a sunny day, but owing to the smoke and soot, visibility was reduced to 100 yards. Our dugouts were shaking and crumbling like a house of cards. By 11:30 A.M. 180 tanks broke through to the stadium of the Tractor Plant. By 4 P.M. the troops were encircled but still fighting.

By midnight it was clear to General Chuikov that the Germans had surrounded the tractor plant and that fighting was going on in the workshops.

> We reckoned that the Germans had lost 40 tanks during the day and in the Tractor Plant there were 2,000 German dead. We also suffered very heavy losses during the day. During the night 3,500 wounded soldiers and officers were taken across the Volga; this was a record figure.

After the tanks had broken through the Russian defenses, the German 389th Infantry Division moved into the mile-long hive of shops. The workshops became slaughterhouses; the glass in the long skylights was shattered and mingled on the floor with pools of blood and awkwardly twisted bodies, German and Russian.

The conflict moved into lesser buildings, some of them dark and cavernous. Here is one German account of fighting inside a factory:

The captain came up and told the men they had to clear the factory of the Russians inside, probably factory militia.

Of course there was no question of argument. With dry mouths, we moved forward into the factory buildings, which were littered with hundreds of large objects—ideal for snipers and as bad as possible for us. The relatively large size of our force was in no way reassuring. Even if we overwhelmed them in the end, each bullet they fired was bound to hit someone, and if I should be the only casualty in a victorious army of a million men, the victory would be without interest to me. The percentage of corpses, in which generals sometimes take pride, doesn't alter the fate of the ones who've been killed. The only leader I know of who finally made a sensible remark on this point, Adolf Hitler, once said to his troops, "Even a victorious army must count its victims."

. . . The first two sheds were empty. Perhaps our prisoners had been telling the truth. But our orders were to check the whole place. Our group surrounded the entire factory complex and then began to move toward the center. We passed through a series of enormous barnlike buildings which seemed to be on the point of collapse.

The wind was blowing hard and the buildings echoed with sinister creaking sounds. Otherwise everything was quiet except for the occasional clatter made by one of our men deliberately shoving aside some metal object or overturning a pile of crates.

Eight of the men moved into the darkness of a building littered with clutter. There were no windows and no light. They heard a series of clicking noises, but the wind was blowing and filled the air with banging. No one took any special precautions. From outside they could hear the shouts and cries of fighting. Suddenly the shed in which these men were fighting was filled with the noise of explosions. A half dozen flares thrown from somewhere up high lit the darkness. Almost simultaneously four of the Germans were hit and screamed with pain. Two more collapsed on the floor, while the others staggered toward the door. One infantryman felt his gun shudder in his hands. It had been hit in the butt by a bullet that took a piece out of it.

There were two Germans still in this shop, and they began to try to convince the Russians there were more. The Russians were now firing at every movement. Bullets were flying around the shop. The infantryman bit his lip to keep from screaming. Suddenly he heard a scratching noise behind him, somewhere between a pile of objects and an upright support. He froze against a large glazed pipe behind which he was hiding. The noise of fighting outside kept him from distinguishing any sounds clearly.

Some sense told him that danger was very close. He was certain that someone had moved on the other side of the barrier that concealed him.

Suddenly he saw a man no more than five yards from him. Then a second man appeared behind the first, crawling toward a pile of boxes. Although the two were in shadow, the infantryman recognized that they were in civilian clothes, and the first one was wearing a cap. He was large and appeared to be strong.

The man moved a few steps away. The infantryman raised his gun until it was pointing at the man. He knew there was one bullet left in the barrel so he did not have to move the bolt. He tightened his nerves, trying to suppress the trembling of his arms. He knew that at the slightest sound the other man would shoot. There was a lot of noise outside, which divided the man's attention.

The infantryman's gun was now level, and his finger was on the trigger. He hesitated. It was not easy to kill a man in cold blood unless one was heartless or numb with fear. The man began to move slowly toward the infantryman's hiding place. He could hear the man breathing. As he approached, the man sensed something. He hesitated. Then a sudden brilliant light blinded him and he collapsed in the dust, his belly torn open from the shot that the infantryman had fired.

The infantryman felt as though he was sinking into a black void. He could not believe he had killed the man and waited for the blood to begin flowing from beneath the body.

Suddenly a piece of the wall collapsed. The German soldiers outside had pulled off a segment of the corrugated sheeting, and the glare of daylight came into the building. It diminished the importance of everything that had happened in there.

The captain came in with a dozen soldiers. They began to fire up into the rafters near the roof, and the firing was answered by Russian machine guns. Bodies began to fall out of the rafters. The Germans set up a heavy spandau machine gun outside and blasted the roof away. Full daylight came into the building, the firing continued, and one by one the Russians dropped and lay still on the factory floor. The place filled up with German soldiers, and the struggle for this shop was over. They formed up and marched on, singing:

Maerkische Heide
Maerkische Sand.
Sind des Freude,
Sind mein Heimatland . . .

Marching on grassland
Marching on sand
Without joy
Outside my homeland . . .

26

Eight thousand Russian commandos of the Soviet 37th Guards Division and several thousand armed factory workers met the Germans, and in the next forty-eight hours five thousand of them were killed or wounded. Whole sections of the factory went up in smoke and flames and debris as the Stukas bombed. General Zholudev, commander of the division, was buried up to his neck in debris by a direct shell hit on his command post. Down on the Volga, General Chuikov's bunker was under intensive fire from artillery, and thirty men were killed around the bunker that day. At the northwest corner at the Barrikady factory the Russian 308th Division, or what was left of it, was pushed inside the machine shops, and its commander was cut off from the troops for hours.

The Germans had managed to capture the tractor plant that day, and north of it there were only a handful of Russian troops left. The Germans attacked again on October 15, "the day of decision." Russian losses were mounting alarmingly. In two days two divisions had lost 75 percent of their men. That night another regiment crossed the Volga and came into the fighting. But the real help came from the Russian artillery, the guns of the Volga flotilla of war craft, and the Shturmovik planes of the air force, which were attacking German troops, although they suffered very heavy losses.

On the night of October 17 Stalingrad still held out, much to General Paulus's discomfort. General Chuikov had a visit from General Yeremenko that night, and Yeremenko promised him ammunition—one day's supply. Chuikov erupted and more was promised.

With the Germans so near, Chuikov had to move his headquarters back down south, to a ravine near Mamayev Hill, inside the Volga cliffs, one thousand yards from the hill. This tiny area was all that remained of central Stalingrad in Russian hands.

But Yeremenko was satisfied that Chuikov was keeping his nerve under the most difficult of circumstances. In three days he had lost thirteen thousand men, a quarter of his force.

On October 19 the Germans continued their attack, but it was apparent that both sides were nearly exhausted. German prisoners indicated that morale in their army had dropped to a new low. The Russians were scraping the barrel for manpower. But there were some positive changes for the Russians. Russian aircraft were now dominating the night sky over Stalingrad, much to the surprise of the Germans. Stalin had ordered all available planes to the area. Here is a German reaction from a 6th Army officer, in a report to Army Group B:

The untouchable nightly air dominance of the Russians has increased beyond understanding. The troops cannot rest, their strength is used to the hilt. Our personnel and material losses are too much in the long run. The Army asks Heeresgruppe to order additional attacks against enemy airports day and night to assist the troops fighting in the front lines. . . .

27

By September the battle for Stalingrad had caught the attention of the world. Russian propangandists helped establish the image of a beleagured population fighting gamely against heavy odds, and folk heroes were created. One was twenty-year-old Tania Chernova, who began as a partisan and then joined the Red Army as a soldier. She came to the east bank of the Volga and boarded a barge to take her to Stalingrad one night in September. The barge was hit in midstream by bombs from the Luftwaffe, and Tania and two Russian soldiers swam for their lives and took refuge in a sewer, worked their way up into the city, and emerged from a manhole. They were discovered by the Germans, but escaped and found their own lines. Tania trained as a sniper, lived in foxholes, slept curled up beside strangers, and ate with a spoon she kept in her boot. Soon she was used on special missions.

One night she and five men were assigned to dynamite a German headquarters near the Red October plant. They passed through the Russian lines to the headquarters located in a half-destroyed apartment house. The patrol went up the stairs. Tania was in the rear. The five men disappeared around a corner, but a German saw her and shouted at her to raise her hands. Instead she kicked him in the groin, cracked his face on her knee, twisted his right arm under him, and started to choke him. One of her patrol came back and bashed in the German's head with a rifle butt. Then they carried out the mission of dynamiting the building.

Another folk hero was Vasili Zaitsev, a soldier with the Russian 248th Division from Siberia. He was so skillful a shot that he became a sniper, and in one ten-day period killed forty Germans, each with a single shot. The Soviet newspaper correspondents got the story and Zaitsev became a folk hero. As the story goes, the Germans learned of his fame and called in Standartenfuehrer SS Heniz Thorwald, the head of the German sniper school at Zossen, to deal with Zaitsev. Thorwald came to Stalingrad, where the Russians soon learned of his presence, and then, so it was said, began a feud that would become famous.

Standartenfuehrer Thorwald spent several days this September surveying the no-man's-land between Mamayev Hill and the Red October plant. German intelligence had secured the publicity about Zaitsev, and the major was equipped with information about the Russian's techniques, while the Russian had never seen the German and knew nothing about him. Zaitsev became aware of his antagonist's existence because two Russian snipers were shot dead and the work was that of an expert. Zaitsev and another soldier laid a trap for the German. For days they watched the trenchline. Zaitsev concluded finally that the German had his hiding place under a sheet of iron next to a pile of bricks in no-man's-land. He tested the theory by hanging a glove on a piece of wood and raising it as though it were a hand. Somebody drilled a hole through the center of the glove. That must be his man.

Next morning Zaitsev and his companion found a place where the afternoon sun would be at their backs and where they had a good view of the piece of sheet iron. The other soldier fired a shot at the sheet iron to arouse the German sniper's interest, and then they waited. In late afternoon Zaitsev focused his telescopic sight on the sheet iron. A piece of glass glinted in the sun. The other Russian soldier raised his helmet over the parapet. The German fired, and the Russian soldier pretended to be killed. Standartenfuehrer Thorwald raised his head to see what had happened and Zaitsev shot him between the eyes.

These stories of heroism were matched every day by the heroism and sacrifice of the ordinary Russian soldier.

North of Mamayev Hill, the Germans were still triumphing. They had taken the tractor plant and broken into the Barrikady. They had occupied the western end of the Red October factory.

But in the center of the city, small groups of Russians still held out, and on October 20 at "Pavlov's house," the handful of Russians holed up in the building fired on four German tanks that came up with a column of infantry, putting one tank out of action and scattering the infantry so that the whole group ducked for cover. The Russians were not licked yet.

PART IX
GENERAL PAULUS'S LAST OFFENSIVE

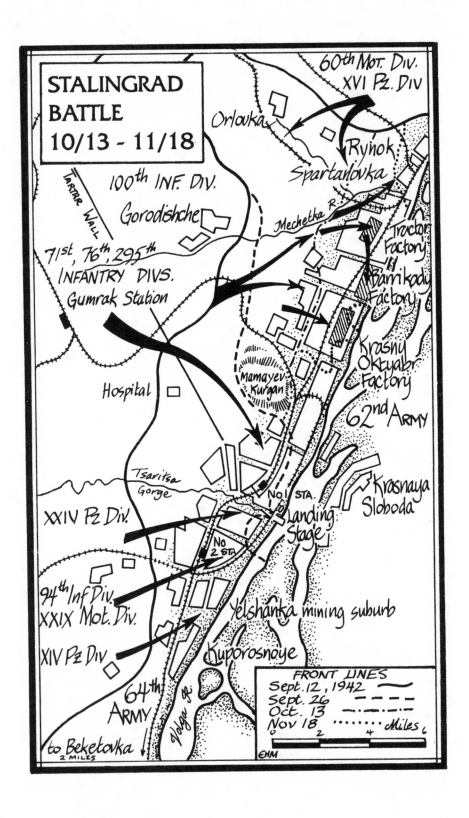

STALINGRAD
BATTLE
10/13 - 11/18

60th MOT. DIV.
XVI PZ. DIV

Orlovka

Rynok

Spartanovka

TARTAR WALL

100th INF. DIV.

Gorodishche

Mechetka R.

Tractor
Factory

71st, 76th, 295th
INFANTRY DIVS.
Gumrak Station

Barrikady
Factory

Hospital

Mamayev
Kurgan

Krasny
Oktyabr
Factory

62nd ARMY

Tsaritsa
Gorge

NO. I STA.

Landing
Stage

Krasnaya
Sloboda

XXIV PZ DIV.

NO
2 STA.

94th Inf Div.
XXIX Mot. Div.

Yelshanka mining suburb

XIV PZ DIV

Kuporosnoye

64th
ARMY

Volga R.

to Beketovka
2 MILES

FRONT LINES
Sept. 12, 1942 ———
Sept. 26 — — —
Oct. 13 —·—·—
Nov 18 ·········· Miles
0   2   4   6

EHM

28

On October 14 Hitler suspended virtually all German offensive activity on the Eastern Front except at Stalingrad. He wanted that city more than any other place.

The Russian 62nd Army weathered the supreme crisis of that day. On the fifteenth the Germans gained ground everywhere. German tanks and infantry surrounded the tractor factory and Spartakovka. They cut the 62nd Army in two and very nearly captured its headquarters, but the 62nd Army survived, and by the night of the sixteenth the exhausted German divisions saw their drive halted.

General Paulus had called on Army Group B for all the reinforcements they could give him. Hitler had sent reinforcements from the Replacement Army in Germany. There were no more replacements for Paulus. Now he would have to move troops from the quiet sections of the army front to the fighting front. It was the only way he could keep going.

Meanwhile the Russian 138th Division arrived in Stalingrad, along with a new organization of workers, thrown rapidly together. Both went to reinforce the Barrikady factory area. The German attack of October 21 and 22 brought them into the Red October and Barrikady factories. But to do this, Paulus's operations were eating up his infantry strength at the rate of a division every five days. By October 23 the Germans held the tractor factory and most of the Barrikady factory, and the Russians were holed up inside the dead furnaces of the Red October factory, with the Germans at the other end of the foundry.

In the Barrikady factory the tall smokestacks rose above a mass of wreckage. Freight cars lay shattered on the sidings, and shell holes gave the building walls a surrealistic look. On the ground German soldiers crouched in their shell holes, and overhead, *katyusha* rockets screamed, then plunged to earth like comets. In the buildings Russian snipers picked off individual Germans as they ran from hole to hole.

The Germans never changed their tactics. On October 25 the 100th Division was to attack in the Barrikady area along a railroad embankment. They waited for the Stukas to pave the way for them, but when the Stukas came, their bombs fell almost on the Germans and were of virtually no use. The attack failed.

On October 25 the Germans captured the center of Spartakovka. The 6th Army nearly reached the Volga here, but was finally pushed back. On October 26 the 100th Division attacked again. This time the artillery put up the heaviest barrage the infantrymen had ever seen, and it blasted the Russian positions. The shelling lasted half an hour. When it stopped, the German soldiers jumped up and ran across the railroad tracks and onto the cliff. They were between the Barrikady plant and the Red October factory, less than four hundred yards from the Volga. This meant that the last remaining Russian ferry landing on the western shore was under direct fire from German machine guns.

German squads plunged into this no-man's-land, and the men of the 100th Division broke into cheers. They were sure the Russians were finished and the battle for Stalingrad was over.

In a Barrikady factory shop a German squad was setting up their radio when one member of the squad reported Russians on the upper floor of the battered building. The Germans threw satchel charges, but the Russians hurled them down the stairs, wounding several Germans. Night came and the Germans were so tired they decided to leave the Russians alone for the night. They slept, exhausted, and the Russians made no sound.

In the morning the German squad called on the radio for reinforcements. It was a full day before the new men arrived. All this while the Russians were quiet upstairs. Across the street German snipers holed up and began firing single shots at the upper story of the building. The Germans on the ground level heard screams and then silence. A few hours later they moved cautiously up the stairs and smashed the door of the locked room. Seven Russians lay on the floor. All of them were dead. The Germans went back downstairs and went back to sleep.

Once again the Russians reached into the manpower barrel and came forth with reinforcements for the 62nd Army, the 45th Infantry Division. Two battalions reached the fighting area before dawn on October 27. They went into the line between the two factories with orders to stop the Germans. They held firmly until evening, when their left flank was forced back a hundred yards. The cost had been awful: half the men of the two battalions were gone in one day's fighting. More reinforcements were on the way to the Russians, but the question was: Could General Chuikov hold out for another day?

The Germans held nine-tenths of the city, and the other tenth was under heavy fire. The Russians were still on Mamayev Hill, and they held a few buildings and a narrow strip of the bank of the Volga, several miles long, but only a few hundred yards wide. This bridgehead was very uncertain indeed. Fighting continued until October 30, but the German attacks grew weaker. The 62nd Army had survived, by what seemed a miracle, but was actually a triumph of grim determination and willingness to sacrifice lives.

In the great bend of the Don River, the commander of the German XI Corps was encharged with holding the left flank of the 6th Army, which he could not do with his three divisions except by sacrificing the position at the river bend at Kremenskaya.

Because of the scattering of German troops, the Soviet 65th Army crossed the Don and established itself in a deep bridgehead on the southern bank of the river. Every day the Russians made some sort of attack on the German positions, just to harry them.

What the Germans here noticed in late October and early November was that the Russians were bringing up troops and weapons to the Don almost continuously, to place them in position against the XI Corps and the Romanian 3rd Army, which adjoined the corps on the left.

These reports were confirmed by aerial reconnaissance. Since the end of October, General Paulus had been getting these reports and passing them on to Army Group B, and the army group had informed Hitler's headquarters that the Russians were deploying on the flank. On this flank stood the XI Corps, the Romanian 3rd Army, and then the Italian 8th Army and the Hungarian 2nd Army.

But Hitler preferred not to believe such reports. Instead, he put his trust in a document prepared by the army staff which indicated the Russians could not have any important reserves left. But when the Romanians asked for reinforcement by panzers, Hitler listened, and sent the XLVIII Panzer Corps, which included one German and one Romanian panzer division. It was not very well equipped or up to full strength. Moreover, elements of the division had been lying camouflaged on the Don Front for weeks, camouflaged under reeds in pits in the ground and covered with straw. In that period mice had gotten into the tanks to build nests and had nibbled at the rubber insulation of the electrical wires. When the division was told to move out, and the 204th Panzer Regiment was ready to move, only 39 of 104 tanks would start up, and another 34 tanks broke down from electrical failures on the march. The Romanian 1st Panzer Division had 108 tanks, but most of them were Czech models, vastly inferior to the Russian tanks.

At the end of October, General Paulus issued a proclamation to the troops.

> The summer and fall offensive is successfully terminated after taking Stalingrad. The 6th Army has played a significant role and held the Russians in check. The action of the leadership and the troops during the offensive will enter into history as an especially glorious page.
>
> Winter is upon us. The Russians will take advantage of it. It is unlikely that the Russians will fight with the same strength as last winter.

29

Indeed winter had arrived suddenly early in November. October had been warm, if rainy, but then the temperature sank below the freezing point and grew colder almost every day. The grass turned brown. The ground froze hard. But this year the Germans had winter clothing, which was coming through the supply chain from Kharkov four hundred miles away.

Private Guy Sajer, an Alsatian whose mother was German, was assigned to a battalion guarding supplies that were coming along the rail pipeline in Russia for the Stalingrad Front.

> At this moment [he said], the Reich was making an immense effort to protect its soldiers from the implacable hostility of the

Russian winter. There were enormous stores of blankets, special winter clothing, made of sheepskin, overshoes with thick insulating soles and uppers of matted hair, gloves, hoods of double catskin and portable heaters which operated equally well on gasoline, oil or solidified alcohol, mountains of rations in specially conditioned boxes and thousands of other necessities. It was our duty, as convoy troops of the Rollbahn, to deliver all this to the front lines where the combat troops were desperately awaiting us.

Private Sajer's company was ordered to take fifteen trucks to join a long road convoy on its way to Stalingrad. First they had to roll out barrels of gasoline and alcohol to fill the gas tanks and radiators, crank up the engines, and shovel many cubic yards of snow in the dark. When the fifteen trucks were ready, they set out, following a bumpy snow-covered track. One of the trucks skidded into a ditch, and it took half an hour to get it out, which they did with manpower. Finally they reached the assembly point and joined the regiment. There they stopped for a lecture from an officer.

The lecture pointed out that even a victorious army had to accept death and casualties, and that our role as a convoy unit was to carry, at whatever cost, and despite all the hardships, which the High Command thoroughly recognized, the food, munitions, and matérial the combat troops required. Our convoy, by any means available, had to reach the bank of the Volga, so that von Paulus could continue to wage his victorious battle. One thousand miles separated us from our destination, and we hadn't a moment to spare.

The convoy moved along the main highway. Road gangs must have been working around the clock, because the road was clear, but the snowbanks on either side were nearly twelve feet high.

Then they came to a hill, and from the top they could see soldiers ahead moving snow with shovels. Their section bogged down, and all the men had to shovel snow. There were not enough shovels, so they used boards and even big serving platters. A sergeant had the bright idea that they could flag down a train and recruit some Russian labor to do the job, and he led Sajer's detail to the rail line. They tried to stop several trains to get help, but none of the trains would stop. They walked down the tracks for about an hour. No trains came. It was growing colder all the time. They saw a hut alongside the rail line and headed for it. Then came a puff of white smoke, and the sergeant dropped and loaded his rifle. One of the men staggered and fell with a stupefied expression on his face. The sergeant's gun cracked, and snow from the roof of the hut shot into the air. The sergeant jumped up and ran forward, telling the others to cover him. The soldiers aimed toward the woods beyond the hut and began to fire their weapons. Bullets whistled by their ears. The sergeant stood up and threw a grenade. One of the planks of the hut disintegrated. The sergeant continued to fire his automatic rifle into the hut, and two figures rushed out the door and ran for the woods.

The sergeant looked in the hut as the other soldiers came up, and they all saw a gaunt, bearded man in civilian rags. He was wounded in the hand and somewhere under his tunic, for blood was running from his collar.

The sergeant put his gun away and told his men to take care of the partisan. The soldiers carried the wounded man outside. He groaned and said something unintelligible to them.

Another train came up and this one stopped. Three soldiers heavily muffled in reindeer-skin coats got off. One of them was a lieutenant. He demanded an explanation why the train had been stopped. The sergeant said he was looking for labor to help with snow removal. The lieutenant said this train was carrying only the wounded. The sergeant said they had two wounded. They picked up the wounded German.

"Where is the other one?" asked the lieutenant.

"Over there by the hut."

The lieutenant looked at the bearded man. "Who's this?"

"A Russian, Mein Leutnant. A partisan."

"So. Do you really think I'm going to saddle myself with one of those bastards who'll shoot you in the back anytime—as if war at the front wasn't enough?"

The lieutenant shouted at the two soldiers who were with him. They walked over to the partisan lying in the snow. Two shots rang out.

Then the lieutenant and the wounded German and the two soldiers got on the train. The others went back to their trucks and stayed the rest of the night. The next morning they started forward again. They reached Kiev. They headed toward Stalingrad, which was more than one hundred miles away. And soon they were making the last half of the round trip, with other convoys heading the way they had come to deliver supplies to Paulus and the 6th Army.

＊ ＊ ＊

What Paulus wanted was to take Stalingrad immediately, and he continued to call for reinforcements. Hitler released five battalions of combat engineers to the 6th Army, hoping they could provide the necessary punch to finish the task. (Pioneer was the German term for the units.)

These troops appeared on the Stalingrad scene on November 7, just across from the Barrikady factory, three thousand troops specially trained in demolition and destruction. They were assigned to capture Russian strongholds: a chemist's shop that had been turned into a stronghold and the "Commissar's House," which had also been fortified by the Russians. These two points dominated the Volga bank and represented the major points of resistance in the area.

30

Hitler expressed perfect confidence in the future. On November 9 he returned to his house in Berchtesgaden, having just made a speech saying that "no power on earth will force us out of Stalingrad."

That day the Pioneer battalions tried to put emphasis on Hitler's words with an attack. They assembled in the Barrikady at the eastern end. The factory had been the scene of intense fighting just a few days before, and the Russians had been pushed out. But they had left mementos behind, as the Germans learned to their surprise and shock. The Pioneers were bunched up in the rooms, waiting to attack, and one of them tripped a booby trap. It exploded and killed eighteen of the Pioneers. The remainder crowded together and tried not to touch anything.

It was after three o'clock in the morning when the German artillery began a barrage against the Russian lines. The Pioneers moved out then. They attacked and captured the chemist's shop, but when they got to the Commissar's House, they found that every window and door had been sealed up, and from peepholes the Russians fired at them. It was daylight before they broke their way through some of the sealed apertures. The Russians retreated to the cellar, and the Germans tore up the floor and dropped satchel charges and Molotov cocktails down. Soon the cellar was quiet and they announced the capture of the Commissar's House. Other engineers rushed down to the bank of the Volga, but when they got there, every man but one was either dead or wounded. A patrol was sent down to help, and within three hours all but three men had become casualties.

In five days the combat engineers lost one thousand men, and the five battalions were combined into one. The Russians who had defended this area were now confined to a shrinking bit of land on the shore four hundred yards wide and one hundred yards deep. The 138th Russian Division had been reduced to a few hundred men.

The Russian high command was not unhappy. As General Chuikov was fond of saying, "Time is blood." The defenders of Stalingrad were doing just what Stalin wanted them to do. They were occupying the German attention, while the buildup of troops on the German 6th Army flanks continued.

General Jodl gave Hitler new reports which showed the Russians massing troops northwest of Stalingrad and also south of the city, where the Romanian 4th Army was covering General Hoth's 4th Panzer Army.

In Stalingrad, although Paulus claimed to have taken the city, he was planning another offensive against the factory district. It began early on the morning of November 11 and involved seven German divisions attacking on a three-mile front east of the gun factory. Four hours before daylight the drive began. General Paulus arrived at the forward command post at ten o'clock. He heard that the attack was moving slowly. After five hours of fighting, Paulus committed his reserves and reached the Volga in the Red October factory area. The Russian forces of the 62nd Army were split into three parts. Soviet casualties were high as usual, but the Russian command had the feeling that this was Paulus's last fling.

On the evening of November 12 the German attack lost its punch, and the 62nd Army began to counterattack. In Stalingrad a rumor spread that it would not be long now: the Red Army was about to launch a major offensive, the greatest yet, against the Germans.

General Richthofen's 4th Air Fleet attacked the Russian bridgeheads at Kletskaya and Serafimovich on the Don River. They knocked out several Russian pontoon bridges. The Russians responded by building new bridges, with the surface just below that of the river, so they were invisible from the air. On November 12 Richthofen confided to his diary that the Russians were building up their forces to attack the Romanians and that artillery pieces were now showing up in the emplacements. He wondered when the offensive would begin, but like the other Germans, Richthofen did not really worry much about the offensive, because he, too, was convinced that the Russians were nearly finished as fighters.

The Luftwaffe was having great difficulty in getting air intelligence because of the bad weather, but on November 13 a reconnaissance plane flew over a mile-long column of Soviet tanks moving west at three hundred feet, and there was no arguing with the findings.

General Zhukov and Red Army Chief of Staff Vasilevsky visited the buildup area in the south and looked over General Vatutin's offensive capability in the Southwest Front. On November 15 Stalin telegraphed Zhukov that everything was prepared in Moscow and Zhukov could set the date for the beginning of the offensive anytime from this point on. Zhukov and Vasilevsky conferred and agreed that the attack should begin in the north on November 19 and in the south a day later. It was to be called Operation Uranus.

Hitler's reaction, when he saw the Soviet buildup on Paulus's flanks, was to urge Paulus on to strong action to capture every bit of the city.

"The difficulties of the fighting at Stalingrad are well known to me," Hitler told Paulus by radio November 16, "but the difficulties on the Russian side must be even greater just now with the ice drifting down the Volga. If we make good use of this period of time we shall save a lot of blood later on. Therefore I expect that the commanders will once again fight with their usual dash in order to break through to the Volga, at least at the ordnance factory and the metallurgical works, and to take these parts of the city."

Paulus relayed Hitler's urgings to his commanding officers on November 17. The next day the Germans renewed the attack on Stalingrad in a driving cold rain. They gained ground. It seemed as though the Germans would be able to win in this last offensive. Perhaps twenty-four hours more would give them real control of Stalingrad. What Hitler said was quite correct: the Russians were having great trouble with the ice that clogged the Volga, and the ice had cut off communication with the east bank of the river. The command was reduced to supplying the slender bridgehead from the air, and the airdrop target was so small that many of the supplies fell into the river or into German hands.

The Russian defense at this point was reduced to three bridgeheads. In the north was the small bridgehead held by General Gorokhov's men.

Near the Barrikady factory was a bridgehead of about a half a square mile, held by Colonel Lunikov's men. Finàlly there was the main bridgehead, about five miles long. General Rodimtsev's men held the left flank, a strip of land a few hundred yards wide. The greatest depth of the bridgehead, east of Mamayev Hill, was a mile.

General Chuikov's command post was inside the Volga cliffs, east of Mamayev Hill. All the Russian positions were under German artillery fire, and most of them were exposed to German machine guns. As one German officer wrote:

> We have fought during fifteen days for a single house, with mortars, grenades, machine guns and bayonets. Already by the third day fifty-four German corpses were strewn in the cellars, on the landings, and the staircases. The front is a corridor between burnt out rooms; it is the thin ceiling between two floors. Help comes from neighboring houses by fire escapes and chimneys. There is a ceaseless struggle from noon to night. From story to story, faces black with sweat, we bombard each other with grenades in the middle of explosions, clouds of dust and smoke, heaps of mortar, floods of blood, fragments of furniture and human beings. Ask any soldier what half an hour of hand-to-hand struggle means in such a fight. And at Stalingrad, it has been eighty days and eighty nights of hand-to-hand struggle. The street is no longer measured by meters but by corpses.
>
> Stalingrad is no longer a town. By day it is an enormous cloud of burning, blinding smoke; it is a vast furnace lit by the reflection of the flames. And when night arrives, one of those scorching, howling, bleeding nights, the dogs plunge into the Volga and swim desperately to gain the other bank. The nights of Stalingrad are a terror for them. Animals flee this hell; the hardest stones cannot bear it for long; only man endures. . . .

So near, yet still so far. The German 6th Army was on the Volga, and only these few pockets of resistance still held out. But the 6th Army was exhausted. To Hitler, Stalingrad was the world's assessment of German power. Stalingrad had assumed the importance given to Verdun in World War I. To withdraw from Stalingrad was to Hitler unthinkable. His generals might suggest that he consider the military expediencies. He chose to consider the world political implications.

It has been suggested that part of Hitler's mind-set was produced by the figures he was fed by General Paulus. In his eagerness to secure reinforcements Paulus had exaggerated the Russian strength at Stalingrad all the way along. What were reported as divisions were often only regiments or even battalions, but the reports indicated figures about five times those that actually existed. This reporting convinced the general staff that the Germans were wearing down the Russian armies faster than they were doing in fact. It also convinced Hitler that the Russians could not have any significant reserves left and that he was very near to victory through Russian exhaustion.

During the first two weeks of November he had many reports of Russian military buildup in the northwest and south of Stalingrad, but he chose to minimize them. On November 17 Hitler ordered General Paulus to capture Stalingrad as quickly as possible. That day he left his country house in Bavaria for Berlin. The next day he was completely occupied with discussions and preparation for the German seizure of the French fleet at Toulon, following the Allied invasion of North Africa a few days earlier.

And then on the morning of November 19, 1942, Hitler learned of the Soviet offensive to entrap the German 6th Army in a pincers. At 7:30 the Russian artillery on the Southwest Front and the Don Front started to fire. Operation Uranus had begun.

PART X
THE TRAP

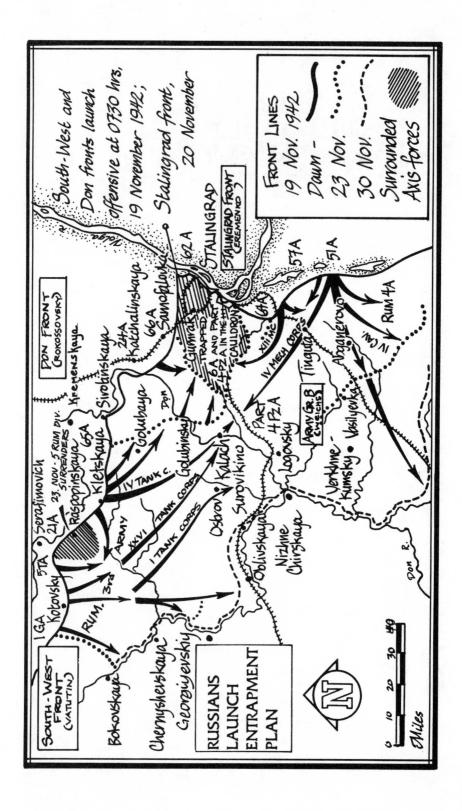

South-West and
Don fronts launch
offensive at 0730 hrs,
19 November 1942;
Stalingrad front,
20 November

FRONT LINES
19 Nov. 1942 —
Dawn —
23 Nov.
30 Nov.
Surrounded
Axis forces

DON FRONT
(ROKOSSOVSKY)

Kremenskaya
Sirotinskaya
24A
Katchalinskaya
66A
Samofilovka
62A
STALINGRAD
STALINGRAD FRONT
(EREMENKO)

23 Nov.- 5 RUM. DIV.
SURRENDERS
Golubaya
Don
65A
Raspopinskaya
Kletskaya

Serafimovich
21A
1 GA
Kobovsky
5TA
RUM. 3rd
XXVI ARMY
IV TANK C.
Golubinsky
TANK CORPS
I TANK CORPS
Osков
Kalach
Surovikino
GUMRAK
TRAPPED
6A AND PART
4 PZ IN THE
CAULDRON
6A
PART
4 PZ
IV MECH CORPS
XIII MC
Tinguta
Abganerovo
Rum 4A
57A
51A
IV CAV.

SOUTH-WEST
FRONT
(VATUTIN)

Bokovskaya
Chernyshevskaya
Georgiyevsky

RUSSIANS
LAUNCH
ENTRAPMENT
PLAN

Logovsky
ARMY GR. B
(WEICHS)
Verkhne-
Kumsky
Vasilyevka

Obliwskaya
Nizhne
Chirskaya
Don R.

N

0 10 20 30 40
Miles

31

The Soviet offensive on November 19 was signaled by the firing of the *katyusha* rockets. Then the field artillery joined in, thirty-five hundred guns and mortars in three narrow breakthrough sectors. Fog and snow made it impossible for the Russian gunners to correct their fire properly, but they banged away at the Romanian defenses. The guns shifted their aim to the center of the defense, and the attacking force of tanks and infantry moved up to the edge of the Romanian defense pattern. At 8:48 that morning the last gun fired, and two minutes later the Russian tanks and infantry began to move.

By midmorning the wind began to disperse the fog, and Soviet aircraft took off to survey the battlefields. The Romanians of the Romanian 3rd Army fought gamely, although their equipment was outmoded and heavy weapons were scarce. But the Russian offense was not as strong as it should have been, and progress was slow until the Russian commanders decided to use their mass of tanks.

The Soviet 5th Tank Army struck from the Serafimovich area, against Ferdinand Heim's weak corps. The Soviets here used two armored corps, one cavalry corps, and six rifle divisions. On their left the Soviet 21st Army struck from Kletskaya with one armored corps, one cavalry corps, and six rifle divisions.

The Russian tanks wheeled around after they pierced through the Romanian lines and attacked from the rear. This brought panic to the

Romanian infantry, who were not experienced in fighting against tanks. By noon, whole divisions of Romanian troops were fleeing westward. The Russians thrust west toward the Chir River, southwest, and south. But then the main Russian force headed southwest, toward the rear of the German 6th Army. Here they ran into General Heim's XLVIII Panzer Corps.

Army Group B ordered the German tanks to attack to the northeast, but they had only begun to move when Hitler interfered and ordered the tanks to attack to the northwest. The confusion created thus enabled the Russian armored spearheads to penetrate thirty miles through a gap at Blinov. By midafternoon the Romanian 3rd Army had virtually collapsed, and the Russians went streaming through. That night Army Group B ordered General Paulus to stop all offensive operations in the Stalingrad area and take three panzer divisions and an infantry division out of Stalingrad to meet the Russian attack on the 6th Army left flank.

On the morning of November 20 the Stalingrad Front joined the offensive. Two Russian armies broke through the Romanian line along the chain of lakes south of Beketovka. The Romanians immediately fled, and at nightfall the German high command wrote off the Romanian VI Corps as a total loss. General Hoth, commander of the 4th Panzer Army, wanted to pull the Romanian VII Corps back on the army's right flank. Army Group B was afraid to let them move because they might panic and go into a rout.

On that morning of November 20 the XIV Panzer Corps and the four divisions from Stalingrad shifted to the west side of the Don and prevented the Russian 21st and 65th armies from creating a pocket west of the river, but they could not stop the major envelopment. The only obstacle in the way of the Russian 5th Tank Army was the XLVIII Panzer Corps and what was left of the Romanian 3rd Army. But the XLVIII Panzer Corps was very nearly trapped until it managed an escape to the west bank of the Chir River. It did delay the Russian advance for twenty-four hours, but then the Russians advanced; their tanks moved toward Kalach, while the Russian cavalry and rifle divisions advanced along the line of the Chir River.

By the end of November 20 the 4th Panzer Army was cut in two, with the German IV Corps and the 29th Motorized Division trapped in the pocket that was forming around Stalingrad. The 4th Panzer Army was unable to stop the advance on Stalingrad or the Russian advance southwest along the left side of the Don.

The Russians were moving to close the pocket. It was seventy miles from the Serafimovich bridgehead to the bridge at Kalach, and a few miles more to the 6th Army railhead at Chir Station. In between the Chir and the Don were hundreds of commands, supply dumps, hospitals, workshops, all the bits and pieces that keep an army going. They all merged into one rolling movement south, trying to escape the Soviet tanks.

Hitler on November 20 created a new Army Group Don. Into it went the 6th Army, the Romanian 3rd and 4th armies, and the 4th Panzer Army. The commander was Field Marshal Fritz Erich von Manstein.

Hitler at that moment was vacationing at his villa in Bavaria. He was completely surprised by the Russian offensive and did not know what to do except one thing: under no circumstances would he allow the 6th Army to retreat from Stalingrad. General Jodl suggested that Stalingrad be evacuated, but Hitler would not hear of it. He issued orders that night to General Paulus to hold fast, in spite of the encirclement. He also ordered two panzer divisions and one mountain division to reinforce Paulus, and promised two infantry divisions to come later. These were all he could find.

On November 20 the German 29th Motorized Division engaged and halted the Soviet 57th Army, but eighteen miles south the Soviet 51st Army broke through the Romanian VI Corps.

That same day General Paulus sent a dispatch to Army Group B suggesting the withdrawal of the German 6th Army from Stalingrad to positions one hundred miles southwest, on the lower Don and Chir rivers. General Weichs, the commander of Army Group B, forwarded the dispatch with his own strong endorsement to OKW headquarters in Rastenburg.

Hitler received the messages and was furious. On the afternoon of November 21 he sent a message to Paulus ordering him to hold at Stalingrad. "Keep railroad line open as long as possible. Special order regarding air supply will follow."

So at least Hitler was promising to supply Stalingrad by air if need be. But when General Richthofen heard this, he telephoned General Albert Jeschonnek, who was Marshal Goering's deputy. "You've got to stop it," Richthofen said. "In this filthy weather we have here there's not a hope of supplying an army of 250,000 men from the air. It's stark staring madness."

As if to emphasize the madness, that night the temperature fell to below zero.

The 29th Motorized Infantry headed for the Russian spearhead to do battle. But on November 21 came orders for Army Group B to break off the attack and adopt a defensive position to protect the southern flank of the 6th Army. The 29th Division was detached from the 4th Panzer Army and attached to Paulus's 6th Army along with IV Corps. It was two days before anybody informed General Paulus of this.

Meanwhile the Soviet 51st Army, after some hesitation, had reached Kalach on the Don on November 22 as the German and Romanian front broke up over a length of fifty miles in the north and thirty miles in the south. Into the breach Zhukov poured six armies. The Russian cavalry cut the western railroad from Kalach in several places.

The big bridge at Kalach had been prepared by the Germans for demolition, and a platoon of engineers was on duty on November 23 in case they got the order to destroy the bridge.

Late that afternoon, tanks could be heard approaching from the west. The lieutenant commanding the engineers thought they were Russians, but he was reassured when the first three vehicles turned out to be Horch personnel carriers with 22nd Panzer Division markings. The lieutenant assumed that this was a reinforcement for Stalingrad and told his men to lift the barrier. The personnel carriers stopped on the bridge and sixty Russian soldiers got out. They killed most of the engineer platoon, captured the rest, removed the demolition charges, and twenty-five tanks passed over the bridge and drove southeast, where that evening they made contact with the 14th Independent Tank Brigade from the 51st Army. The Russian forces had linked up. A quarter of a million Germans were trapped in the pocket. The turning point of the war had arrived.

THE STALINGRAD MINEFIELDS

In the battle of Stalingrad the Russians prepared minefields for nineteen areas of troop concentration: thirteen antitank centers, in all twenty-three minefields. They laid ten thousand mines of various kinds and put out obstacles, land mines, and booby traps. The official Soviet staff study of the battle says Russian engineers made a total of seventy-three passage-ways through minefields, thirty-five to four hundred meters wide, and removed twelve thousand mines. When they began the Stalingrad offensive on November 20, 1942, several hours before the troops

(*continued next page*)

> *(continued from preceding page)*
> attacked, the engineers, "under a reinforcing cover of submachine
> guns, light machine guns, and heavy machine guns of the rifle units,
> started clearing the minefields and scattered barbed wire entangle-
> ments of the enemy. In three and a half hours the engineers made
> sixty-four passageways and drew out and disarmed more than five
> thousand enemy mines. Where they were not able to construct
> passageways, they planned thirty-seven of the most convenient routes
> for bypassing the minefields."
>
> That is the official version, but there was more to it. After the war
> was over, in the first meeting between Marshal Zhukov and General
> Dwight D. Eisenhower, the latter marveled at the difficulties the
> Russians must have had with the German minefields. How did they
> manage them? Ike asked.
>
> "If we come to a minefield," Zhukov explained, "our infantry attack
> exactly as if it were not there. The losses we get from personnel mines
> we consider only equal to those we would have gotten from machine
> guns and artillery if the Germans had chosen to defend the area with
> strong bodies of troops instead of minefields."
>
> And it was true. Usually these troops were members of punitive
> battalions, arrested by the NKVD for attempted desertion or some
> other military crime. They were often promised absolution from their
> crimes if they survived, but sometimes they were marched out at
> gunpoint. The SS also had punitive battalions of German soldiers, and
> they, too, were used in such dangerous work as mine clearance.

A group of German soldiers had just been given leave, and they
boarded a bus for Chir, where they expected to take trains to get back to
Germany. In a few hours they returned to their post, to report that the
Russians held the Kalach bridge and they could not get over the Don.
They, too, were trapped.

The main supply depot for the German 6th Army was located at Bolshe
Nabatov, 30 miles south of Kletskaya. Quartermaster Binder hurried
there to save the eight hundred cattle he had collected to feed the 6th
Army through the winter. He assembled a convoy and brought it east to
Stalingrad before the Russians could get to Bolshe Nabatov. In the next
few days Binder crossed the Don many times, salvaging what he could for
the army and getting it to Stalingrad. Although the Russians had entered

the whole curve of the Don, and had passed through Bolshe Nabatov, they had contented themselves with shooting up a few buildings and then had gone elsewhere.

The Russian troops of the Stalingrad Front and the Southeast Front had joined up, encircling the 6th Army between the Volga and the Don. In four days the Romanian 3rd Army had lost seventy-five thousand men, and the entire heavy equipment of five divisions plus thirty-four thousand horses.

During the successful weeks of September and October, General Paulus had caused to be built a new winter headquarters for the 6th Army at Nizhne Chirskaya. This headquarters had excellent communications links to Army Group B and the Fuehrer's headquarters. On November 21 Paulus transferred his headquarters from Golubinskaya on the Don to Gumrak near the Stalingrad fighting front. At the same time he took a trip to Nizhne Chirskaya, which was outside the pocket, to meet General Hoth and discuss the situation and also to be in touch with various headquarters. When Hitler discovered where Paulus was, on November 22 he sent an insulting message to Paulus, ordering him back to Gumrak.

General Paulus again made an effort to save his army. In a message to Army Group B on the night of November 22 he reported:

"The Army is encircled. The South front is still open east of the Don. The Don is frozen over and can be crossed. There is little fuel left; once it is used up, tanks and heavy weapons will be immobile. Ammunition is short. Provisions will last for six more days. Request freedom of action. The situation might come to abandonment of Stalingrad and the northern front." Again the message was passed to Hitler. He refused to address the problem.

"Sixth Army must know that I am doing everything to help and to relieve it. I shall issue orders in good time," he said.

That night Army Chief of Staff Kurt Zeitzler and Luftwaffe General Jeschonnek were at Hitler's Berghof, trying to persuade Hitler to give up the idea of an airlift. It was impossible, they said. Hitler did not believe them, and he called Goering, who then called Jeschonnek and told him not to oppose what Hitler wanted to do.

On November 23 Paulus sent a new message to Army Group B:

"Murderous attack on all fronts. Arrival of sufficient air supplies is not believed possible, even if weather should improve. The ammunition and fuel situation will render the troops defenseless in the very near future."

There was no reply to this message.

* * *

Between the Chir and Kletskaya on the Don, the last Romanian outposts were either slaughtered or surrendered. Several thousand Romanians headed south to the safety of the lines of General Heim and the XLVIII Panzer Corps. Without Hitler's permission Heim was moving south to the banks of the Chir and safety. Here Heim was arrested by Hitler's order and sent back to Germany to stand trial for not stopping the Russians.

On the night of November 23 Paulus added another message, this one a personal appeal to Hitler.

Mein Fuehrer:
Ammunition and fuel are running short. A timely and adequate replenishment is not possible.
I must forthwith withdraw all the divisions from Stalingrad itself and further considerable forces from the northern perimeter.
In view of the situation I request you to grant me complete freedom of action.

Hitler received those messages from General Paulus when he returned to Rastenburg that day. The telephone lines to 4th Panzer Army and 6th Army had been cut, but Hitler managed to reach Paulus by radio and reiterated his demand that the 6th Army stand fast. He spoke again that night about an airlift.

32

General Paulus did not know it but that night of November 23 General Walther Seydlitz-Kurzbach, commander of the LI Corps, ordered the 94th Infantry Division to retreat from its position in the northeastern sector of the pocket. He and his troops referred to the pocket as *der Kessel*, the Cauldron.

THE CAULDRON

On November 19 the Russians launched their Operation Uranus, whose purpose was to surround, trap, and destroy the German 6th Army. Within a week they had compressed the German and allied forces into an area one hundred miles square, bounded on the east by Stalingrad and on the west by the curve of the Don River. The perimeter formed a rough quadrangle. Around it the Russians concentrated seven armies and two thousand field guns.

The Germans were trapped in what they called *der Kessel*, the Cauldron. It was, however, so large an area that at first the concept of entrapment escaped many of the soldiers.

They would soon learn . . .

The general's idea was to force Paulus's hand by starting the retreat, in the hope that the units on both sides of the 94th would stampede and the exodus would spread throughout the 6th Army. The troops of the 94th blew up their ammunition dumps and burned their documents, and orders were given to pull back. One officer observed that this would mean the loss of one-third of the division. As it turned out he was an optimist.

When the 94th Division started to draw back, it was attacked by the Russian 62nd Army. The men of the 94th Division were caught in the open, and the toll exacted was enormous. By dawn of November 24 the 94th Division ceased to exist. The other German units did not follow suit, but held.

Inside Stalingrad the Luftwaffe radio informed Hitler of the withdrawal of the 94th Division. No one told General Paulus, until Hitler descended on him in absolute rage. On the morning of November 24 he sent Paulus a direct order under the heading *Fuehrerbefehl*, which meant the highest priority of dictatorial decree. It ordered Paulus to establish a fortress by hedgehog defense and hold the Volga Front and the Northern Front at all costs. Again Hitler said supplies would come by air.

So Paulus was denied any freedom of action. The 6th Army would remain in Stalingrad.

On the morning of November 24 Goering arrived at Fuehrer headquarters in his private train. He met with Zeitzler and Hitler.

Hitler wanted to know if the Luftwaffe could supply the 6th Army by air.

"Fuehrer," said Goering, "I announce that the Luftwaffe will supply the 6th Army from the air."

Zeitzler asked Goering if he knew what that meant: how many sorties the Luftwaffe would have to fly every day.

Goering said he did not know but his staff did.

It would take five hundred tons of supply landed every day, even if the Germans slaughtered every horse inside the Cauldron.

"I can manage that," said Goering.

"It's a lie," said Zeitzler. Goering reddened and clenched his fists. Hitler intervened.

"The Reichsmarschall has made his announcement, and I am obliged to believe him," he said. "The decision is up to me."

Hitler and Goering emerged from the room smiling. Orders went out that day for the 4th Luftflotte to begin flying three hundred tons of supply a day into Stalingrad immediately. Goering would make more planes available and then the tonnage would increase to the five hundred minimum that Paulus required.

Even as Goering made the promise, it was apparent to all the operating officers of the Luftwaffe that what he promised could not be. Then why did the Reichsmarschall do it? The speculation was that Goering knew he had lost Hitler's confidence in matters relating to the Luftwaffe with his failure to conquer the British Royal Air Force in 1940. Here was his chance to recover lost prestige. The promise was based on nothing at all. Goering had relinquished his day-to-day authority over the Luftwaffe to Jeschonnek and General Erhard Milch. He did not actually know what was going on in the daily operations. So it was easy for him to make the blithe promise.

As for Hitler, he believed because he wanted to believe. The promise meant that Hitler would not have to face the hard decision of extricating the 6th Army and admitting failure.

So the decision was made that changed the fate of the 6th Army and made Stalingrad the turning point of the war.

Still furious with Paulus, Hitler proceeded to strip him of some of his authority but not responsibility. He sent a message to Army Group B, putting the northern part of the Stalingrad area under General Seydlitz. He did not know that Seydlitz was responsible for the defection of the 94th Division.

Seydlitz would be responsible directly to Hitler, but this did not affect Paulus's overall responsibility for everything in the 6th Army.

33

In the days since the penetration of the Romanian line, General Zhukov had moved 134 divisions across the Don, 12 from the Beketonskaya bridgehead and 22 from Kremenskaya. Their tanks had turned westward, probing into the straggling elements that made up the German rear. Their infantry had turned east to build an iron ring around Stalingrad.

Zhukov's artillery kept the whole pocket under bombardment from his big guns on the east bank of the Volga.

The Soviet intention was to keep the pressure on the Germans and to be sure to maintain contact so that they would know the first signs of a German effort to break out of Stalingrad's Cauldron. But Zhukov did not want to take any action that might push the Germans into doing this, so they waited, on their ring of steel.

On November 23 and 24 men labored mightily to bring in battery after battery of 76mm guns across the frozen steppe. By the evening of November 24, when Field Marshal Manstein arrived at the headquarters of Army Group B, the Russians had one thousand antitank guns in position in an arc that ran from Vertyachi in the north around to Kalach, then eastward, and to the Volga. The extrication of the 6th Army from Stalingrad was going to be a serious battle proposition. Zhukov had no such grandiose plans as Stalin was likely to devise. He had secured the agreement of the Soviet Military Council (Stavka) that the aim of this operation was the destruction of the German 6th Army, and that having destroyed it, they would have made sure that the Germans would never again be able to launch a major offensive operation in the east. The whole operation was confined to a quadrangle less than one hundred miles square bounded by Stalingrad and the eastern corner of the Don bend. In this area the Russians had concentrated seven of the nine reserve armies they had built. There would be no wasteful and repetitive attacks as in the past. Zhukov was determined to use his two thousand guns around the 6th Army as an unbreakable chain, and not to allow anything to distract him. As of the end of November, he had concentrated ninety-four divisions and brigades against the German 6th Army, and only forty-nine units against the 4th Panzer Army and the Romanian 3rd Army, and only twenty of these latter units were actually in line. He had given up the offensive in the Chir River sector to concentrate on Stalingrad.

But also on November 24 Paulus had a ray of hope in a message from Field Marshal Manstein, who had just assumed command of Army Group Don. Manstein said he would do everything possible to relieve the 6th Army. But the army must form up in order to clear a supply channel to the southwest.

Here at least was something concrete.

Manstein hoped to make a two-pronged attack. One attack would be a diversion from the west, aimed at Kalach. This should draw Russian units. Meanwhile the main attack would start at Kotelnikovo, seventy-five miles south of Stalingrad. The forces would not have to cross the Don, but only two small streams, and most of the way it was open steppe, thirty miles of flatland reaching to the southern perimeter of the pocket. When the relief force reached the Mishkova River, Manstein hoped Paulus would break out with his army and link up.

Manstein began assembling his forces, the 6th and 17th Panzer divisions fresh from Germany, the 16th Motorized Division, and the 23rd Panzer Division. He did not know that the 23rd had only two dozen tanks left. To protect his flanks he would use what was left of the Romanian armies.

XVII Corps held the line from the Chir to the north, and the Romanian 3rd Army, which was now only a name—its headquarters was German and so were most of the units in the line—held the area south to the confluence of the Chir and the Don. In the 4th Panzer Army sector the whole, including two Romanian corps remnants, was designated Armee Gruppe Hoth.

In the last few days of the month the transports of German troops for the relief of Stalingrad began to arrive.

In Stalingrad the German soldiers cheered when they heard that Manstein was coming to save them. But he could not come immediately. And for the immediate future they had to depend on Marshal Goering's promise that the Luftwaffe could supply the 6th Army.

On November 24 General Richthofen sent his fighters and bombers on sorties against the Russian troop columns and troop concentrations. They destroyed a few isolated tanks. But Russian fighter planes were seriously interfering with the supply airlift, which had started. The Russian air forces had been told to concentrate on shooting down transport planes around Stalingrad. Richthofen had to move some of his fighters into

Stalingrad itself, which meant they, too, had to be supplied by his air force. Richthofen had to admit that "we have not been able to master the Russian fighters absolutely and of course the Russians can attack our forward airfields any time they like."

No matter what Goering said, Richthofen knew it was going to be out of the question for the Luftwaffe to fly in enough supplies to maintain the 6th Army's fighting strength, let alone to increase it. Richthofen believed that if the 6th Army would be given orders immediately to fight its way out of the Cauldron, it could make it. But if the orders were delayed . . .

On November 25 all the three-engined Ju-52s available were employed in flying in supplies, but this meant less each day. On November 24 the 4th Luftflotte had forty-seven Ju-52s, but twenty-two were lost. On the twenty-fifth another nine were shot down.

"We have thus been able to fly in only 75 tons instead of the 300 tons directed from above. We simply have not got the transport aircraft to do it," said Richthofen.

Luftwaffe General Jeschonnek, who was the real operational chief along with General Milch, knew that Goering did not know what he was talking about when he said he could airlift five hundred tons or even three hundred tons of supply per day. But Goering was still the chief of the Luftwaffe, even though for months his duties as economic czar of Germany had taken his mind off the air force.

What was needed was seven hundred tons of supply a day for the 6th Army. They could provide two hundred tons within the Cauldron for a while.

"Impossible," said Jeschonnek.

"We can do it," said Goering.

Hitler chose to believe Goering rather than Jeschonnek and Zeitzler, so there was nothing to be done by Richthofen but try, knowing from the first that it was a lost cause.

But Richthofen felt impelled to speak up. On November 25 he made "urgent representations" to Jeschonnek and Zeitzler to back him in asking Hitler to let Paulus fight his way out of the trap and to get Goering to agree to back them. The trouble was that Goering was in Paris and could not be reached. Jeschonnek and Zeitzler tried to help, and Richthofen's recommendation was submitted to Hitler. The dictator listened to what was said and then said no. He would not countenance leaving the Volga. If he once left the Volga, he would never get it back again, he said.

Richthofen sighed in desperation. "I disagree," he said. "But orders are orders and we'll do our best to carry them out. The tragedy is that no local commander on the spot, even of those who enjoy the Fuehrer's confidence, can any longer exercise any influence. As things are, we commanders—from the operations point of view—are now nothing more than highly paid NCOs!"

It was apparent that the hopes of the 6th Army now depended on two factors: the relief expedition that was going to be mounted by Manstein, and the supply of the 6th Army by the Luftwaffe. Thus the operations of the Luftwaffe were one key to 6th Army salvation.

At this time, Richthofen had 550 bombers, 350 fighters, and 100 reconnaissance planes, plus his niggling supply of transports. Obviously the transport issue would have to be resolved by Goering and many more transports allocated to Stalingrad. But to protect them, Richthofen would have to use his warplanes, which were inferior in number to the Russian 1,250 planes of the 8th, 16th, and 17th Air armies.

At the end of November the Russian air forces were given a new mission. On November 26 observers noted the vast increase in the number of supply missions being flown by the Germans, so that day Zhukov told the air forces they were to destroy the ability of the Luftwaffe to supply Stalingrad. Before he smashed the Germans he would starve them. This, then, because the primary mission of Soviet air. It would be the key to the destruction of the 6th Army.

PART XI

THE CRISIS: DECEMBER 1–15

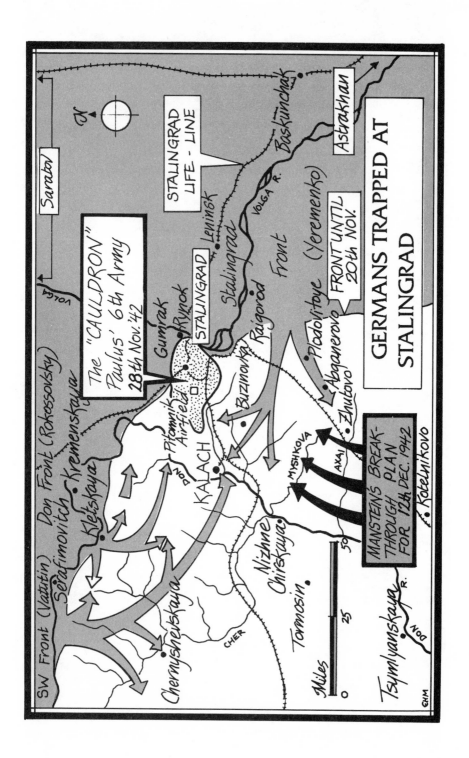

GERMANS TRAPPED AT STALINGRAD

SW Front (Vatutin)
Don Front (Rokossovsky)
Serafimovitch
Kremenskaya
Kletskaya
Chernyshevskaya

Saratov
VOLGA R.

The "CAULDRON"
Paulus' 6th Army
28th Nov. '42

Gumrak
Rynok
STALINGRAD
Pitomnik Airfield
Buzinovka
KALACH
DON
Nizhne Chirskaya
Tormosin
CHER

STALINGRAD LIFE - LINE

Leninsk
Stalingrad
VOLGA R.
Raigorod
Front
Astrakhan
Baskunchak

Pladovitoye (Yeremenko)
Abganerovo
Znutovo

FRONT UNTIL 20th Nov.

MANSTEIN'S BREAK-THROUGH PLAN FOR 12th DEC. 1942
MYSHKOVA
AXAI
Kotelnikovo

Tsymlyanskaya
DON R.

Miles
0   25   50

CRM

34

On November 23 Moscow announced triumphantly that Russian forces had won a great victory in the bend of the Don, and that the Germans were now entrapped in Stalingrad.

That news convulsed the world. Even Hitler and Dr. Goebbels had to let some inkling of the truth get out, although the face they put on it was that the matter was of no importance and the situation would be rectified quickly. The army high command announced that the Russians had broken through the German lines northwest and south of the 6th Army.

But the very vagueness of the German communiqué seemed to be proof, in Germany and elsewhere, that something had gone very wrong with Hitler's war in Russia.

By November 28 the iron ring around Stalingrad had closed.

To convince the world that a great victory had been achieved, Stalin let up on censorship enough for foreign correspondents to see what had happened in the bend of the Don. The American United Press correspondent Henry Shapiro was allowed to make a trip to Serafimovich, the headquarters of General Vatutin's Southwest Front, which had sent the spearhead south to Kalach.

Shapiro traveled by train to a point about one hundred miles northeast of Stalingrad. He saw nothing but destruction wherever he went. The railroad lines had been bombed heavily by the Luftwaffe, all the stations had been destroyed, and the military commands and railroad personnel were now operating from dugouts and ruined buildings. But the trains were running and carrying a constant stream of troops and arms to the west. Traffic was continuous, day and night.

Shapiro left the railroad and proceeded by car. It was the same. Everywhere he saw destruction but a new feeling of hope and pride in the Russians that he had not seen before.

"By the time I got to Serafimovich, the Russians were not only consolidating the ring around Stalingrad, but were now making a second ring. It was clear from the map that the Germans at Stalingrad were completely trapped, and could not get out. I found among the soldiers and officers a feeling of confidence the like of which I had never seen in the Red Army before."

The Russians let Shapiro see what he wanted to see. He encountered thousands of Romanians, wandering around the steppe, cursing the Germans and waiting to be taken over as prisoners of war, so they would be fed. Some of them appealed to the Russian peasants, who tended to regard them as kindred. Anyone who was not a German got Russian sympathy. The Germans got nothing but hatred and, now, scorn.

Shapiro observed that except for a handful of Iron Guardsmen, the equivalent of the Nazis in Romania, the Romanian soldiers were glad to be out of the war. It was Hitler's war, they told him.

When correspondent Shapiro moved to Stalingrad, the more prisoners he saw and the more Germans.

"The steppe was a fantastic sight; it was full of dead horses, while some horses were only half dead, standing on three legs and shaking the broken one. It was pathetic, ten thousand horses had been killed in the Russian breakthrough. The whole steppe was strewn with these dead horses, and wrecked guns and tanks and trucks and half-tracks, and no end of Romanian and German corpses. The Russian bodies were the first to be buried. The civilians were already coming back to the villages, most of them wrecked. Kalach was a shambles with only one house standing."

German prisoners that Shapiro saw were "mostly young fellows and very miserable." The temperature was thirty below zero, but they had only tunics—no greatcoats—with blankets wrapped around their necks. The Russians had sheepskin coats, warm gloves, boots, and all the accoutrements for a cold winter.

General I. M. Chistiakov, whom Shapiro saw at his headquarters in a village near Kalach, predicted that Stalingrad would be taken by the end of December.

35

On the night of November 28 Zhukov was visiting the Kalinin Front headquarters when Stalin telephoned him from Moscow and asked him to give some thought to the best means of liquidating the trapped German forces inside the Cauldron. The next morning Zhukov wired his analysis.

The Germans, he said, would not try to break out until they received relief either from Nizhne Chirskaya or from Kotelnikovo. They would hold on the Don Front and launch a relief expedition from one of those two places. Therefore, the Russian army must be prepared to throw the relief force back, no matter whence it came. That meant two tank groups, each of at least one hundred tanks, must be put aside in reserve for that purpose.

Moreover, as soon as possible the German forces should be split. This would require two thrusts, one toward Bolshaya Rossoskha and the other in the direction of Dubininsky and Hill 135. Elsewhere the Soviet forces should take defensive positions and operate only to exhaust the Germans, without exhausting themselves. After the trapped German forces had been cut in half, the weaker half should be eliminated and then the Russians should strike with all available units against the Stalingrad Cauldron and destroy the 6th Army.

When Stalin received this appraisal, he was already deep in plans to prevent the Germans from moving forces from Army Group Center to the defense of Stalingrad. Stalin wanted to launch a new offensive on the Western and Kalinin fronts against the Rzhev salient.

36

On November 30 General Richthofen's 4th Luftflotte pressed into service forty Heinkel-111 bombers to augment the handful of Ju-52 transports that were available on short notice to fly supplies into Stalingrad. From their fields outside the besieged circle it took the German planes almost an hour to fly to Pitomnik inside the circle. Their mechanics and handlers swarmed over the aircraft as they landed, unloading the supplies and bringing aboard the wounded for shipment to hospitals in the safe zone.

Everything that could be left in Stalingrad was left. The crews even siphoned extra gas from the plane tanks for the planes and vehicles in Stalingrad.

To Paulus this was a hopeful beginning, but it was illusory. The next day a weather front moved in, and for two days there were virtually no relief flights at all.

In Germany the Luftwaffe was stretching to assemble a fleet of Ju-52s to carry out Marshal Goering's promise to Hitler. The 20th, 21st, and 23rd Transport groups were preparing to move to the Stalingrad area.

At that moment the operating potential of the Luftwaffe was fair enough. General Richthofen had around Stalingrad an extensive network of airports, with five big aerodromes in the vicinity of the Cauldron—fields at Stalingrad, Gumrak, Basargino, Bolshaya Rossoskha, and Voronopovo. The shallow depth of the Russian encirclement seemed to make it possible to fly in both directions on short notice.

This factor should have also made it very difficult for the Russian fighters. By the time they got the word of a supply mission, and got their planes in the air to attack, the mission had usually landed. At this time the Germans were flying in supplies in small groups of planes, traveling at five thousand to ten thousand feet altitude, without fighter protection.

Nevertheless, General Richthofen made sure all his supply bases were well covered by antiaircraft guns. He also had the engineers get to work building emergency landing strips here and there.

As of December 1 the Russian 8th and 16th Air forces were assigned to the destruction of the Stalingrad airlift. The Russians brought up a fighter division and a ground support division, to airfields west of the pocket. In two days they changed the nature of the battle of the air, concentrating on the supply planes, and shot down twenty-eight aircraft, most of them the slow Ju-52s. From that time on the number of supply planes shot down increased to thirty and forty per day.

From the beginning Richthofen tried to convince Hitler that this idea of air supply was bound to fail. He sent a staff officer to Fuehrer headquarters. Hitler received the staff officer, for he had great respect for Richthofen, and he heard everything the officer said about the weather, about the shortage of aircraft, about the growing strength of the Russians' fighter force.

He heard, but he did not listen.

When the officer was finished, Hitler said that Goering had promised to deliver the supplies and that the 6th Army must be supplied and must remain in Stalingrad. That was all there was to it.

By December 8 the Russian forces were ready to attack. The attack was to begin on December 10. German defenses were to be assaulted between Bolshoye Kropotovo and Yarygino. Sychevka was to be seized by December 15.

During the early days of December, Field Marshal Manstein put his efforts to assembling the force to relieve the 6th Army. In the first week, Army Group Don was holding its front with a ragtag mixture of units formed up on short notice from headquarters staffs, noncombatant units, and Luftwaffe personnel. Most of these troops had no infantry training and knew nothing about close combat. They were short of antitank weapons and heavy artillery, but they managed to hold the bridgehead at the confluence of the Chir and the Don.

It was to this area that Manstein directed the first of his reinforcements. The remnants of the XLVIII Panzer Corps were brought south from Veshenskaya, and three new divisions were brought to the line of the northern Don. Best of these was the 11th Panzer Division, which had been in reserve since October. Other fresh divisions were the 6th Panzer, the 62nd and 294th Infantry, and a Luftwaffe division and a mountain division.

This new force, called the Hollidt Force—under General Karl Hollidt—would stand fast on the flank and only attack when the 4th Panzer Army drew level with the bridgehead at Nizhne Chirskaya. This action would then give the 6th Army two routes for escape, either to the west or to the south.

To reinforce General Hoth's 4th Panzer Army, Manstein secured from Hitler the 6th Panzer Army from Rostov and the LVII Panzer Corps from Army Group A.

In the meantime, the Hollidt detachment was threatened by a part of the Russian 5th Army. On December 7 and 8, however, the Russians were met by the 11th Panzer Division at State Farm No. 79, and the Russian threat was broken up by the German tanks. After that the 11th Panzer Division was employed to defend the bridgehead at Nizhne Chirskaya.

There it engaged in another battle with the Russians and lost many of its tanks. After that battle, in which the Russians were also driven off, the 11th Panzer Division strength was reduced by about half. It dug in.

The main relief column was concentrated at Kotelnikovo in the south. On December 10 Manstein informed Paulus that the column would move in twenty-four hours. Hitler was pleased. He told Manstein that he was confident the old position on the Don would soon be regained and that the first phase of the Russian winter offensive had been brought to an end "without a decision."

Manstein planned a three-phase operation:

1. He would attack from Kotelnikovo to the northeast.
2. The German elements along the Chir would attack out of the Chir bridgehead.
3. The 6th Army would break out to the south.

The final phase of the Manstein plan was not revealed to Hitler. The dictator believed that Manstein would deliver the supplies to Paulus and then set up in Stalingrad, to break the Russian ring and defeat the Russians. Manstein did not want to disabuse him, because he did not want one of those "stand fast" orders that Hitler was now issuing, which paralyzed all operations.

On December 12 the mission to relieve Stalingrad started off with the 23rd Panzer Division leading the way. The fighting force was the LVII Panzer Corps, with parts of two Luftwaffe divisions and on the flanks the re-formed Romanian 4th Army. Behind this striking force came a motley collection of eight hundred trucks with three thousand tons of supplies for the 6th Army. The vehicles were French, Czech, Russian, English, and American as well as German.

On December 13 and December 14 they moved north, making good progress against the Russian 51st Army, which had been reduced by recent fighting to about half its authorized strength. The ground was frozen hard, icy, with a covering of snow. It looked perfectly flat from the air, but this was illusory, for the snow covered many deep gorges and gullies across the route, and the drifting snow hid many small units of

Russians, battalion size or less, who were quiet in the daytime but rode out at night. Thus the Germans were harried by Russian cavalry and small track units by night. Even so, they moved on, and by December 15 the relief force was nearing the Aksai River.

37

The Stalingrad Cauldron was thirty miles wide and twenty miles long. Outside were the Russians, on every side, with the Volga River on the east. In the middle were five corps headquarters, and on the perimeter five divisions manned the line.

In the north, close to the Volga, were the 16th and 24th Panzer divisions. On the west were the 160th Motorized Division and the 113th Infantry. In the northwest were the 76th, 44th, and 384th divisions. At the far west was the 376th Division, or what was left of it, and the 3rd Motorized Division. On the south were the 29th Motorized Division and the 297th and 371st Infantry divisions. In reserve inside the pocket but uncommitted were the 14th Panzer Division and the 9th Antiaircraft Division, two Romanian divisions, and one regiment of Croatians.

In Stalingrad itself were the 71st, 79th, 100th, 295th, 305th, and 389th divisions, all of them bloody and battered, which had come so very close to winning the Battle of Stalingrad in October.

General Paulus had moved his headquarters to Gumrak on the steppe, four miles west of Stalingrad. The headquarters was established in twelve earth bunkers near the railroad station. Paulus lived in a bunker that was twelve feet square with six feet of frozen soil on top. The bunker was furnished with rude wooden tables and benches, made on the spot. It was heated by a homemade clay stove. Blankets were hung across the doorways to keep the wind out and the heat in. The vehicle park was away from the bunkers, so that from the air all that could be seen on the steppe was an occasional wisp of smoke.

December 1. The Germans in the Stalingrad pocket were already on half rations. As General Paulus had warned Hitler, by November 23 the army

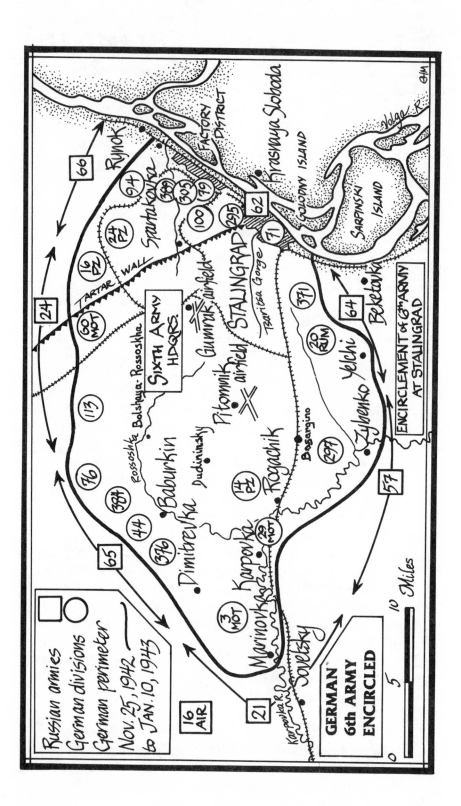

had only six days of food supply. The reason was that the Russian offensive had immediately cut them off from their railhead on the Chir and their nearby warehouses. Quartermaster Binder had made many trips to the warehouses. He had avoided the Russians and saved much, but they were already slaughtering the draft animals, three hundred horses a day.

On December 2 the Russians attacked from the south against the 297th Infantry. The attack was beaten off. It had not been anything serious. The Russians were just testing the defenses and making the Germans expend precious ammunition.

On December 3 the Russian high command adopted another plan for battle, Plan Saturn. It was the result of Stalin's questions to Zhukov and Zhukov's answers at the end of November. This plan called for the liquidation of the Germans in Stalingrad, and then the Germans in the bend of the Don, and finally the cutting off of the German forces in the Caucasus.

On December 4 the Russians attacked from the north and northwest against the 44th Division. The 14th Panzer Division was rushed in from reserve to help stop the attack. One German regiment lost five hundred men.

Then suddenly the Russians were gone. Again, it had not been anything serious. The Russians were following Zhukov's orders, more or less.

But such was the hatred of the Russian soldiers for the enemy that they could not always be restrained. In this fighting, for example, all the troops holding one position had been shot, stripped of their clothing, and left naked in the snow like slaughtered animals.

Elsewhere along the perimeter, it was almost quiet, but never safe. Snipers patrolled both sides of the line, and woe to the man who stuck his head up over the parapet or was seen running across the snow.

The action, such as it was, almost all turned out to be testing for Stalin's Plan Saturn. The Russians learned that they would have to strengthen their forces around Stalingrad if they wanted to carry it out. So new units were ordered up to the Stalingrad area, including the 2nd Guards Army under the command of Lieutenant General Rodion Malinovsky.

On the Volga the fighting continued in the old familiar places, on Mamayev Hill, in the Barrikady factory, in the Commissar's House and several other houses nearby. The Germans held the houses by day but the Russians infiltrated at night, and the battle went room-to-room. Every morning the corpses piled higher in the rooms, and there was no one to bury them.

38

When General Paulus saw the figures for the day's airlift on the night of December 7 he was encouraged. For the first time, the Luftwaffe had brought in nearly three hundred tons of supplies. But they were not to repeat that performance until December 19. The average tonnage turned out to be under one hundred.

On December 12 at the daily Hitler leadership conference in Rasten-burg the Fuehrer was briefed on the Stalingrad airlift. The figures given him were very impressive; they concerned the numbers of flights that had taken off to deliver supplies to Paulus. But what they did not reflect was the number of aborted missions and plane losses. The Russians noted with satisfaction that on December 10 and 11 they had destroyed eighty-nine German planes, most of them transports.

Because of the failure of the airlift, rations in the Stalingrad Cauldron were cut and cut again, until the whole army was on one-third the normal rations. Combat units were slaughtering their war dogs. Dober-man pinscher stew was delicious, one lieutenant said. Horse steaks, horse roast, stewed horse, and horse soup became gourmet fare. The officers and the noncoms got most of it, the common soldiers very little.

Every day the fighting capacity of the 6th Army went down a little more. As Paulus knew very well, hungry men are not good fighting men. But there was nothing to be done except wait for Manstein's relief expedition. That hope buoyed the Germans in Stalingrad, and though hungry, they fought very hard. General Chuikov paid them tribute:

"They continued to live in hopes and put up a desperate resistance, often literally to the last cartridge. We practically took no prisoners, since the Nazis just wouldn't surrender."

By December 12 the Germans of Stalingrad were tightening their belts and going hungry, but they were exhilarated by the word that Manstein had started north. At the 6th Army command post at Gumrak, General Paulus had ten radio operators monitoring the wavelengths hoping for news from Manstein. The Russians jammed every channel, and if there were messages, none of them got through.

That night of December 12 the Russians attacked along the 62nd Army front, in the factory area, and the center of the city.

General Chuikov—still in the dark as to the plans of his superiors—kept fighting as he was ordered to do. He had not received reinforcements since the beginning of the Soviet offensive in November. As for supplies, they were being delivered from the east bank of the Volga to the Russian fighting men on the west bank by launch and by liaison plane. It would be another week before the Volga froze over and the sleighs could travel across the ice.

"The streets and squares continued to be deserted," General Chuikov said. "Neither we nor the Germans could act openly. Whoever stuck his head out or ran across the street was inevitably shot by a sniper or tommygunner."

The hand-to-hand slaughter inside Stalingrad went on and on.

PART XII
MANSTEIN'S DRIVE

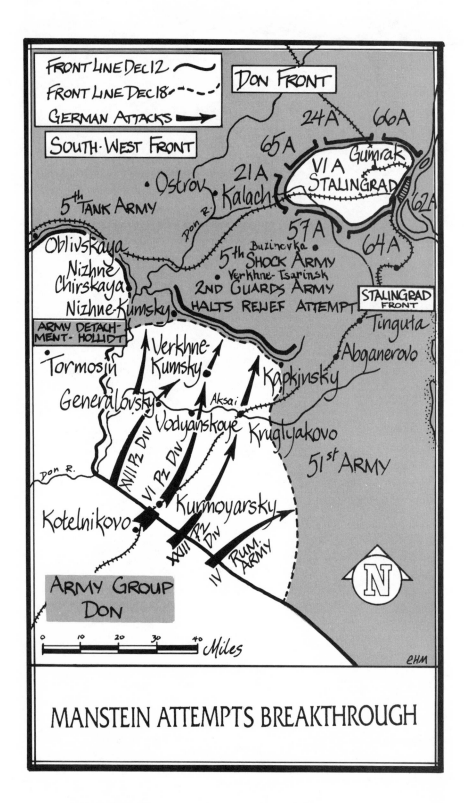

MANSTEIN ATTEMPTS BREAKTHROUGH

39

When Field Marshal Manstein launched his relief expedition to Stalingrad on the morning of December 12, he took the Russians completely by surprise. General Yeremenko telephoned Stalin and told him that he feared the Germans would hit the rear of the Russian 57th Army, which was sealing off the southwestern edge of the Stalingrad pocket. If Paulus were to strike from inside the pocket at the same time with his 200,000 fighting troops, there was nothing to prevent his breaking out.

It was only hours before the Russian high command was aware of the Manstein move. Russian Army Chief of Staff Vasilevsky happened to be visiting the headquarters of the 51st Army at Verkhne-Tsarinsk that day along with Commissar Nikita Khrushchev. Vasilevsky telephoned Marshal Rokossovsky and told him that he wanted to divert the 2nd Guards Army from the Don Front to the Stalingrad Front to stop Manstein. Rokossovsky objected. The matter was referred to Stalin, who refused to make an immediate decision.

Meanwhile, driving along the railroad, the Germans advanced against the Russian 51st Army, which had been greatly weakened in the fighting of November.

The Germans had a sixty-mile march to the southern edge of the pocket. It started very well. The 11th Panzer Regiment of the 6th Panzer Division hit elements of the 51st Army on the first day, and they fell back to the east.

After the first few days of good weather, the skies clouded over, visibility was reduced to a ceiling of five hundred feet, and the Luftwaffe was grounded. When the column reached the Aksai River, Manstein found that the ice on the river was only solid enough to carry foot soldiers, not tanks. But there were two bridges, at Shestakovo and Romashkin, where the railroad from Caucasus crossed the river.

Zhukov had sent 120 tanks and two infantry divisions with tanks and artillery to defend the Aksai River crossings.

With air support from the Luftwaffe, the advance continued rapidly. In three days the Manstein force had advanced 25 miles and then crossed the Aksai. Following conversations with Yeremenko, who continued to air his fears, Stalin demanded that the general hold with whatever he had. He acceded to Vasilevsky's request for the 2nd Guards Army on the morning of December 13, but it was several days before that army could get into action.

While this series of events occurred south of Stalingrad, to the west, on the Don, the Russians on December 16 launched an offensive of their own, aimed at cutting up the force Manstein had assembled at Verkhni-Mamon. Two army groups under Generals Golikov and Vatutin were involved. They moved on a front of thirty miles on both sides of the Don. For a change, the Russians had excellent air support. In the first few days their aircraft flew four thousand missions in support of the troops.

Most of the troops in this area belonged to the Italian 8th Army, with one German division and two battalions of another. The German reserve was the 27th Panzer Division, but it was equipped with repaired tanks for the most part, tanks that had already seen their better days.

The ice on the Don was so thick that the Russian tanks could cross as they wished, and during the daylight hours thick fog covered the battlefield. The Italians were not used to this sort of weather or this sort of fighting, and many units panicked. Five Italian divisions were decimated, as well as a brigade of Black Shirts, Mussolini's counterpart of Hitler's fighting SS. The Italian army of 250,000 men was cut in half.

News of this Russian thrust was conveyed to Manstein that night. It was clear that something very serious had occurred. The responsibility was not Manstein's but that of Army Group B, but the threat to his flank was very real, as was the threat to the German forces in the Caucasus.

At the same time the German position on the lower Chir River began to crumble under Russian attack at Nizhne Chirskaya, where the

Russians had thrown in four infantry divisions and driven the Germans back to the west bank.

That night they threw in more troops. The 11th Panzer Division was again called to help, but it was apparent that the whole of the Hollidt detachment was about to be pushed out of the Chir bulge.

The two "Luftwaffe divisions" had turned out to be straw soldiers. This whole idea of infantry of the Luftwaffe was Hermann Goering's, and the Luftwaffe had neither the system nor the officers to conduct proper training for field troops. Thus the Luftwaffe field divisions were nothing more than men with guns, men who did not know how to use their weapons in battle. In this fight they were virtually wiped out.

The good news for Manstein on December 18 was that the 17th Panzer Division had arrived on the fighting front at the Aksai, and the German strength there was considerably greater than the Russian. If the 4th Panzer Army could open the ring, and the 6th Army's eleven divisions came out, the balance of strength would be tipped to the Germans.

The fighting north of the Aksai was as violent as any that had gone before anywhere. The 6th Panzer Division was trying to reach Verkhne-Kumsky. The Russians had prepared a network of rifle pits that made it almost impossible for the tanks to advance.

And the Russians would not surrender. The Germans brought their tanks to the trenches and fired from point-blank range. After a long afternoon Soviet armor arrived, and the Panzers retreated to the village. The Mishkova River was still ahead, and the weather was not helping any. It seemed to be growing colder by the hour, but the Germans were determined to drive northward and they kept going.

Still, Manstein faced difficulties. Hitler had no enthusiasm for the 6th Army breakout, nor did Oberkommando des Heeres, the army high command. Even Paulus, who had earlier talked of breakout, was strangely silent on the subject now that Hitler had ordered him to stand fast.

The general made an inspection tour of the front that day. What he saw at the XIV Panzer Division quarters appalled him. His men moved like robots in the snow. Their faces were red and the cheekbones stuck out. Their eyes were sunken and vacant. This was one of the two best fighting units on the Eastern Front? No one could now believe that. It was questionable in Paulus's mind whether his men had the ability or the will to break out of the pocket.

He went back to the command bunker at Gumrak to await developments. Perhaps he would learn something new about Manstein's plans and progress.

That day Manstein sent a message to General Zeitzler at OKH asking him to take immediate action to initiate the breakout of the 6th Army toward the 4th Panzer Army.

That night, December 18, Major Eismann, the intelligence officer of Army Group Don, was sent into the Stalingrad pocket to see General Paulus and tell him what Manstein wanted him to do.

During the night he drove from Novocherkassk to Morosovosk, and there took off from the airfield in a Fieseler Storch reconnaissance plane an hour before dawn. He arrived at Gumrak airfield just before eight o'clock on the morning of December 19 and was taken to Paulus's bunker. Waiting for him were the general, his chief of staff, General Schmidt, two corps commanders, and the chief quartermaster and the chief of operations of the 6th Army.

Major Eismann gave Manstein's views. Paulus now turned evasive. There were many difficulties and risks in an attempt to break out of the pocket, said the general. Then the chief of operations and the quartermaster spoke up. It sounded to Eismann as if he were listening to carefully rehearsed set pieces. But when questioned by Eismann, both officers finally admitted that "in the circumstances it is not only essential to attempt a breakout at the earliest possible moment, but entirely feasible."

After all this, General Schmidt had his say. He was an ardent Nazi, and since Hitler had said "hold," he had no other course in mind.

"It is quite impossible to break out just now," said General Schmidt. "It would be an acknowledgment of disaster. Sixth Army will still be in position at Easter. All you people have to do is supply it."

The discussions continued all day. From time to time gunfire shook the dugout.

During the afternoon a very bad lunch was served, as if to emphasize the truth of what Major Eismann was contending, that time was running out. But General Paulus seemed bent on blaming his troubles on the failure of Manstein to get supplies to him and the failure of the Luftwaffe to bring supplies in by air.

The major offered three alternatives:

1. Break out and link up with the 4th Panzer Army.
2. Break out without linkup.
3. Hold out.

General Paulus said he would think about them, but by the end of the day it was apparent to the major that Paulus was not going to make any effort to break out of Stalingrad.

Major Eismann returned to Manstein to announce that his mission had been a failure. However, Paulus was still of two minds and was, in fact, making preparations for breakout. He assigned one regiment the job of leading the breakthrough and told the men to get ready. He moved armored combat groups into the southwest sector of the perimeter. He called on his combat engineers to plow and keep clear the road network around the pocket. He assigned two road construction battalions to deactivate the minefields when the time came.

Manstein had the news that General Hoth had passed the Aksai line and moved as far as the Mishkova.

That afternoon Manstein telegraphed General Zeitzler: "I now consider a breakout to the southwest to be the last possible means of preserving at least the bulk of the troops and the still mobile elements of the 6th Army."

By nightfall he had not had an answer. Manstein then sent a message directly to Paulus using a radio circuit that could not be monitored by the Russians. What followed was a teleprinter conversation between generals.

First, Manstein asked for Paulus's comments on the Eismann report. Paulus gave them:

1. Break out to link up with 4th Panzer Army was possible only with tanks. The infantry did not have the strength. This would take all the armored reserves.
2. Break out without linkup. This would result in heavy losses. Before it could be done, the 6th Army must have sufficient food and fuel to improve the condition of the troops. The infantry divisions were almost immobilized because horses were being slaughtered to feed the men.
3. Hold out. This would depend on the Luftwaffe bringing in supplies as promised. The scale of one hundred tons a day was totally inadequate.

Then General Paulus added: "Further holding out on present basis not possible much longer."

Manstein then responded, and Paulus and his staff stood at the teleprinter and read the messages as they came in.

M.: When at the earliest could you start alternative 2?

P.: Time needed for preparation three to four days.

M.: How much fuel and food required?

P.: Reduced rations for ten days for 270,000 men.

M.: 4th Panzer Army attack has reached the Mishkova River.

P.: Enemy forces have attacked 6th Army combat groups assembled for breakout, in southwest corner of perimeter.

M.: Stand by to receive an order.

Order

To Sixth Army:

(1) Fourth Panzer Army has defeated the enemy in the Verkhne-Kumsky area with LVII Panzer Corps and reached the Mishkova sector. An attack has been initiated against a strong enemy group in the Kamenka area and north of it. Heavy fighting is to be expected there. The situation on the Chir front does not permit the advance of forces west of the Don towards Stalingrad. The Don bridge at Chirskaya is in enemy hands.

(2) Sixth Army will launch "Winter Storm" as soon as possible. Measures must be taken to establish link-up with LVII Panzer Corps if necessary across the Donskaya Tsaritsa in order to get a convoy through.

(3) Development of the situation may make it imperative to extend instruction for Army to break through to LVII Panzer Corps as far as the Mishkova. Code name: Thunder Clap. In that case the main task will again be the quickest establishment of contact, by means of tanks, with LVII Panzer Corps with a view to getting convoy through. The Army, its flanks having been covered along the lower Karpovka and the Chervlenaya, must then be moved forward toward the Mishkova while the fortress area is evacuated section by section.

Operation Thunder Clap may have to follow directly on attack Winter Storm. Aerial supplies will, on the whole, have to be brought in currently, without major buildup of stores. Airfield of Pitomnik must be held as long as possible.

All arms and artillery that can be moved at all to be taken along, especially the guns needed for the operation, and to be ammuni-tioned, but also such weapons and equipment as are difficult to replace. These must be concentrated in the southwestern part of the pocket in good time.

(4) Preparations to be made for (3). Putting into effect only under express order Thunder Clap.

(5) Report day and time of attack. (2).

All day long on December 19 Manstein had been trying to get Hitler's approval of this plan, but Hitler did not reply to his messages.

At 8:30 that night General Friedrich Schultz, chief of staff to Army Group Don, and General Schmidt, chief of staff to 6th Army, were again conversing by teleprinter.

General Schmidt reported that Russian attacks in the southwest were engaging most of the 6th Army tanks and part of its infantry. "Only when these forces have ceased to be tied down in defensive fighting can a breakout be launched. Earliest date, 22 December."

On the morning of December 20 General Paulus visited the crisis centers of the pocket. All day the fighting continued in many sectors. His interest was in the threats to the southwest, where he might break out. He did not go to the Volga, where he knew what was happening: the fighting in the streets was going on and on.

Because he did not go to the Volga, the general was spared a sight that would become more and more common. An officer of the 576th Regiment at the Barrikady gun factory was detached to join a unit west of Stalingrad, and began walking down the road.

It was thirty below zero. He noticed a man sitting on the side of the road in the snow, not moving. He recognized the soldier. It was a man of his regiment. He asked the man if he was tired, and the man nodded. The officer and his orderly helped the soldier stand up and supported him. When they came to an aid station, they took him to a doctor. An hour later he died. Starvation.

Back at the Barrikady gun factory the soldier's comrades were ripping up the wooden flooring of the room they used as barracks, and building tiny fires. The flooring was oil-soaked from years of industrial use, and the fires produced a black greasy smoke that pained the lungs, smoke that turned every man's face to soot.

On that afternoon the chiefs of staff held another teleprinter conversation.

Schmidt:

As a result of losses during the past few days manpower situation on the western front and in Stalingrad is exceedingly tight. Penetrations can be cleared up only by drawing upon the forces earmarked for Winter Storm. In the event of major penetrations, let alone breakthroughs, our Army reserves, in particular the tanks, have to be employed if the fortress is to be held at all. The situation could be viewed somewhat differently if it were certain that Winter Storm would be followed immediately by Thunder Clap. In that event, local penetrations on the remaining fronts could be accepted provided they did not jeopardize the withdrawal of the Army as a whole. In that event we could be considerably stronger for a breakout towards the south, as we could then concentrate in the south numerous reserves from all fronts.

But being a loyal Nazi, General Schmidt had persuaded Paulus not to move until Hitler's permission for the 6th Army breakout—Operation Thunder Clap—had been secured.

General Schultz then appealed to Schmidt:

Dear Schmidt: The field marshal believes that 6th Army must launch Winter Storm as soon as possible. You cannot wait until Hoth has got Buzinovka. We fully realize that your attacking strength for Winter Storm will be limited. That is why the Field Marshal is trying to get approval for Thunder Clap.

He appealed again to 6th Army to get going: There were three thousand tons of supply waiting for them. The 4th Panzer Army would provide towing vehicles. Thirty buses had been laid on to handle the 6th Army wounded. Everything, it seemed, had been considered.

But Hitler would not budge. He would not give permission to evacuate Stalingrad. "I will not leave the Volga," he said over and over again.

And Paulus, chivied by the loyal Nazi Schmidt, would not go against his Fuehrer's orders, even though in Stalingrad real starvation had set in. The men were eating mice and anything else that moved.

The airlift was becoming a fiasco, although the men of the Luftwaffe were sacrificing their lives every day. Thirty percent of the flights to Stalingrad ended in disaster, usually with the loss of the plane and its crew and the supplies that would never be delivered. Russian fighters were taking a greater toll, but the principal enemies were the weather and lack of service to the aircraft. In the intense cold, if a man stuck his hand on a metal part, they welded together, frozen. It was so cold that the bolts and fasteners on aircraft left out overnight would not work. Under these circumstances many planes crashed.

Such was the hurry and the disorganization of the airlift that it was not being supervised at the loading end by trained quartermaster personnel. The planes were loaded with whatever happened to be delivered to the airport. One shipment of condoms, millions of condoms, was delivered. Four tons of spices were delivered. Several thousand right shoes came in, but no left shoes.

Many of the soldiers were now too weak to stand guard. The fighting efficiency of the 6th Army was down to perhaps 25 percent of its strength. There was very little fuel. In fact, General Schmidt, when asked for a figure, told Manstein that the 6th Army had only enough fuel to move twenty miles, and the 4th Panzer Army was thirty miles away.

In a heated discussion with General Zeitzler about the 6th Army, Hitler put his finger on the problem. He had the fuel report in his hand.

"What do you want me to do?" he demanded of Zeitzler. "Paulus can't break out and you know it."

40

On December 21 Manstein reported to Hitler that the 4th Panzer Army had reached a point about thirty miles from Stalingrad, but was being heavily engaged by Russian tanks and infantry and could make no more progress. Chief of Staff Zeitzler tried to get approval for the breakout, but Hitler said the 6th Army could break out only if it could also hold Stalingrad on the Volga.

This nonsense convinced many of those around Hitler that his obsessions were now in charge and that he was incapable of making a rational decision.

By December 23 the situation was becoming more complicated by the success of the Russian drive on the Chir west of Stalingrad. The danger was so great that Manstein had to move one of 4th Panzer Army's three divisions to the west to the lower Chir to protect the flank and prevent further breakthrough by the Russians. General Hoth sent his 6th Panzer Division. But that action so weakened his drive toward Stalingrad that the prospect of further progress was nil.

The 6th Panzer Division could not move west in time to stop one particular tragedy that affected the future of the 6th Army directly. At dawn the German air base at Tatsinskaya, about two hundred miles west of Gumrak, was under fire from Russian artillery.

The attack had been expected ever since the beginning of the Russian drive in the west, and General Richthofen had asked Hitler time and again for permission to move the transport planes stationed here, but Hitler had refused. The German troops who were coming would take care of the enemy, Hitler said. This morning General Martin Fiebig, the commander there, watched as Russian shell fire began to blow up his Ju-52s.

His officers pleaded to be allowed to get the planes into the air. Fiebig said he needed authority. Besides, the field was socked in that morning with fog. But the shelling continued, and the planes continued to burn.

Finally General Fiebig could stand it no longer and gave permission to get the planes off the field. The pilots rushed to their aircraft, and motors began to race. Soon Ju-52s were hurrying into the air.

They took off from all the runways in thorough confusion. Two planes collided and erupted in balls of flame. But scores of them got into the air and climbed above the field.

At a little after six o'clock in the morning T-34 tanks began to appear on the field and the last of the Ju-52s roared away as the Russians took control. Of the 180 planes on the field, nearly 60 were lost.

On Christmas Eve the 4th Panzer Army had to withdraw behind the Aksai River in the face of heavy attack by reinforced Russian units. That day other Russian reinforcements crossed the Volga from the east, armed with new tanks and guns, to join General Chuikov's 62nd Army. They replaced the remnants of the Russian troops who had held the foothold on the west bank of the Volga for the past two months.

General Chuikov held forth in his command post, toasting his old comrades in vodka and smoking endless cigarettes. Then those officers headed across the Volga to rest camps, taking the two thousand survivors of the twenty thousand who had come to fight at the tractor factory and the Red October plant.

In the Red October plant, tattered and weary German soldiers gathered to celebrate Christmas around a Christmas tree that someone had carved from wooden crates. Their Christmas Eve feast was a slice of horse meat, a piece of bread, and extra cigarettes. Someone produced some rum and a little wine. Two of the officers argued the merits and demerits of suicide.

The men manning the guardposts listened to propaganda broadcasts from the Russians, calling on them to lay down their arms and surrender. They would be treated humanely and they would even meet some Russian girls. Most of the soldiers smiled. It was just Russian propaganda.

Quartermaster Binder went to church service that night, walking along the frozen road, passing the mounds of unburied bodies. That night he wrote home: "During the past weeks all of us have begun to think about the end of everything. . . ."

Christmas morning opened with an attack on the Cauldron by the Russians in the southwest. The principal target was the sector held by the 16th Panzer Division. The Germans fought resolutely, but there were too many Russian tanks, and the German 88mm guns ran out of ammunition. They blew up the guns and retreated to the second line of resistance.

That afternoon they counted casualties. Their losses and those of the Russians had been shocking. That night the attack was the subject of General Schmidt's nightly teleprinter conversations with Army Group Don. He lied to General Schultz about the success of the German counterattack but admitted the Russians had taken an important hill in the sector. He asked General Schultz if the 4th Panzer Army was still holding on the Mishkova River. Schultz lied that it was.

That night General Schmidt supervised the writing of the day's entry in the army war diary: "Forty-eight hours without food supplies. Food and fuel are nearing their end . . . the strength of the men is rapidly decreasing. . . ."

On their shortwave radios some German Stalingrad units picked up a special Christmas broadcast prepared by Dr. Goebbels for the home front. The broadcasters took the audience from Germany, to France, to Norway, Tunisia, and Greece. "And now," said the announcer, "here is Stalingrad."

A joyful chorus of soldiers' voices filled the airwaves.

Everyone in Stalingrad recognized it as ersatz. Probably the others were, too.

December 26. In the nightly teleprinter discussion General Schmidt reported that Stalingrad had received forty-one air transports that day carrying seventy-one tons of supply. They had only enough bread for two days, food for one day, and no fat. On December 27 they would ration out the last of the fuel. General Paulus had just been waiting for Christmas to pass to cut the ration again. From now on each man would receive two ounces of bread per day, soup without fat for luncheon, soup for dinner, with a can of meat when it was available.

That night the teleprinter conversations ended. Russian tanks captured the relay stations west of the pocket. From this point on, communication could be maintained only by a handful of field radio sets, and the messages would have to be coded because the Russians would be listening.

41

Field Marshal Manstein was still trying to convince Hitler to order the 6th Army breakout, although it was very late. He explained the consequence that had come of Hitler's diverting one of his divisions to the Chir.

> This measure means dropping for an indefinite period the relief of Sixth Army, which in turn means the Army would now have to be adequately supplied on a long term basis. In Richthofen's opinion no more than a daily average of 200 tons can be counted on. Unless adequate supplies can be assured for Sixth Army the only remaining alternative is the earliest possible breakout of Sixth Army at the cost of a considerable risk along the left wing of Army Group. The risks involved in this operation, in view of the Army's condition, are sufficiently known.

As everyone knew, the army's condition was much worse than that. The supply airlift was only producing about eighty tons a day, and that not every day. When the weather was too bad, more planes crashed and fewer got through. As all the generals agreed, the only solution was for Paulus to break out.

Paulus, however, would not move without Hitler's permission, and Hitler would not give that permission. Everything else—all the discus-

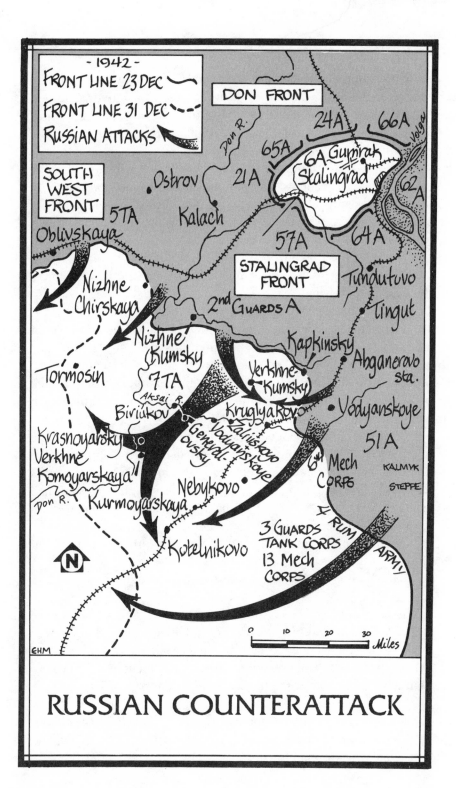

RUSSIAN COUNTERATTACK

sions of the amount of fuel on hand and the amount needed, the condition of the army—was as nothing because Hitler refused to act. Even by Christmas 1942, it was probably too late to have saved the whole army in a breakout. But most of the 270,000 men of 6th Army in the pocket could have been saved.

Hitler ignored Manstein's warnings and continued to believe that the 6th Army was safe inside its "fortress" and that it would hang on until spring. He had many other matters on his mind just at this moment, not the least of which was the Soviet drive on the southwest, which threatened the German troops in the Caucasus as well as Stalingrad. On December 28, as the 4th Panzer Army was stalled behind the Aksai River, and the 6th Army refused to break out of Stalingrad, the Russian forces in the west were moving.

General Vatutin reported to Stalin that in two weeks his forces had destroyed seventeen divisions, most of them Italian, and seized their supplies. They had taken sixty thousand prisoners and killed sixty thousand enemy soldiers. The Germans and their allies continued to stand fast along the line from Oblivskaya to Verkhne-Chirsky. In the Morozovsk area the Russians captured many men of the German 11th Tank Division and the 8th Airborne Division.

But the troops sent by General Hoth were holding the line of the southern Don. Aerial reconnaissance showed troops moving into the northern Donets area, and the Russians began to believe the Germans were preparing this as a main line of defense. For now, the Russians had to content themselves with containing the Germans on the west of Stalingrad, and not pursuing Stalin's greater dream, to cut off the troops in the Caucasus and eliminate them after the 6th Army was destroyed at Stalingrad.

So by the end of 1942, Zhukov assessed the situation:

The successful strikes of the Southwest and Stalingrad Fronts against the enemy forces in the areas of Kotelnikovo and Morozovsk finally sealed the fate of von Paulus' forces encircled at Stalingrad. Our troops in a brilliant execution of their assignment broke up von Manstein's attempt to reach the trapped Germans.

As the year came to an end, the Russians had reached a line that ran from Novaya Kalitva through Voloshino, Millerovo, and Morozovsk, and threatened all the German forces in the Caucasus.

But first there was the German 6th Army to deal with. At the end of December Stalin decided he would put this task in the hands of a single commander, and he chose General Rokossovsky with his Don Front. General Yeremenko was ordered to transfer his 57th Army, 64th Army, and 62nd Army to Rokossovsky, his Stalingrad Front was renamed the Southern Front and sent off to fight the Germans in the Rostov area, and Rokossovsky began preparations to wipe out the Germans in Stalingrad. Rokossovsky had 212,000 men, 6,500 guns, 250 tanks, and 300 aircraft to do the job.

STALINGRAD WINTER

Perhaps it was the humidity generated by the Volga, perhaps it was the wind across the steppe, but the cold of Stalingrad that winter was excruciating. In a day the temperature would run up and down 25 degrees or more. One morning it was -20 degrees, and then it dropped to -30. By afternoon it was -35 degrees. Evening brought a fall to -40 degrees and the dark of night took the thermometer down to -44. One of the correspondents who later visited Stalingrad described the intensity of the cold:

Your breath catches. If you breathe on your glove a thin film of ice immediately forms. We couldn't eat anything, because all our food—bread, sausage, and eggs—had turned into stone. Even wearing valenki [felt boots] and two pairs of woolen socks, you had to move your toes all the time to keep the circulation going. Without valenki, frostbite would have been certain, and the Germans had no valenki. To keep your hands in good condition you had to clap them half the time or play imaginary scales. Once I took out a pencil to write down a few words. The first word was all right, the second was written by a drunk, the last two were the scrawl of a paralytic; quickly I blew on my purple fingers and put them back in the fur lined glove.

And in this weather German and Russian soldiers fought each other.

PART XIII

STARVATION

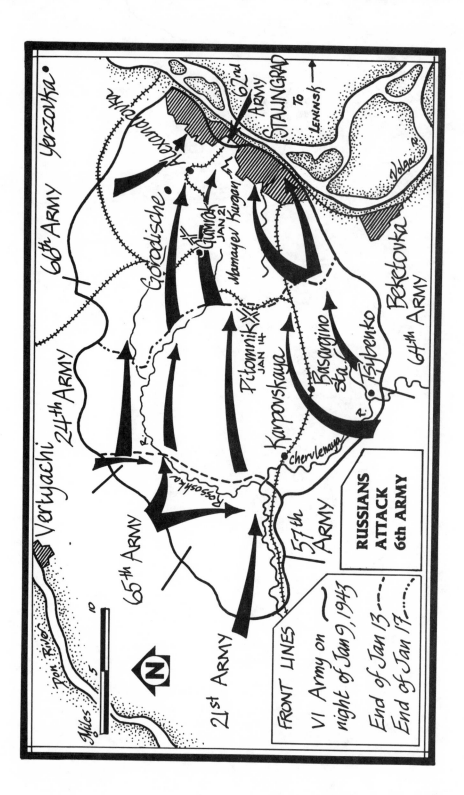

Yerzovka •

Alexandreuka

66th ARMY

62nd ARMY
STALINGRAD
To Leninsk →

Volga

Gorodische •

Gumrak
JAN 21

Mamayev Kurgan

Pitomnik
JAN 14

Vertyachi

24th ARMY

Don River

Basargino Sta.

Tsybenko

Bektovka

64th ARMY

Karpovskaya

Rossoshka

Chervlenaya

57th ARMY

65th ARMY

Miles
5   10

N

21st ARMY

RUSSIANS
ATTACK
6th ARMY

FRONT LINES

VI Army on
night of Jan 9, 1943

End of Jan 13 ----
End of Jan 17 ......

42

New Year's Eve, 1942. On the Mishkova Front, General Hoth's 4th Panzer Army had fought a desperate battle, trying to maintain the Stalingrad corridor after all the rebuffs. The decision to dispatch the 6th Panzer Division west to fend off the Russian drive toward the Caucasus had sealed the fate of the 6th Army.

Now General Hoth did not have the strength to advance farther. It was all he could do to fend off the superior Russian forces and maintain his mobility. All that Paulus could possibly do now would be break out and save a part of his forces, if he so chose. But since Hitler still refused to authorize the breakout, the 6th Army was anchored in Stalingrad.

At this point Manstein stopped thinking about saving the 6th Army. It was necessary instead that they hold out and that they engage the half million Soviet troops in the ring around Stalingrad. Otherwise these Russian armies could be turned south, and the whole German force in the Caucasus would be lost.

The role of the 4th Panzer Army was to slow the Russians in the south, and General Hoth was doing that with great skill. The 4th Panzer Army managed to get across the Mishkova River in one place near Nizhne Kumsky and surrounded several Russian units of regimental size. At the nearest point the 4th Panzer Army was still only 22 miles from the 6th Army perimeter. But the general advance had ended several days before, and now the Russians had driven the main force of the 4th Panzer Army back sixty miles below Kotelnikovo, the starting point of the relief mission. No longer could the men of the 6th Army see the gun flashes in the south that brought them hope.

So it was also on the west. The Germans had been pushed back twenty-five miles from the Nizhne Chirskaya bridgehead, and the besieged forces in the pocket could no longer see their gunfire either. The nights were growing very dark at Stalingrad.

On the night of December 31 General S. S. Biryuzov, the chief of staff of the Russian 2nd Guards Army, was working late in his office. An officer hand-delivered an invitation from General Pavel M. Rotmistrov, commander of the Russian VII Tank Corps, to a New Year's Eve party.

General Biryuzov at first felt angry. To hold a celebration in the middle of a campaign seemed most improper. But then he considered the matter. The ebullient Rotmistrov was no mean fighter, and he had already made a reputation for himself in the past three weeks of battle. General Biryuzov decided to go to the party.

When he got to Rotmistrov's quarters in Kotelnikovo, he found all the senior officers there, including Army Chief of Staff Vasilevsky. They were standing about a Christmas tree, with vodka glasses in hand. On a candlelit table nearby was a real feast: all kinds of cheese from France and Holland, French wines, butter and bacon from Denmark, and tinned fish and jams from Norway. All these delicacies were in packages stamped "For Germans Only."

General Rotmistrov apologized. "Not all my men can read German," he said, "so when they found this stuff they took it all. But we'll have to give the candles back to Hitler, so that he can light them in mourning for his 6th Army."

Next day the front was stirred by action once again. In the daylight hours the Germans in Stalingrad fought the Russians. At night they fought the mice and rats. All the human and horse meat piled up around the battlefields inside the pocket had caused the rat and mouse population to explode and the rodents to become bolder and bolder.

The German soldiers attacked the rats with knives and spades and rifle butts. The rats attacked the soldiers while they slept. One infantryman with frostbitten feet lost two toes to a rat one night and did not even know it until the morning. An officer from OKW who had been sent to Stalingrad to report what was going on told that story in his report, along with other horror tales. But his reports were dismissed at Fuehrer headquarters as defeatist. Marshal Goering even had the temerity to suggest that the Russians had stolen the officers' radio transmitter and were using it. Nobody thought of checking to find out if the officer was there and what he was saying might be true. The "loyal" officers had a way of handling such problems. In one infantry company a man went to sleep and did not wake up; the same night two men on a trench-digging detail stumbled, fell down, and did not get up. When their lieutenant reported the deaths to the captain in command of the company, he was told to list them as "killed in action." That is what he did.

The Russian bridgehead on the west side of the Volga was growing stronger every day. The river was frozen solid, and hundreds of trucks crossed daily bringing American food, plenty of ammunition, and all the warm clothing anyone would need. The Russian equivalent of the USO began to send actors, ballet dancers, and musicians to the Stalingrad Front to entertain the troops.

AMERICAN AID TO THE RUSSIANS

When the war began in 1939 the United States was extremely suspicious of Russian attitudes, and the attack on Finland brought American antipathy to such a high level that a volunteer corps of Americans was formed to fight the Russians. But when Hitler attacked Russia in the summer of 1942 the American attitude changed overnight, and Russia became "our gallant ally." Lend Lease to the Russians began in August 1941, four months before the U.S. entered the war. By November 1941 President Roosevelt had granted the Russians a loan of a billion dollars to finance Lend Lease deliveries. The amount of assistance kept growing. By the fall of 1942 the Americans planned to deliver 4.5 million tons of supply to the Russians by the spring of 1943.

American policy toward Russia was far more open handed than British policy. The British warned the Americans that Stalin would take over all of Eastern Europe unless checked, but Roosevelt wanted Stalin to enter the war against Japan, and to join the United Nations organization which he believed would curb Russian ambitions.

(continued next page)

(continued from preceding page)

Therefore American policy began to diverge sharply from British policy in 1943 and continued to diverge until the end of the war in Europe.

From the beginning of the attack on Russia, Stalin called for Allied assistance and a second front to be established in Western Europe to take the pressure off the Russians. Thereafter he was unremitting in his clamor for that second front, and was unimpressed and ungrateful when the Americans and British gave him his second front in North Africa, in the autumn of 1942. Throughout the war Stalin and his officials kept pressing for more Allied assistance, but told the Russian people virtually nothing about it. Still, the appearance of American jeeps and trucks and aircraft could not be denied, and the Russian people had a pretty good knowledge of the extent of American and British assistance during the war.

On January 1 Hitler issued his New Year's message to General Paulus and the men of Stalingrad: "You and your soldiers should begin the new year with a strong faith that I and the German Wehrmacht will use all strength to relieve the defenders of Stalingrad and make their long wait the highest achievement of German war history."

Some believed. Many others were beyond hope. Anyone who ate his thumbnail-sized piece of bread knew that the airlift was a failure. Once in a while the Luftwaffe managed to deliver two hundred tons. Many days they did not deliver anything at all.

The principal supply field, Pitomnik, lay inside a network of highways that were kept clear of snow by herculean effort from the combat engineers. They marked the edges of the roads with round stakes. Only the observant noted that those stakes were the legs of horses. They were easier to find than wooden posts.

The weather was so cold that the snow-removal equipment would hardly operate. On blizzard days the engineers wore gas masks to prevent frostbite. Nor could all their effort be directed at road clearance. They also had to dispose of the wrecked transports that littered the field, victims of Russian fighters and Russian antiaircraft. The Russians had placed hundreds of antiaircraft batteries outside the pocket on the flight lines from the German supply fields to Pitomnik.

At Army Group Don headquarters in Novocherkassk, Field Marshal Manstein now did not want Hitler to change his mind or the 6th Army to attempt a breakout. He was completely occupied by the peril 400 miles south of Stalingrad where Army Group A was isolated in the foothills of the Caucasus Mountains. The Russian troops in the west were being urged by Stalin to move into the "Great Saturn" operation, which was to drive to Rostov and cut off the German 1st Panzer Army and the 17th Army, creating another Stalingrad.

As the year opened, the entire German army in Russia was in peril. The front was now twelve hundred miles long. The top half, running from the Baltic to Orel, was static and had been for months. It was in the south that the fate of the German adventure in Russia would be decided.

In the first week of January 1943 Manstein's forces were divided into three segments, none of which could help the others. Since the 6th Army was surrounded, the mobile German strength in Russia was cut in half. This is why Stalin was so eager to wipe out the 6th Army. In the southeast Army Group A was vulnerable to Russian encirclement, which Stalin was planning. Manstein's Army Group Don had lost almost half its effectiveness in the fighting of the last few weeks. The western half was now built around a handful of fighting groups.

For the first time since the beginning of Operation Barbarossa, the Russians had the stronger army, although they were short on competent leadership.

Zhukov was trying to cut the Germans off in the south, but one-third of his force was still battling Paulus, unable to overrun the Stalingrad Cauldron. In that sense, then, although Paulus was in peril, and he was losing one man every seven seconds, his army was still of value to the Reich.

Just now, in the first week of January, Manstein's attention was focused on the specific problems of extricating Army Group A from the Caucasus. His method was to leave General Hoth's 4th Panzer Army in position south of Stalingrad, with freedom to pull back gradually toward Rostov while keeping open the line of retreat for Army Group A. But this, too, depended on the ability of Paulus to hold out for one more month.

Hoth was doing a magnificent job of fighting a delaying action, moving a little bit toward Rostov and stopping to delay the Russian again.

Hitler watched, and he grew annoyed. This was not his way of fighting war. He recalled that he had saved the German armies in Russia in the previous winter with his "stand fast" policy, when all the generals had wanted to retreat.

Hoth must stand firm, he said. Manstein got that message on January 5 and promptly offered to resign his command. "Should this headquarters continue to be tied down," he telegraphed Hitler, "I cannot see that any useful purpose will be served by my continuing as commander of Army Group Don."

Hitler backed down. Hoth's campaign of evasion and attack went on.

Hitler did not expect to evacuate the Caucasus. This would be just too much, added to the desperate plight into which the 6th Army had gotten. The Fuehrer talked about contracting the front, but leaving a "balcony" from which he could later undertake the capture of the Russian oil fields. He wanted to hold Novorossisk, which would confine the Russian Black Sea fleet to one port (Batum) and supply Kleist's Army Group A across the strait from the Crimea. Later he could return in triumph to the Caucasus.

Manstein wanted to have all those divisions of Army Group A to strengthen Army Group Don. Kleist wanted to keep them. Hitler could not make up his mind, so the command structure was never clarified.

While Manstein wanted Army Group A to move fast, Kleist said he would need 155 trains to do so and then 88 more trains to build up his Kuban bridgehead.

This was the greater problem for the Germans, as the Russians prepared to move against Rostov and cut the Germans off. And Stalin was waiting impatiently for the destruction of the 6th Army at Stalingrad.

43

On a trip to Stalingrad authorized by the Soviet authorities war correspondent Alexander Werth stopped off at Leninsk, the railhead thirty miles from Stalingrad. This was the end of the line; from here he must travel to Stalingrad by road. Leninsk, he found, was a bustling place, relatively undamaged, full of soldiers and supply trains.

He encountered a pretty girl from Stalingrad, a medical statistician at the hospital. She told him her dreams of a postwar life, when Stalingrad would be beautiful again, and she and her friends would go for holidays to the Caucasus. That day came the word that the Germans were pulling out of the Caucasus. So the Stalingrad girl's dream was not a wild dream after all.

After the failure of the 4th Panzer Army to relieve the 6th Army in December, Zhukov increased the rate of transfer of armored forces and mechanized forces toward the south, but he continued to retain half a million men around Stalingrad. Therefore, he had to go slow in the drive against the Germans in the Caucasus because only his 2nd Guards Army was strong enough to do the job assigned to it.

Nadya, the girl from Stalingrad, would have to wait a little while to see the Caucasus again.

In this first week of January the Russians published a detailed (and highly exaggerated) communiqué on the results for the first six weeks of the Russian offensive. Small matter that the claims were overindulgent. The world still knew that the Russians had dealt the Germans a striking defeat, and the world could sense that Hitler was dead wrong when he made the claim that the Russian offensive had run down without the loss of much by the Germans.

What was true was that the Germans still had the façade of strength and power in Russia. They were still ensconced on the Volga. They were still in the Caucasus. They still threatened Leningrad. But at the same time, the Germans no longer had the strength to exploit any of these positions. They were in deadly peril in Stalingrad, and the danger in the Caucasus was very great although not immediate.

The next few weeks would tell the tale.

During the first week of January the troops of the Don Front under Generals Rokossovsky and Nikolai Voronov were preparing for the final attack on Stalingrad. On a line seven miles long they installed seven thousand field guns. Hundreds of *katyushas* were brought in and hundreds of T-34 tanks wheeled along outside the perimeter of the pocket, in view of the Germans. Rokossovsky made a trip to the Volga and conferred with Chuikov. He outlined the attack that he would make from the west, north, and south, and called on Chuikov to make a simultaneous attack from the east to keep the Germans from escaping down or across the Volga.

The main thrust of the attack would be made by General Batov's 65th Army and General Chistiakov's 21st Army. They would try to split the encircled German force. General Zhadov's 66th Army and General Galanin's 24th Army would attack from the north, and the 57th and 64th armies would attack from the south. The effect would be that of a nutcracker, and something would have to give.

But because the Russians knew that the Germans were still very powerful within the pocket, and that the process of defeating them would be extremely costly in terms of lives and material, they made one last attempt to avoid the battle. On January 8 General Voronov, on behalf of the Red Army supreme command, and General Rokossovsky, commander of the Don Front, called on the Germans to surrender.

Under a white flag of truce, three Russian representatives walked through the German lines on the morning of January 8 and delivered an ultimatum to the 6th Army:

> The German Sixth Army, formations of the 4th Panzer Army and units sent to them as reinforcements have been completely surrounded since November 23. The German troops rushed to your assistance have been routed, and their remnants are now retreating towards Rostov. The German air transport force which kept you supplied with starvation rations of food, ammunition and fuel is frequently compelled to shift its bases and to fly long distances to reach you. It is suffering from tremendous losses to its planes and crews and its help is becoming ineffective.
>
> Your troops are suffering from hunger, disease and cold. The severe Russian winter is only beginning. You have no chance of breaking through the ring surrounding you. Your position is hopeless and further resistance is useless.

Everything the Russians said except the last were true, but General Paulus was not listening. He had been advised that the Russians were coming and he refused to see them. He now knew that Hitler expected him to hold out as long as humanly possible.

The Russians delivered their ultimatum to a junior officer. Voronov and Rokossovsky offered "an honorable peace" to the Germans. Arms, equipment, and munitions were to be turned over to the Russians in an organized manner and in good condition.

Life and safety guaranteed to all soldiers and officers who cease hostilities; and upon the termination of the war their return to Germany or to any country the prisoners of war may choose.

All prisoners may retain their uniforms, insignia, decorations, and personal belongings and in the case of high officers, their sidearms. All prisoners will be provided with normal food, and all in need of medical treatment will be given it.

The ultimatum stated that General Paulus's representatives were to travel by car with a white flag to the Russian lines at ten o'clock on the morning of January 9. If the ultimatum was rejected, "the Red Army and Air Force will be compelled to wipe out the surrounded German troops. . . ."

Paulus submitted the Russian ultimatum to Hitler, and again asked for freedom of action. It was refused again, but this time on different terms. Hitler seemed to have accepted the inevitable now and told Paulus that "every day the army holds out helps the entire front." What that meant was that as long as the 6th Army tied up hundreds of thousands of troops at Stalingrad, Army Group A in the Caucasus had a better chance of escaping a Russian trap. At Fuehrer headquarters they were still talking about a relief expedition, but now one that would bring three new panzer divisions from France. They could not arrive before February. So, what miracle would descend to save Paulus and the starving men of the 6th Army between January 9 and February?

The Russians waited through January 9. But when no answer came at eight o'clock on the morning of January 10 the Russian *katyushas* and guns along the southern and western sides of the pocket began to speak, seven thousand strong. The Russians had prepared well. In some places the density of guns and mortars reached 170 per kilometer. At the same time as the artillery barrage, Russian planes were bombing the German positions near the center of the pocket.

The barrage lasted an hour, and then the Russian tanks and infantry began to move. At the airfield in Pitomnik shells fell on the runways and hit squads unloading supplies from the planes of the airlift. Quartermaster Binder had just brought a column of trucks to take supplies back to Stalingrad, and the column was disrupted there on the airfield.

The Russian bombardment continued, here and there. T-34 tanks burst through the perimeter in the middle of the front. The German 376th and 384th divisions simply disappeared as the center of the front vanished. The Russians headed down the valley of the Karpovka River. The Russian aim was to drive the Germans across the open steppe to Stalingrad.

In the southwest, where the Germans had developed an exposed salient, the 29th Motorized and 3rd Motorized divisions tried to hold, but the 3rd was hit in the flank and had to pull back beyond the Rossoshka River to reorganize. The Russians turned their force against the 29th Motorized Division, and that division began to retreat toward Stalingrad.

The battle continued for three days. The Germans suffered enormous casualties. The 76th Division, for example, was now reduced from its pre-Stalingrad strength of ten thousand men to six hundred men. At the end of the three days, the Russians had cut off the western side of the pocket, about 250 square miles. The only assistance that the 6th Army was getting was coming in by air, at the big aerodrome at Pitomnik, and that field was being reduced to confusion day by day as the Russian attack drew near.

The scene at the airfield was noisy and busy. A plane would land, bumping along the snow-covered runway. It would skid to a stop and the ground crews would rush out in trucks to begin the unloading at high speed. Soviet artillery would bombard the area blindly if the gunners thought there was any activity. Soviet fighter planes would swoop down from overhead to bomb and strafe the German planes and the ground crews. Roving groups of the T-34 tanks appeared on the airfield every day, shooting up the planes on the ground.

The problem of getting the supplies unloaded was nothing compared to the problem of getting the wounded out. They had been brought by truck and cart to the field and lay in stretchers or sat waiting in a tent for a place on a plane. There were so many of them, and many who were not authorized to go, that General Schmidt issued a special order: no man would be allowed on a plane unless he had an order signed by General Schmidt himself.

But even this did little good. The airfield piled up with wounded, and when a plane came in, the rush was on. The walking wounded would run to get a place. Military police with drawn pistols tried to sort out the real wounded from the deserters, and they shot a man occasionally. But they did not stop the rush. They looked beneath the bandages and sometimes found no wounds. They checked documents and found one highly placed officer who had written his own orders to evacuate. They checked one sergeant with a foot wound and found gunpowder burns, which meant he had shot himself in the foot. All these people were sorted out (the penalty for a self-inflicted wound was death), but still there were too many wounded for the planes.

Finally, for each plane the loading would finish and the pilot would taxi to take off. Sometimes there was a last-minute rush to get aboard, which confused matters more. Several times soldiers clung to the tail of the plane, and took off, only to fall to their death when their freezing hands lost their grip.

44

Allied newspaper correspondents were allowed to visit General Malinovsky's 2nd Guards Army command, south of the pocket. They asked him questions about the drive to crush the 6th Army. The marshal's answer was blunt: "Stalingrad is an armed prisoners camp and its situation is hopeless."

On January 12 General Paulus issued orders to his men to stand fast at their positions and not retreat. That day he sent congratulations to the 44th Austrian Infantry Division, which was holding the approaches to the airfield at Pitomnik. The soldiers were running out of ammunition, and that day they saw the Russians overrun one heavy-machine-gun position after the gunner had fired his last belt of ammunition.

That night the 1st Battalion of the 134th Infantry Regiment held its position with some help from two antiaircraft guns which they turned level. The next morning they had to withdraw and leave the guns behind. They had captured jeeps, but they had no fuel to run them. One gun after another was blown up.

On the following night the commander of the battalion drove back to Pitomnik to examine the situation. He passed the wrecked aircraft along the road and the dead horses and the dead vehicles. Pitomnik field was a mass of wreckage by that time. Two dressing stations were crammed with wounded men, some of them being hit by incoming Russian shells. And all the while aircraft were coming down, unloading, loading up, and flying off again.

But not all Paulus's command were standing so firm. Some were paying no attention to him and looking for opportunities to surrender to the Russians, but because the Russians were moving so fast, they did not have time to take prisoners. New regulations regarding the treatment of prisoners had been issued at the first of the year and given wide publicity, obviously in the hope of persuading the Germans at Stalingrad to give up. But these regulations were ignored by many of the Russian commanders. They did not have the time or the inclination to deal gently with their German enemies.

Paulus sent an emissary by air to Manstein to plead for more food. The mission was a total failure. The Luftwaffe could do no more. Only seventy-five transport planes were left in operating condition. More than four hundred transports had been shot down or wrecked on the airlift. The Luftwaffe was running out of planes.

That day Paulus sent a special emissary to see Hitler. The excuse was to deliver the 6th Army war diary to Fuehrer headquarters before it was too late. The officer was to try to get through to Hitler, to convince him of the desperate state into which 6th Army had been flung.

Not all Paulus's men were paralyzed with desperation, however. Virtually all of them knew that the end was near, that there was no possibility of survival of the army, but many vowed to stand fast. Some of these were Nazis, but many were not, like the noncommissioned officer who wrote a last letter home advising his wife quietly about the future.

I am sure that you will keep me in your mind and that you will tell the children everything when the proper time has come. You should not mourn my death. Should you ever feel that fortune wants to give you a hand, do not fail to grasp it. You will have to live on your own. I am sure that everything will continue. You will have to take a job and take care of the little ones. I shall carry you in my heart until the last moment. You will be with me until I take my last breath.

By the end of the fourth day, eight divisions on the western side of the pocket had been destroyed, and only one, the 29th Motorized Division, had any appreciable strength left. Although they had only a few tanks left, after dark they staged a counterattack and the surprised Russians fell back. The remnants of the 29th Motorized Division regrouped and retreated toward Stalingrad.

The Pitomnik airfield was captured by the Russians on January 14, and the Germans were now reduced to airdrop for supplies. A light plane could still land at Gumrak airstrip but not a Ju-52. The airlift was virtually at an end, and so were the hopes of the men of Stalingrad. There were eighty thousand fewer of them now, those fourscore thousand men killed in the first few days of the Russian drive to split the pocket. The perimeter had contracted sharply to the east, and the whole central section had been torn off. The ring was closing in.

45

The fall of Pitomnik airfield to the Russians meant the end of the airlift, because Gumrak field could not accommodate the transports and was too small even for fighters. But General Paulus and his officers would not accept the inevitable. They lengthened the runway of the Gumrak airfield and then declared that it was safe for Ju-52s to land. The Luftwaffe men knew better. On the day the Pitomnik airfield fell, six Me-109 fighters took off and flew to the safety of Gumrak. Five of them crashed, either overshooting the short runway or crashing in the debris of the field. The sixth plane circled and disappeared to the west, landing safely at a field outside the pocket.

What was to be done with the wounded now? Thousands of them had been evacuated in the air supply planes, and the doctors continued to believe that planes would come for them. The medical facilities were moved to Gumrak airfield, and doctors worked eighteen hours a day treating the mutilated bodies of the wounded.

The patients lay on cots, on floors, and in trucks outside the aid stations and hospital. When truck drivers came up with a load of wounded and were waved off by the MPs, who said there was no room, the truck drivers often abandoned their trucks, and the wounded usually froze to death within a few hours.

On January 16 Paulus told Manstein by radio that the Gumrak field was now perfectly usable. Manstein asked the Luftwaffe and they said the field was a death trap for anything larger than a Storch.

Paulus screamed. The Luftwaffe was making excuses, he said. The landing field had been extended, the ground support staff had been put together. He asked Hitler to intervene and force the Luftwaffe to continue to deliver supplies and take out the wounded.

On January 19 a Luftwaffe officer came to Gumrak to survey the field and settle the argument. He saw the wrecks of a dozen planes littering the field, forcing pilots to use only a part of the runway. The runways were pockmarked with bomb craters that had not been properly filled. The field was covered with snow.

The officer met with Paulus and his staff, and they berated him for the failure of the Luftwaffe to get supplies through to them. It was four days since some of Paulus's men in forward positions had had anything to eat. They were reduced to boiling the bones of dead horses, cutting open the frozen heads and eating the frozen brains.

Paulus was now reduced to fantasy. He scored Goering for ever saying that he could supply the 6th Army through the winter. If Goering had said no, Paulus now said, he would have broken out a long time ago. Nobody reminded him that a long, long time ago Richthofen, Manstein, and others had warned him that the Luftwaffe could not live up to Goering's promise.

Paulus's indignation produced results. The Luftwaffe began flights into Gumrak, the operations officers shaking their heads at the impossibility of it and the danger. But on January 15 General Milch had taken personal charge of the airlift, and he decreed that it should go on, no matter the cost to the Luftwaffe.

The airfield at Tatsinskaya, which was the closest supply point for the Germans to airlift to Stalingrad, fell to the Russians in mid-month; thereafter, supplies had to be airlifted from Rostov and Novocherkassk, which were more than two hundred miles from the surrounded area.

The Ju-52s began to land at Gumrak. The He-111s, which demanded a longer landing space and had weaker landing gear, could not.

The Ju-52s would come in with their cases of goods, and the ground crews would dash to unload. The wounded lay in tent shelters or in the open, waiting for the blessed airplane that would take them to safety. When the plane was empty, the rush would begin. The military police would hold the doors at gunpoint while the stretcher cases were loaded, piled on top of each other all over the floor. Then the walking wounded and the men, mostly officers, who had somehow secured one of the clearances from General Schmidt, or had faked it, would clamber aboard, pushing and shoving and shouting. The planes would start bumping across the ground at increasing speed, with clouds of snow blowing back from the propellers. A wheel would drop into a shell crater with a crash, and if the plane was lucky, the undercarriage would hold together. Otherwise it all ended there in a ground loop on the field.

On one such mission, after a wheel dropped into a crater, the pilot cut the engines, turned around, and returned to the starting line. He then insisted that he must take two thousand kilograms of weight off the plane. That meant twenty men would have to get out. The plane stopped, and no one volunteered to leave. Kicking and screaming, twenty men were taken off the aircraft, and the plane started up again.

Other aircraft carried off hundreds of men who were not wounded and not sick, whose papers were in order. These were specialists, valuable personnel who were being sent out of the pocket to go back to Germany and form new divisions and fight again. Some of the generals went out—General Erwin Jaenecke, who was badly wounded with sixteen shrapnel holes in his body, and General Hans Hube—and lesser officers, one of them carrying General Schmidt's will.

These officers somehow crammed themselves into the Ju-52s. One of the transports came in as Russian shrapnel was spraying the airport. The pilot unloaded, and loaded up, and tried to take off. He could not. Men had jumped up on the wings of the plane and were holding on to anything they could grasp. They did not realize that it was hopeless, and suicidal. The transport ran down the runway, picking up speed. One by one the unwelcome riders fell off and fell back into the slipstream and onto the ground. The plane took off, and the others fell. The plane streaked away to the south, to Rostov and to safety.

West and north of Gumrak the Russians were threatening this airfield, too. T-34s were close enough to shell the runways.

From Salsk, 220 miles from Stalingrad, the Germans were still sending transport planes to brave the dangers of Gumrak. But many of these flights were now ending in crashes. Correspondents interviewed some German airmen who had been lucky enough to survive them. Most of them were upset by the suicidal missions they had been asked to perform. Only a handful of Nazis in the Luftwaffe (which had more than its share) believed that the defeat of Germany was impossible.

Several western war correspondents were allowed to follow the route taken by the retreating 4th Panzer Army, south of Stalingrad, and join the 2nd Guards Army in its pursuit. They spent a few days at Kotelnikovo. Edgar Snow and Alexander Werth were billeted in the small wooden cottage of an elementary-school teacher. She described life in five months of occupation by the Romanians and the Germans. Five German soldiers—members of a tank crew—had been billeted in her house, and she and her son and the grandmother had lived in the little kitchen. The Germans had not been brutal.

"They weren't so bad, those five Germans, but they thought we were just their slaves," she said. "In other houses they behaved much worse, and the Romanians were terrible—wouldn't leave the women alone. There was a lot of rape in the town. I didn't hear of anybody being shot, but thirty or maybe fifty people were taken away by the Germans."

On the last night, she said, the Germans had set out to burn the town. They set fire to all the public buildings. But then the Russians came up in pursuit, and the Germans left Kotelnikovo in a hurry.

The correspondents continued to follow the trail of the 4th Panzer Army. They went to Zimovniki, sixty miles down the Stalingrad-Caucasus line that General Hoth was taking. The Germans were still fighting a rearguard action, and gunfire could be heard clearly in the little town.

The street signs were still in Romanian or German, and on the pedestal of the Lenin statue there was only half a leg still standing. The big clubhouse had been used as a barracks for the Germans. The whole floor was covered with bundles of straw on which they had slept. The rostrum was still decorated with fir branches and the tables and the heaps of straw were littered with what looked like the remains of a Christmas party—dozens of empty wine and brandy bottles, mostly French, empty tins and German cigarette and biscuit cartons. Here also lay a pile of magazines, one of them showing German soldiers basking in deck chairs on a verandah overlooking the Black Sea and carrying a touristy article about "*Der herrliche Kaukasus und die Schwarzseekueste.*" The magazine was only three weeks old, so they had already been making themselves at home in the Caucasus. Now they were beating it from the Caucasus as fast as their legs would carry them.

The correspondents went to the little park behind the clubhouse, and there saw Russian soldiers digging a common grave for Russians who had been killed at Zimovniki only two or three days before. There were perhaps eighty Russian corpses, placed in rows, frozen in attitudes, some of them sitting up, some with their arms wide apart, some with their heads blown away. Some were bearded men. Some were young boys with open eyes.

The middle of January was marked in the Stalingrad area by an unseasonably mild spell. The temperature rose above freezing, not enough to unfreeze the mounds of bodies in Stalingrad, but enough to make the cold a little less torturous.

At Rastenburg, Hitler was talking happily of the SS Panzer Corps, which was moving toward Kharkov to assemble by mid-February. He promised everyone it would be ready to drive the 350 miles to Stalingrad to relieve Paulus.

Field Marshal Manstein met with General Richthofen for dinner, and as they dined they talked about the war. They agreed. "We both feel the same," Richthofen wrote in his diary, "that we are like a couple of attendants in a lunatic asylum."

Manstein's concern was the three great gaps that had opened in the German front. By January 15 all that was preventing total disaster for the Germans was the existence of the Stalingrad pocket that was still tying down nearly half a million Russians and their T-34 tanks.

On January 17 the Russians completed the first phase of their attack on the Stalingrad pocket, stabilizing along a line that ran from Rossoshka on the north to Voronopovo Station on the south. The Stalingrad pocket had been reduced by half.

If it were not for Stalingrad, Zhukov would have Rokossovsky's army and all the other armies to throw against the Germans around Rostov. The first great gap in the German line was west of detachment Hollidt, a small German force centered on Millerovo which was vulnerable on the left after the collapse of the Italian 8th Army. With a little more power the Russians could drive south toward Rostov, or southwest toward the Sea of Azov. Either way they would cut the Don-Dnieper railroad, the only supply line for the entire German army in the south.

The second gap was in the Don River valley, where the Hollidt detachment and the 4th Panzer Army were pushed back along two lines, one west and the other southwest. With a little more strength the Soviets could make flanking attacks against the rear of either German force, or strike Rostov.

Between these last two points, only the 16th Motorized Division stood in the gap that threatened the rear of the German armies in the Caucasus.

As January 15 passed, even Hitler now admitted that the only force keeping the Russians at bay was the continued existence of the 6th Army in Stalingrad. But that army's position was now pitiful; it was no longer a fighting force. It was a mass of something over two hundred thousand men, starving, staggering, too weak even to pull a cart or a gun carriage. Each day hundreds of men died. Yet in its suffering it was protecting the rest of the German army in Russia.

How long could this go on?

Not long. Field Marshal Manstein knew. He hoped it could go on long enough for him to convince Hitler that something had to be done to get the German forces out of the Caucasus before it was too late. It was all up to Hitler. Manstein's greatest fear was that Hitler would acquiesce to the withdrawal from the Caucasus only when it was too late.

The second half of January opened, with the abandonment of the Chir position by the Hollidt detachment. General Hoth was retreating steadily, river valley to river valley, keeping the tanks concentrated against Soviet attacks down the Don and Manych River valley.

The Russians were moving against and around the 4th Panzer Army, and one marauding force approached to within a mile of Manstein's headquarters at Novocherkassk before it was turned back.

Just before the beginning of January, Hitler had finally approved a withdrawal of Army Group A to the Kuma line, but that was three hundred miles east of Rostov. That way, said Hitler, they could go for the Caucasus again in the spring of 1943.

What Manstein wanted was the 1st Panzer Army. If he had that, he could draw back to the Donets and defend that line. Hitler had not agreed to this. He continued to talk about resuming the offensive in the spring, not realizing that with the end at Stalingrad in sight he would never again have the strength for an offensive, and that the Russians, who were building power every day, now had the initiative. Hitler did not yet recognize that his ultimate problem was to prevent the Russians from driving straight through into Germany. This would be the result if Stalingrad fell precipitately.

46

The headquarters of German Army Group Don was permeated by a great sense of urgency. On January 17 the Russians captured Millerovo, which offered a new threat in the south, but Hitler still would not allow the retreat of Army Group A from the Caucasus. By the end of the third week of January, one German detachment, having extricated 14,000 troops from encirclement near Millerovo, was in line behind the Donets. The Hollidt detachment had also gained the riverbank and was now 165 miles from Stalingrad. The 4th Panzer Army had set up a defense on the Manych Canal between the Don and Pryloetarskaya and was now 195 miles from Stalingrad. Neither force could get there no matter what happened.

But at this point no one outside Stalingrad cared. The 1st Panzer Army's flank reached the 4th Army east of Salsk. That was what was important to Manstein. He was now worried about saving the 1st Panzer Army, not Paulus's 6th.

In Stalingrad the airlift was suspended for several hours on January 17 because a pilot radioed back to Rostov that when he tried to land at Gumrak he saw German troops retreating past the field. But this was in error, and by the end of the day, the flights were resumed.

That same day, January 17, the Russians completed the first stage of their squeeze on the pocket. The area of the pocket had been reduced about two-thirds, but General Rokossovsky had not achieved his aim, which was to press the Germans into the confines of Stalingrad alone. The reason was faulty intelligence. Rokossovsky had gone into the battle believing that the German force had been reduced to eighty thousand men. Instead, he had faced 200,000 fighting men, not all of them effective, but still a much larger force than expected.

The western part of the remaining pocket was still studded with hundreds of pillboxes and other firing points. The Germans had been given months to prepare their defenses and they had done well with them. The Soviet report on January 17 said that they had destroyed 1,260 pillboxes and fortified dugouts, 75 fortified observation posts, and 317 gun or mortar batteries. They had captured or destroyed 400 aircraft, 6,600 tanks, and 16,000 trucks. The had killed twenty-five thousand

Germans, but taken only seven thousand prisoners, and many of these were Romanians. That figure was indicative of the continued high morale of the Germans. In spite of the hopeless situation of the 6th Army, most of the soldiers remained obedient to orders.

Now General Rokossovsky made another offer of surrender to General Paulus. Several of Paulus's generals were in favor of accepting, but Paulus still had no authority to do so, and when he asked Hitler again, silence was his answer.

The German high command was sunk in confusion. Hitler approved a new draft of 500,000 men and on January 17 ordered all leaves for forces in the east canceled. The men must return immediately to their units. But the suddenness of the order and the condition of rail transport to the east made it impossible for the transport officials to move the men in good time. The trains backed up. The stations were jammed with men trying to get back to their units. The whole eastward movement of men and supplies slowed to an agonizing crawl.

On January 19 Russians on the Voronezh Front continued to make progress. Vauyki Vrazavo fell to the Russians, and the Hungarians were driven from Ostrogozhsk. On this front the Russians took fifty thousand prisoners, but only twenty-five hundred of them were Germans. The German allies were bearing the brunt of the attacks.

General Rokossovsky regrouped along the Rossoshka-Voronopovo line for four days. Meanwhile in the west, the 2nd Hungarian Army began to fall apart under Soviet attack, but the fact that it could hold at all was immensely helpful to the armies of the south. The Red Army advance on the Voronezh Front was slowed because there were not enough troops.

On January 21 all the commotion about the viability of Gumrak airport came to an end. The Russians captured it, and the Germans were now completely cut off from the outside world. On January 22 General Rokossovsky began the second stage of Operation Koltso, the destruction of the Stalingrad pocket and the 6th Army. The Russian 57th Army Infantry broke through along a three-mile front on the railroad, reached Voroponovo Station, and marched eastward with their battle flags flying in triumph.

There was no way the gap could be closed. The troops on the west had run out of ammunition, and there was not enough gasoline to enable anyone to bring it from another sector.

The ultimate disaster was about to descend on the 6th Army in Stalingrad.

THE WARLORDS: HITLER VS. STALIN

Hitler and Stalin were both experienced soldiers. Stalin's experience in the Russian Civil War was in command, while Hitler's was only as a frontline corporal.

But in matters of strategy Hitler was light-years ahead of his opponent. The Russian dictator and his sycophants began fighting the Germans with a kind of "continuous front" warfare. The moment that Stalin assumed command of the war, after the first week of fighting, he ordered a general attack by Russian forces which they were neither ready for nor in position to execute. As a result, army after army was decimated, and before the Germans had reached Minsk they had captured hundreds of thousands of Russian prisoners and wrecked three Russian armies. Stalin's response to this disaster was to fling more armies into frontal assaults that always lost.

When Zhukov, then chief of staff to Stalin's army, tried to persuade Stalin to modern methods of warfare, Stalin would not listen. Zhukov argued that in the south the Russian armies had to retreat beyond the Dnieper River to avoid encirclement and capture. Stalin exploded. How dare Zhukov suggest this. It would mean the surrender of Kiev to the enemy. Zhukov then offered his resignation. He would go to the front, even as a divisional commander.

Stalin said if he felt that way, he did not need Zhukov, and replaced him with Marshal Shaposhnikov, who was politically reliable, but too sick to function.

Stalin continued his bullheaded and disastrous leadership. When the Germans struck on June 22, they had only 3 million men in the field as compared to the Russian army's 4.2 million plus border guards and NKVD special units in the west. But after a month of calamitous Stalin decisions, the Germans had the upper hand in manpower. In two battles, Smolensk and Kiev, the Russians lost one million men. In the next six months hundreds of thousands of Russian lives would be lost because of Stalin's obstinacy.

In August, with the Germans pressing on Leningrad, Marshal Voroshilov and party boss Andrei Zhdanov set up a Leningrad Military Council to coordinate the defense. Stalin descended on them in rage.

(*continued next page*)

(continued from preceding page)

He had not authorized such an act. He suspected them of trying to break Leningrad away from the USSR. He sent Molotov and Malenkov to Leningrad to check up and dissolved the council. Voroshilov and Zhdanov were reprimanded, and the defense of Leningrad was set back by months. Not until Zhukov came did affairs grow any better.

It was not until Moscow in the winter of 1941 that Stalin began to learn at all, and then his progress was very slow. Even then his suspicions of his generals continued. Not until Stalingrad was he even willing to trust Zhukov, whom he had assigned the defense.

Hitler, on the other hand, conceived a master plan that was both daring and decisive when he began the assault on Russia. In spite of the fact that the opening was delayed a month in the spring by events in the Balkans, the German timetable was still sound. Hitler struck on three fronts: north, south, and in the middle. The attack was every bit as successful as he had expected it to be. The strategy worked, and Hitler's appreciation of dynamic warfare as opposed to Stalin's positional tactics brought victory after victory and hundreds of thousands of prisoners.

But Hitler finally faltered. The assault on Moscow was abandoned for critical weeks, when it could have carried the city in the summer sun. Fearful that he was losing momentum in the Caucasus, Hitler stripped the center army of its striking power. Thus he lost the chance to take Moscow before winter and disrupt the entire Soviet government. He was audacious, but not audacious enough.

After the defeat before Moscow in the winter of 1941–42, Hitler showed another flash of brilliance when he ordered his German troops to stand and hold even at the cost of being surrounded. Several armies were indeed surrounded, but they stood fast, and were supplied by the Luftwaffe, and when spring came they fought their way out of the encirclements and were strong enough to mount new offensives.

But then Hitler miscalculated. While Stalin was learning by constant defeat, Hitler could not see that the Russians were winning the battle of time and production. The new T-34 tanks were coming off the lines in the thousands, and new Russian fighter planes were

(continued next page)

(*continued from preceding page*)
coming to the front. Hitler did not have the resources to launch offensives on three fronts as he had done the previous year, but he would not give up the pattern.

In the end, Army Group North was forced to remain stagnant while Army Group Center and Army Group South carried the battle. Hitler completely underestimated the Russian ability to rebound and bring in new reserve units. He wanted too much, both Stalingrad and the Caucasus in one season. And so he ended up winning neither, and at Stalingrad the war turned against him.

PART XIV

THE FALL OF STALINGRAD

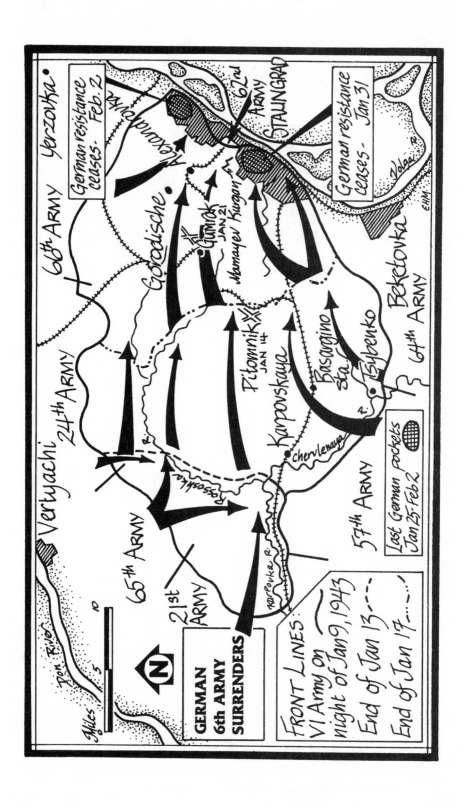

47

On January 20 Hitler called up from the Eastern Front the Death's Head Panzers, who only two weeks before had been told they would remain in Germany. Hitler now said they would be needed in Russia in February.

One reason the Death's Head was so sorely needed was that there was almost total collapse of the Axis armies. On December 22 these armies were all placed under German control, with the euphemistic announcement that the Italian, Romanian, and Hungarian generals were being freed of operational duties so that they could reorganize their forces.

On January 22, realizing that the German forces in the Caucasus had retreated to safety and were not immediately threatened, General Paulus asked for permission to surrender.

"Absolutely not!" thundered Hitler. Field Marshal Manstein backed the Paulus request with all his prestige and authority, but Hitler would not budge. On January 23 Paulus added the argument that his ammunition was almost all gone, and repeated the request. Hitler refused again. The 6th Army must fight on to give the German forces time.

Time for what, Hitler did not say.

On January 24 the chief of operations of the 6th Army sent a message to Manstein to explain the situation of the army.

> Attacks in undiminished violence are being made against the entire western front which has been fighting its way back eastward to the Gorodische area since the morning of the 24th in order to form

a hedgehog in the tractor works. In the southern part of Stalingrad the western front along the city outskirts held on to the western and southern edges of Minima until 4 P.M. Local penetrations were made in that sector. The Volga and northeastern fronts are unchanged. The conditions in the city are frightful, where twenty thousand unattended wounded are seeking shelter among the ruins. With them are about the same number of starved and frostbitten men and stragglers, most of them without weapons, which they lost in the fighting. Heavy artillery is pounding the whole city area. Last resistance along the city outskirts in the southern part of Stalingrad will be offered on January 25 under the leadership of energetic generals fighting in the line and gallant officers around whom a few men still capable of fighting have rallied. The tractor works may possibly hold out a little longer.

When Manstein had that report, he put in a telephone call to Hitler. Since the 6th Army was no longer able to tie down any appreciable Russian force, he said, would Hitler please order Paulus to surrender and save the lives of those who were left? They were still promised honorable terms. If they did not accept them, who knew what would happen to the remnants of the 6th Army.

Hitler would not relent. The 6th Army must continue to hold Stalingrad.

General Zeitzler made another attempt, using Major Coelestin von Zitsewitz, who had been for several weeks Zeitzler's personal representative in Stalingrad. The chief of staff had sent the major there just after the Russians began their encirclement of the city, and Zitsewitz had been reporting faithfully ever since.

Most of his reports had been rejected by Hitler and Goering, because they told the truth of the worsening of conditions in the city and the rest of the pocket. But Zeitzler had not lost faith, and on January 20 he had ordered Zitsewitz out of the pocket to report to Oberkommando des Heeres. On January 23 Zeitzler took Major Zitsewitz to see Hitler. Here is Zitsewitz's own account of the meeting:

> When we arrived at the Fuehrer's headquarters Zeitzler was admitted at once, while I was made to wait in an anteroom. A little while later the door opened and I was called in. I reported present.

Hitler came to meet me and with both his hands gripped my right hand.

"You've come from a deplorable situation," he said.

The spacious room was only dimly lit. In front of the fireplace was a large circular table with club chairs around it, and on the right stood a long table, lit from above with a huge situation map of the entire Eastern Front. In the background sat two stenographers taking down every word. Apart from General Zeitsler only General Schmundt and two personal Army and Luftwaffe ADCs were present.

Hitler gestured to me to sit down on a stool by the situation map, and himself sat down facing me. The other gentlemen sat down in the chairs in the dark part of the room. Only the Army ADC stood on the far side of the map table. Hitler was speaking. Time and again he pointed to the map. He spoke of a tentative idea of making a battalion of entirely new tanks, the Panther, attack straight through the enemy towards Stalingrad in order to ferry supplies through in this way and to reinforce 6th Army by tanks.

I was flabbergasted. A single Panzer battalion was to launch a successful attack across several hundred miles of strongly held enemy territory when an entire Panzer army had been unable to accomplish this feat.

I used the first pause which Hitler made in his expose to describe the hardships of the 6th Army. I quoted examples, I read off figures from a slip of paper I had prepared.

I spoke about the hunger, the frostbite, the inadequate supplies and the sense of having been written off. I spoke of wounded men and lack of medical supplies. I concluded with the words,

"My Fuehrer, permit me to state that the troops at Stalingrad can no longer be ordered to fight to their last round because they are no longer physically capable of fighting and because they no longer have a last round."

Hitler regarded me in surprise, but I felt that he was looking straight through me. Then he said: "Man recovers very quickly." With these words I was dismissed.

To Stalingrad that night Hitler radioed:
"Surrender out of the question. Troops will resist to the end."

48

The Russians entered Gumrak and set fire to the railroad station. The Germans had stacked corpses up against the outside wall to the level of the second-story windows. The bodies caught fire, and the whole structure became a monstrous pyre burning the hopes of the 6th Army in the snow.

On January 24 and 25 the besieged units on the western side of the Cauldron headed for the last refuge of Stalingrad. They traveled the "Road of Death," five miles of snow, coated with the blood of the defenders and marked by the bodies of those who could not make it. All who could walk or crawl were heading for the city and the protection of its cellars, just about the only points of safety left in the city.

Field Marshal Manstein again tried to argue with Hitler about the fate of the 6th Army. There was no point in the army continuing to suffer now, he said. No point at all.

Hitler would not listen. Each hour that Paulus continued to hold down the Russians around Stalingrad was valuable to the German cause, he said. Besides, the Russians never kept any agreements they made anyhow. The men of Stalingrad would have no chance to survive even if they surrendered. The answer was no.

In Stalingrad now almost every man was thinking: What will happen to me? Will the Russians kill me? Or will they send us into slavery in a Siberian prison camp? None of them expected decent treatment. They could remember how they had treated the Russians for these past eighteen months. Most of them had seen the remains of some of their comrades who had been left to the mercies of the Russians on the battlefield. All they could do was shudder.

As for their homeland, almost 60 percent of them believed the war was lost, and 33 percent were so jaded they had no opinions about anything. Only 2 percent of the soldiers approved of the way Hitler was conducting the war.

After January 24 the fighting in Stalingrad was sporadic and hopeless. The Russians came, moving block to block and house to house, squads of red-faced healthy Russian soldiers in their heavy fur-lined overcoats and thick boots. They moved slowly and carefully, ready to shoot at the slightest motion.

In the minor engagements they tried not to get killed. They came forward. They saw little groups of Germans. Then the shooting stopped. They shouted *"Raus! Raus!"* and watched carefully as the Germans came out of their holes, hands high.

Sometimes a German made a false move and was promptly shot. Sometimes a Russian soldier, remembering, could not resist the urge to strike out at the helpless prisoners.

But mostly the Russians just made the Germans hold up their hands, made them march, and took them away.

In their holes the Germans scratched their lice and chased mice. The lice now seemed more important, and they were assuming a new importance to the medical officers as well. In the enormous impromptu hospital ward called Timoshenko Bunker, down by the Volga, two thousand German wounded had been clustered.

In the beginning this bunker had been made into an underground hospital, with electric lights, running water, and proper sanitation. All that was long gone. The wounded were piled in here now, stinking and sweating, and moaning in pain. The doctors noticed something new in the last few days. Many men were coming down with lung congestion and temperatures running up to 104 degrees. Some were having convulsions. A new problem had invaded the cellars of Stalingrad: typhus. The men of the 6th Army had never been vaccinated against it.

Suddenly, almost overnight, it seemed, General Paulus had become a tired old man. His posture, once straight and military, had become stooped. His uniform bagged and was covered with food stains. His face was lined and unshaven, and he had developed a tick in his right cheek that extended from his eyebrow to his lower jaw. His chief of staff, General Schmidt, was running the army now. Paulus was simply going through the motions. Sixth Army headquarters had moved from the bunkers at Gumrak to the warehouse in the bottom of the wrecked Univermag department store in the center of Stalingrad. Paulus spent most of his time on a narrow cot in his cubicle, sleeping or staring at the ceiling. Once he roused himself.

General Schmidt reported to him that a number of the generals were conspiring to disobey his orders and arrange a mass surrender of the troops. He went to the NKVD prison, where a number of the German generals were housed. He told them they would do nothing of the sort and that they would continue to hold out. Then he turned his back on them and left. The plan to surrender was not discussed again.

Other generals were behaving in different ways. General von Hartman, commander of the 71st Division, walked out to a railroad embankment in full view of the enemy and began firing a carbine toward the Russian lines. A few minutes later he got what he wanted, a Russian bullet in the brain.

General Stempel committed suicide. General Drebber of the 297th Division surrendered to a Russian colonel and sent back a letter to General Paulus saying he was being well treated. Paulus wanted to believe it, but General Schmidt persuaded him the letter was written under compulsion and that the Russians would kill them all if they surrendered.

On January 26 the Russians, advancing from the west, entered the city and met the men of General Chuikov's 62nd Army near Mamayev Hill. On January 28 the Russians divided the city into three sectors. In one sector the Russian XI Corps surrounded the tractor factory; the VIII and LI Corps were in the Mamayev Hill area, and the IV Corps surrounded the downtown business district. Where there were German wounded, and this was everywhere in the city, the doctors placed the most serious cases in the hallways and near the doors, where they would freeze to death quickly. The wounded were no longer getting any food; it was all being saved for the fighting men. Hundreds of the wounded committed suicide, most using pistols and hand grenades.

On January 30, the tenth anniversary of the "Thousand Year Reich," Hitler was supposed to speak to the nation. Instead, he gave the honor to Marshal Goering, who lionized the men of Stalingrad.

"Rising above the gigantic battle like a mighty monument is Stalingrad," he said. "One day it will be recognized as the greatest battle in our history. . . ."

General Paulus sent a message to Hitler congratulating him on the anniversary and swearing that the Stalingrad battle would be a lesson to future generations that Germans never surrendered.

N

TARTAR WALL

Mokraya Mechetka

Tractor Factory

Workers' Settlements

Barrikady Gun Factory

Zaitsevski Is

Road to Gumrak

Mamayev Hill

Red October Plant

Lazur Plant

Downtown Residential Area

Railroad Station #1

DETAIL BELOW

Volga R.

Tsaritsa Gorge

YEREMENKO'S FIRST HQ

Krasnaya Slobodla

Railroad Sta #2 Dar Gova

Grain Silos

Golodny Island

E.H.M.

STALINGRAD

1942

RR STA #1

DOWNTOWN STALINGRAD

NAIL FACTORY

GOGOL ST.

SOLECHNAYA

RED SQUARE

9th OF JAN. SQUARE

GORKY THEATER

UNIVERMAG DEPT. STORE

L-SHAPED HOUSE

PAVLOV'S HOUSE

SOVIETSKAYA ST.

NKVD AND 42nd REGT. HQ

HOUSE OF SPECIALISTS

STATE BANK

BEER FACTORY

TO MAIN FERRY LANDING

RODIMTSEV'S FIRST HQ

Volga R.

*   *   *

The Russians advanced until they controlled nearly all the city. General Roske's 71st Division manned the posts around the Univermag department store. On the afternoon of January 30 Roske told Schmidt that the division could no longer help. Russian tanks were coming toward the department store.

Shortly before midnight, General Paulus slept.

On January 31 Hitler showered promotions on the officers. Paulus was promoted to field marshal. This was a purely Hitlerian ploy, designed to persuade Paulus to commit suicide, because as everyone knew, no German field marshal had ever surrendered.

But that day Paulus surrendered to a Russian lieutenant who came into the 6th Army headquarters. He was taken away in a car to the headquarters of General Mikhail Shumilov, commander of the Soviet 64th Army. There he was offered food from an enormous buffet, but refused to eat until he had been assured that his men would receive rations and medical care.

While the Russians were promising these things, other Russians in Stalingrad were cleaning up the ruins. They set fire to the old Soviet military garrison building which the Germans had converted to a hospital. Hundreds of wounded were burned to death. Russian soldiers wandered around the town taking prisoners and stripping them of their valuables. In a cellar north of Red Square fifty German wounded were doused with gasoline and turned into human torches.

At Fuehrer headquarters in East Prussia Hitler was furious when he learned of the surrender, and vowed that he would not create another field marshal because nobody could be trusted. He would have been proud of General Strecker, the commander of German XI Corps, who was still holding out in northern Stalingrad on February 2. The Russians were very angry at their refusal to quit fighting, and many of them were not allowed to surrender when they ran out of ammunition, but were shot down or clubbed to death. Just before the XI Corps command post was overrun, General Strecker sent a message to Hitler: "Eleventh Corps and its divisions have fought to the last man against vastly superior forces. Long live Germany."

49

In Germany the shock was unmistakable. Dr. Goebbels tried to ignore the Soviet proclamations of triumph that rang across the world. For three days all radio broadcasts were suspended, and all places of entertainment were shut down. Berlin was like a funeral parlor, and the people for the first time sensed that the war was going to be lost. Goebbels spent the time drafting a speech calling on the Germans to engage now in "total war."

On the road from Kharkov, a convoy was stopped by an officer in a three-wheeled motorcycle. The officer had a message. The men were assembled on the snowy highway, and the convoy commander came up. Here is the scene, as described by Private Guy Sajer, one of the soldiers in the convoy:

> He didn't lift his eyes from the ground, and his expression was one of despair.
>
> A shiver of anxiety ran across our shaggy and exhausted faces.
>
> "Achtung. Stillgestanden!" shouted a feldwebel.
>
> We stood at attention. The captain gave us a long look. Then slowly, in his gloved hand, he lifted a paper to the level of his eyes.
>
> "Soldiers," he said. "I have some very serious news for you; serious for you, for all the fighting men of the Axis, for our people, and for everything our faith and sacrifice represents. Wherever this news will be heard this evening, it will be received with emotion and profound grief. Everywhere along our vast front, in the heart of our fatherland, we will find it difficult to contain our emotion."
>
> "Stillgestanden," shouted the feldwebel.
>
> "Stalingrad has fallen!" the captain continued. "Marshal von Paulus and his 6th Army, driven to the ultimate sacrifice, have been obliged to lay down their arms unconditionally."
>
> We felt stunned and profoundly anxious. The captain continued after a moment of silence.
>
> "Marshal von Paulus, in the next to last message he sent, informed the Fuehrer that he was awarding the Cross for bravery with exceptional merit to every one of his soldiers. The marshal added that the calvary of these unfortunate combatants had reached

a peak, and that after the hell of this battle, which lasted for months, the halo of glory has never been more truly deserved. I have here the last message picked up by short wave from the ruins of the tractor factory Red October. This High Command requests that I read it to you.

"It was sent by one of the last fighting soldiers of the 6th Army, Heinrich Stoda. Heinrich states in this message that in the southwest district of Stalingrad he could still hear the sound of fighting. Here is the message:

"'We are the last seven survivors in this place. Four of us are wounded. We have been entrenched in the wreckage of the tractor factory for four days. We have not had any food for four days. I have just opened the last magazine for my automatic. In ten minutes the Bolsheviks will overrun us. Tell my father that I have done my duty, and that I shall know how to die. Long live Germany. Heil Hitler.'"

A man in the ranks began to whimper. His white temples made him look like an old man. Then he quit his rigid posture and began to walk toward the officers, crying and shouting at the same time. "My two sons are dead," he cried. . . .

For the first time I was strongly impressed by the dismal vastness of Russia. I felt quite distinctly that the huge, heavy gray horizon was closing in around us, and shivered more violently than ever.

That is when Private Sajer and his companions knew the war was lost.

AFTER THE SURRENDER

The days of the German surrender at Stalingrad, January 31 and February 1, 1943, were days of resurgence for the Red Army, and everyone in Russia knew it. They had captured a German field marshal and twenty German generals. No German field marshal had ever been captured before—by anybody in the world! The Red Army claimed now to have overnight become the greatest fighting machine in existence.

Stalin declared himself to be a Marshal of the Soviet Union and began wearing a marshal's uniform, which he did thereafter for the rest of his life. He claimed a lion's share of the credit for the victory at Stalingrad.

(*continued next page*)

(*continued from preceding page*)
He ordered costly new medals for the heroes of Stalingrad, including himself.

Russian generals had been as inconspicuous as the Japanese in their baggy uniforms. Suddenly they blossomed out in new gaudy uniforms, which with their medals made them the showiest group of officials in the world. In 1945, Stalin declared himself to be from now on Generalissimo, in addition to Supreme Commander.

His generals noticed that they were now honored and not ordered around by Stalin like errand boys, but the essentially political nature of the Red Army did not change. Every front commander had a political counterpart, just as General Yeremensky at Stalingrad had Comrade Khrushchev to keep him toeing the mark. Stalin never relinquished his overall watchfulness and distrust of his generals.

50

A group of foreign war correspondents was brought to Stalingrad after the surrender. They met several Soviet correspondents who had witnessed the fighting. One of them, who had been in Gumrak during the fighting, told them about it:

> The biggest slaughter of Germans ever. The place is just littered with thousands of them; we got them well encircled, and our katyushas let fly. God, what a massacre! And there are thousands and thousands of lorries and cars, most of them dumped in the ravines; they had neither the time nor the means to destroy them, and thousands of guns. . . . Sixty or seventy percent of the lorries and guns can be repaired and used again. . . .

Another survivor talked of Pitomnik airfield:

> The place is now littered with thousands of dead frozen Fritzes. Before the war Pitomnik was a wonderful fruit tree nursery, the finest

apple, pear and cherry trees were grown there; now everything is destroyed.

He told of finding there a camp for Russian prisoners:

Open air, with barbed wire round it. It was dreadful. There were originally 1400 men there, whom the Germans forced to work on fortifications. Only 102 survived. You might say the Germans had nothing to eat themselves, but the starvation of the prisoners began long before the encirclement. . . .

Correspondent Alexander Werth was one of the visitors. He wrote:

It wasn't quite what I had expected. For a moment I was dazzled by the sun shining on the snow. We were in one of those Garden Cities which the Russians had lost in September. . . . Most of the cottages and trees had been completely smashed. To the right, in the distance, there were large imposing looking blocks of five or six story buildings; they were in reality the shells of the buildings of central Stalingrad. . . . On the left, a couple of miles away, there rose a large number of enormously high factory chimneys; one had the impression that there was over there, a live industrial town, but under the chimneys there was nothing but the ruins of the Tractor Plant. Chimneys are hard to hit, and these were standing, seemingly untouched. . . .

They traveled down toward the Volga past smashed warehouses and railroad buildings. A few frozen Germans were still lying by the roadside. They crossed the rail line and saw railway cars and engines piled on top of each other. The oil tanks, high and cylindrical, were crumpled like cardboard and riddled with shell holes. On the other side of the road they saw a honeycomb of trenches and dugouts and shell holes; beyond was the road, and before them was the road, and before them was the Volga, white and icebound. The temperature was forty below.

The Volga! Here was the scene of one of the grimmest episodes of the war; the Stalingrad lifeline. The remnants of it were still there, those barges and steamers, most of them smashed, frozen into ice.

Now a thin trickle of traffic was calmly driving across the ice; cars and horse sleighs and some soldiers on foot. . . .

They walked down the main street of Stalingrad, running south, between enormous blocks of burned-out buildings toward the other square. In the middle of the pavement they saw a dead German who was running when the shell hit him. His legs still seemed to be running, though one was cut off by the shell, and splintered white bone stuck out through the flesh. The face was a bloody frozen mess, and beside it was a frozen pool of blood.

They went to the Univermag department store, all the upper floors burned out, where General Paulus had surrendered, and they crossed the square to the yard of the Red Army House. Here they had a glimpse of the last days of Stalingrad for the Germans.

In the porch lay the skeleton of a horse, with only a few scraps of meat still clinging to its ribs. Then we came into the yard. Here lay more horses' skeletons and, to the right, there was an enormous horrible cesspool—fortunately frozen solid. And then suddenly at the far end I caught sight of a human figure. He had been crouching over another cesspool, and now, noticing us, he was hastily pulling up his pants, and then he slunk away into the door of a basement. But as he passed, I caught a glimpse of the wretch's face—with its mixture of suffering and idiot-like incomprehension. For a moment I wished the whole of Germany were there to see it. The man was perhaps already dying. In that basement into which he had slunk there were perhaps still two hundred Germans. . . .

The Russians had not yet had time to deal with them. Correspondent Werth's mind leaped back to photographs of Hitler "smirking as he stood on the steps of the Madeleine in Paris and the weary days of '38 and '39 when a jittery Europe would tune in to Berlin and hear Hitler's yells accompanied by the cannibal roar of the German mob. And there seemed a rough but divine justice in those frozen cesspools with their diarrhea, and their horses' bones, and those starved yellow corpses in the yard of the Red Army House at Stalingrad."

CASUALTIES

The total number of casualties of the war in Russia will never be known. Russian statistics, such as they were, turned out to be highly inflated and unreliable, used for propaganda more than for information. Millions of Russian civilians perished or vanished. At Stalingrad alone, nearly 500,000 people were associated with the factory complex before the war. At the end of the Battle of Stalingrad some fifteen hundred civilians emerged from their caves and other hiding places. The rest were either dead or missing.

In less than seven months the Stalingrad dead numbered over three million.

By the spring of 1944, some 5.16 million Russian soldiers had been captured by the Germans. Of that total only 1.053 million survived. Another 200,000 were claimed captured before the end of the war.

As for German prisoners captured by the Russians, there are no accurate statistics. General Halder kept track of total casualties as long as he was in office, and counted 1,670 million on the Eastern Front until September 10, 1942. After that hundreds of thousands were killed in Belorussia, 300,000 in the last campaign, 84,000 at Koenigsberg alone. And that is to say nothing of the allied armies of Italians, Romanians, Hungarians, Croats, Finns, Slovakians, more than a million altogether, very few of whom returned home.

Arctic Ocean

NORWAY

SWEDEN

FINLAND

Murmansk

Archangel

RUSSIA

Ural Mts.

Perm •

Leningrad

Baltic Sea

Moscow

Kuybyshev

Warsaw

POLAND

Kiev

HUNGARY

Kharkov

Stalingrad

Astrakhan

RUMANIA

Rostov

YUG.

BULGARIA

Black
Sea

Caspian
Sea

GREECE

TURKEY

Tiflis

Miles

AXIS TERRITORIES
BEFORE "BARBAROSSA"

LIMIT OF GERMAN ADVANCE
INTO RUSSIA · NOV 1942

PROJECTED EXTENT OF THE
"GREATER GERMAN EMPIRE"

0   100 200 300 400 500

NAZI DREAM OF A
GREATER GERMAN EMPIRE

EPILOGUE

When the Russians sprang their trap in the bend of the Don on November 19, 1942, they caught 330,000 Axis soldiers in it. Units of Germans, Italians, Hungarians, Romanians, and Croatians were surrounded and decimated, and the survivors were made prisoner. Very few of them ever saw their homeland again.

When the Battle of Stalingrad ended in February 1943, ninety-one thousand soldiers, mostly Germans, marched out of the city of Stalingrad to captivity. In the first few weeks of their captivity they were treated without sympathy and thousands died. Tens of thousands had died of hunger earlier, and more died under the Russians. But the major reason for the deaths was typhus. The disease the German doctors had noticed before the capitulation reached epidemic proportions, and fifty thousand men died of it. Later, when the prisoners were moved to Asian prison camps, more died from the journey and from malnutrition.

General Paulus and his senior officers lived near Moscow in comfortable quarters. One reason for their good treatment was the propaganda value the Russians could make of them. But as for the rank and file, there are tales of murder and cannibalism about these times. No matter what promises were made, the German, Italian, and other prisoners did not get enough food. They were put to forced labor, and in the end when the last of the Germans went home in 1955, there were only five thousand survivors. Thus Stalingrad became the burial place of the German 6th Army.

That army was reconstituted in name by the Germans almost immediately after the battle, and a 6th Army continued to fight for the German cause. But it was not the same. Nor was anything else the same. The waste that Hitler created in the summer and fall of 1942 destroyed more than an army. The 6th Army was lost, and so were the Hungarian, Romanian, and Italian armies that had been sent to fight under Hitler. The whole German alliance began to come apart. Most important, so many Germans were lost that after Stalingrad the army in the Eastern Front never regained its strength and faced a constantly growing and constantly improving Red Army.

Stalingrad marked the changeover from the German offensive in Russia to the defensive. Never again was Hitler able to launch a major offensive, although after the German retreat to the Dnieper Field Marshal Kleist managed a counterattack which recaptured Kharkov and gave the Germans several months of time.

THE TIDE OF WAR TURNS . . .

In the German attack on Russia, Stalin had run the gamut from despair that caused him to sequester himself for the first week of war, leaving Russia rudderless, to reckless overconfidence that cost the Russian armies millions of lives. But when the Germans were defeated at Stalingrad, the Russians knew that the war had turned around, and that they would defeat their enemy in time. After that there was no turning back, no hesitation, and the confidence of the Russian people and the Russian armies soared. The banks of the Volga and the Don were the graveyard of German ambitions in Russia.

By the late summer of 1942 the partisan movement was solidly established behind the German lines. Thereafter the partisans' successes began to bolster Russian morale and the newspapers and magazines were full of their heroic exploits. The leaders were called to conferences, and their activities were highly publicized. By the summer of 1943 the partisan movement, because of Nazi brutality, had gained a strong foothold, and thereafter the once-recalcitrant Ukrainians joined wholeheartedly in the war to push the Germans out of the Soviet borders.

Stalingrad came as a real surprise to the Russian high command, although Stalin never admitted it. After the victory as won, there was a good deal of fumbling, because the military leadership was not prepared to exploit their victory. But later in the year the Russians were

(*continued next page*)

(continued from preceding page)
able to launch two simultaneous offensives in the North and the South, to the great surprise of the Germans who were still operating on the theory that the Russian reserves had been nearly used up at Stalingrad. As Stalin reported to the Russian people on February 23, 1943:

"Three months ago, the Red Army troops began an offensive at the approaches to Stalingrad. Since then the initiative of military operations has been in our hands, while the striking force of the Red Army's operations have not weakened. At present in the hard conditions of winter, the Red Army advances on a frontage of 1,500 kilometers and achieves success practically everywhere. In the north at Leningrad, on the central front, at the approaches to Kharkov, in the Donbas, at Rostov, on the Azov, and Black Sea coasts, the Red Army strikes one blow after another at Hitler's troops. In three months the Red Army has cleared the enemy from the territory of the Voronezh and Stalingrad regions, the Chechenno-Ingush, North Ossetian, Kabardion-Balkarian and Krasnodar Territories, the Cherkess Karachai and Adygei Autonomous Regions, and nearly all of the Rostov, Kharkov, and KUrsk regions. The expulsion of the enemy from the Soviet country has begun."

The Russians realized that the Red Army had completely destroyed the German Sixth army, and the Romanian, Hungarian, and Italian armies that had joined Hitler's forces on the eastern front. The Germans had enjoyed an enormous superiority in experience and resources at hand, but in twenty months the Russians had learned to strike and to exploit German weaknesses. The Red Army had begun the liberation of the Ukraine. The danger at this point, Stalin said, was that the poeple would become complacent and there was still an enormous job to be done to free Russia entirely from the boot of Hitler. So far had affairs changed in the war by the spring of 1943 that the Soviet dictator felt that he had to warn the people against overconfidence.

Hitler insisted on another offensive that summer and put together seventeen armored divisions in an attack on the Russian Kursk salient. But the Russians escaped the trap laid by the Germans and then launched their own offensive in the autumn and winter of 1943.

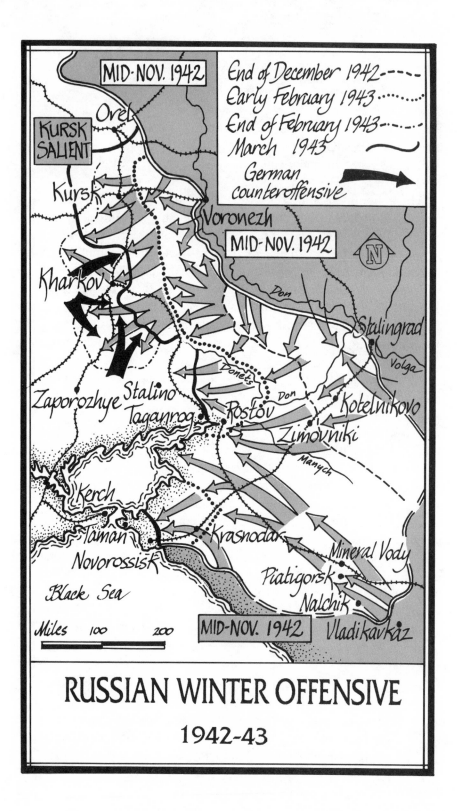

MID·NOV. 1942

End of December 1942 ----
Early February 1943 ·········
End of February 1943 --·--
March 1943

German
counteroffensive

Orel

KURSK
SALIENT

Kursk

Voronezh

MID·NOV. 1942

N

Kharkov

Don

Stalingrad

Volga

Donets

Don

Zaporozhye Stalino
Taganrog

Rostov

Kotelnikovo

Zimovniki

Manych

Kerch

Krasnodar

Taman

Mineral Vody

Novorossisk

Piatigorsk

Black Sea

Nalchik

Miles 100 200

MID·NOV. 1942

Vladikavkaz

RUSSIAN WINTER OFFENSIVE

1942-43

The Germans did best in the north, where they had been on the defensive for months. A number of the German generals interviewed after the war said they thought Germany might have fought the war to a draw, had the generals been allowed to fight in military fashion.

General Werner Tippelskirch put it this way: "The root cause of Germany's defeat was the way that her forces were wasted in fruitless efforts, and above all in fruitless resistance at the wrong time and place. That was due to Hitler. There was no strategy in our campaign."

Fruitless resistance at the wrong time and place. That is the story of the Germans at Stalingrad and the story of the death of the German 6th Army. That army could have captured Stalingrad easily in the late spring of 1942, but was not sent to do so. When it was assigned the task, the Germans did not understand that the Russians had decided to make this the key battle of the war and were willing to throw all their resources into it.

But a major reason for the Russian triumph at Stalingrad was sheer Russian perseverance. Field Marshal Kleist, in assessing the Red Army, had this to say:

> The men were first-rate fighters from the start, and we owed our success simply to superior training. They became first-rate soldiers with experience. They fought most toughly, had amazing endurance, and could carry on without most of the things all other armies regarded as necessities. The Staff was quick to learn from their early defeats, and soon became highly efficient.

As for the Russian leadership, the Germans agreed that in the beginning it was very poor, but that it got better and better as the war progressed. The leading Russian military figure was always Marshal Zhukov, the hero of Stalingrad, and Marshal Konev came to be highly regarded.

STALIN AND ZHUKOV

By the summer of 1942, when Stalin realized that Stalingrad would determine the fate of Russia and that he did not know enough to lead the armies to victory himself, he gave Zhukov a free hand.

General P.A. Belov got the impression that Zhukov was giving the
(*continued next page*)

(*continued from preceding page*)

orders that summer, and Stalin was listening. Alexander Yakolev, aircraft designer who became an intimate of Stalin's in the way that Albert Speer the architect became an intimate of Hitler's, wrote that one day at lunch in the Stalin dacha Zhukov sat down and, like the peasant he was, wolfed down his lunch without a word. Only then did he join the general discussion that was going on at Stalin's table. Stalin never said a word in complaint at the high-handed treatment.

When, after Stalingrad, the war turned around, Stalin resumed his old habit of ordering people around but not Zhukov. The marshal remained as deputy supreme commander of the Russian armies until the end of the war. Just afterward, however, he was relegated to a provincial command. Eventually disgraced, he was only rehabilitated after Stalin's death. Stalin would not defer to anyone for long. After Zhukov had won the war for him, Zhukov was expendable. More than that, Stalin saw him as a threat, and Stalin never countenanced even the suggestion of a threat.

"One of their greatest assets," said General Dittmar, the military commentator, "was their officers' readiness to learn and the way they studied their job."

But the most important asset of the Russians, and it showed nowhere better than at Stalingrad, was what Dittmar called "the soulless indifference of the troops—it was something more than fatalism." He called it "extraordinary stolidity." Another way of putting it was extraordinary willingness to sacrifice. Again and again at Stalingrad the willingness of the Russians to sacrifice and die was shown in the battles for the town and the factories.

As for Stalingraders, they paid in blood for the hard-fought victory. In five months of fighting, the city was 99 percent destroyed. Three hundred factories, forty-one thousand homes, and more than one hundred hospitals and schools had been destroyed. Of the 500,000 inhabitants of Stalingrad, only 1,500 remained. The rest were either dead or scattered across Russia as far as Vladivostok.

Stalingrad was the most important battle of the war against Hitler, and his defeat here paved the way for his final defeat.

But it was more than that. From that first summer day when the planes of the Luftwaffe set out to destroy a city and then destroyed it, until that last German paroxysm in the early days of February, when the last Germans went down fighting in the Red October factory, the battle for Stalingrad added up to more than the sum of its parts.

From some point in the middle of the fight for Stalingrad and its factory complexes the Germans began to realize that here was the proof of what Stalin had said on the anniversary of the October Revolution:

"The German invaders want a war of extermination against the peoples of the USSR. Well, if the Germans want a war of extermination, they shall have it."

Stalingrad was a part of Stalin's fulfillment of that promise, and by the end every German in Russia knew what Stalingrad meant and every German was afraid.

STALINGRAD BEFORE . . .

Stalingrad was conceived in the 1920s and built in the 1930s, the model of a Soviet factory city, with all the amenities of which a communist society would like to boast. This was the way all the new USSR would be in the future, the planners said, and they mortgaged the future to try to build a supercity.

The raison d'être of Stalingrad lay in its position on the Volga, the lifeline of Central Russia and the vital-most trading center for Russia, the Ukraine, the Caucasus, and Kazakhstan. The Communist government gave the place a new importance with the creation of model factories and model factory developments. Single men and women lived in dormitories, but families had their own detached houses, the envy of the workers in the crowded old cities of the Soviet Union. The houses were little wooden cottages with flower gardens and room to plant vegetables. Spaciousness was the key to Stalingrad. The streets were wide and new, and the buildings were concrete examples of the best architecture that the party and the government could find.

Red Square was the political and cultural center of the city, with the party offices and government offices adjoining and across the street the huge Univermag department store, the greatest in the region. Whatever consumer goods were to be found in the region, they would be found in Univermag. The Red Army had its center on the edge of the

(*continued next page*)

(continued from preceding page)

square, and the newspaper *Pravda* was there. The wedding of industry and agriculture was symbolized by the huge grain elevator complex on the river at Tsaritsa Gorge. South of the city center was the mining community, and south of that lay Kuporosnoye. North of the business center, with its boulevards and parks, schools and hospital, and the dreaded NKVD prison lay the factory complex, the pride of the USSR planners. Southernmost of these was the Red October factory, north of it the Barrikady factory, and north of that the tractor factory. Each factory complex boasted its own schools, its own parks, its own housing development, and little provision stations and other amenities. It was by Soviet standards a great achievement, and the cultural wave of Russia's future if the party leaders would have their way.

West of the city were the great communal farms of the Don basin with their thousands upon thousands of acres of waving wheat and their orchards and produce for the cities. Industrial, mining, and agricultural center of the whole enormous region, Stalingrad was Stalin's pride and joy.

AFTER . . .

On February 3, the official day of the capitulation of the Germans in Stalingrad, two planeloads of western war correspondents were flown into the city by the exultant Russian leaders, who were, for once, so proud of their achievement that they relaxed their iron discipline of the press. The temperature was four below zero, but the temperature began falling and ultimately hit thirty below. What the correspondents saw were smashed houses of the garden cities, many, many lonely chimneys, which had once stood above busy buildings, and stood now above piles of rubble, and miles of frozen earth, covered partly by snow, wrecked vehicles and equipment. Along the roadsides and in what had been German and Russian defensive positions, rubble was everywhere. One correspondent was reminded of the Warsaw Ghetto after it had been leveled by the Germans, although in Warsaw the act had been deliberate, the random destruction of the battle worse, and the area of destruction much larger.

(continued next page)

(continued from preceding page)

As for what was recognizable in the wreckage, it was the devil's spoils of war: railroad carriages mixed with bent and broken rusted rails and smashed locomotives and parts of locomotives in the railyard, oil tanks along the river crumpled and battered. The ground was honeycombed by now smashed trenches whose sides had fallen in, and the wreckage of pillboxes and bunkers. Dugouts and shell holes pocked the whole countryside, and the carcasses and partial carcasses of thousands of horses lay frozen and twisted on the ground. Along the Volga the banks were lined with smashed steamers and barges and the hulks of little craft. Mamayev Hill, the scene of the fiercest and longest fighting, was scattered with human bones. Once it had been the central height in a woody park where lovers liked to come in evenings to enjoy the shaded privacy. Anywhere at all, you might come across a body frozen in the attitude of death, or part of a body, sometimes unidentifiable.

The whole area was a wasteland. It looked as though it had been swept by fire and then ravaged by an earthquake and finished off with a volcanic eruption. There was virtually no relationship to what was once human workmanship. This frozen desert was unrecognizable as the corpse of a working city. There was no visible line where the townended and the countryside began. It was all rubble and ruin. If one had to imagine what must be done to rehabilitate Stalingrad, one would have to decide that it was much, much worse than starting from scratch. First the live ammunition, the unexploded hardware, would have to be removed, and this would mean digging down many feet for the big shells and big bombs. Then the whole would have to be leveled, and fill brought in to erase the enormous craters. Topsoil would have to be generated if anything was ever to grow here again, and then the arduous process of engineering and building a new city would have to begin. Yes, it was going to be much, much worse than starting from scratch.

BIBLIOGRAPHY

DOCUMENTS AND REPORTS

Captured German documents in the U.S. National Archives, Washington, D.C.

War diary, German 6th Army. August 1942, January 1943.

War diaries, Festung Stalingrad. December 1942–January 1943.

Daily reports, Army Group Don. November 1942–January 1943.

Operations and situation reports:

VIII Corps, XI Corps, LI Corps, XXIV Panzer Corps.

Infantry Divisions: 44, 71, 76, 79, 94, 113, 100 Jaeger, 295, 305, 371, 376, 384, 389, 397.

Panzer Divisions: 14,16, 24.

Motorized Divisions: 3, 29, 60.

BOOKS

Carell, Paul. *Hitler Moves East*. Boston: Little, Brown, 1964.

Chuikov, Vasili, *The Battle for Stalingrad*. New York: Holt, Rinehart and Winston, 1964.

Clark, Alan. *Barbarossa: The Russian-German Conflict, 1941–45*. New York: Morrow, 1985

Craig, William. *Enemy at the Gates, the Battle for Stalingrad*. New York: Reader's Digest Press, 1973.

Downing, David. *The Devil's Virtuosos: German Generals at War, 1940–45*. New York: St. Martin's Press, 1977.

Erickson, John. *The Road to Stalingrad*. London: Weidenfeld & Nicolson, 1965.

Gilbert, Felix. *Hitler Directs His War.* New York: Oxford University Press, 1951.

Guderian, Heinz. *Panzer Leader.* London: Futura, 1974.

Hitler's Stalingrad Decisions. Berkeley: University of California Press, 1985.

Jukes, Geffrey. *Stalingrad, the Turning Point.* New York: Ballantine Books, 1968.

Karpov, Vladimir. *Russia at War, 1941–45.* New York: Vendome Press, 1987.

Keitel, Wilhelm. *The Memoirs of Field Marshal Keitel.* New York: Stein & Day, 1966.

Liddell Hart, B. H. *The German Generals Talk.* New York: Quill, 1979.

Paulus, Friedrich. *Paulus and Stalingrad.* Edited by Walter Goerlich. Westport, Conn.: Greenwood Press, 1974.

Rotundo, Louis, ed. *Battle for Stalingrad.* The 1943 Soviet General Staff Study. Washington, D.C.: Pergamon-Brassey, 1989.

Sajer, Guy. *The Forgotten Soldier.* New York: Ballantine Books, 1972.

Stalin, Joseph. *The Great Patriotic War.* New York: International, 1945.

Trevor-Roper, Hugh, ed. *Hitler's War Directives, 1939–45.* London: Sidgwick & Jackson, 1964.

Werth, Alexander. *Russia at War.* New York: E. P. Dutton, 1964.

Zhukov, Georgi K. *Marshal Zhukov's Greatest Battles.* Translated by Theodore Shabad. New York: Harper & Row, 1969.

———. *Memoirs.* New York: Delacorte, 1971.

Ziemke, Earl F., and Magna E. Bauer. *Moscow to Stalingrad.* New York: Military Heritage Press, 1988.

NOTES AND ACKNOWLEDGMENTS

I am much indebted to archivists at the U.S. National Archives for assistance in examining the captured German military documents, and to librarians at the Chevy Chase and Bethesda branches of the Montgomery County library. Merrill and Donna Needham steered me to a number of sources and, because I was unable to drive at the time, chauffeured me to many bookstores. I am indebted to Bob Gleason, my editor at Tor, who found me a copy of Guy Sajer's *The Forgotten Soldier*, which evokes the spirit of the German soldier in Russia during the war and indicates the importance of Stalingrad in that war. As always I am indebted to Olga Gruhzit-Hoyt for all sorts of help, from book buying to encouragement and perspicacious editing.

SOURCE MATERIALS

What the Germans were to reap in the aftermath of Stalingrad, they sowed beginning in the summer of 1941 with their total war policy, in which the Russian people were to be treated as *Untermensch,* or subhumans. By starving, murdering, and torturing the people in the occupied zones, the "Master Race" made it certain that when the time came for retribution they would see no mercy. As noted in the story by Edwin Erich Dwinger, even the Germans were astounded at the Russian people's ability to absorb punishment and the willingness of men, women, and children to die for the Russian cause. There should have been a lesson there for the Germans, but they were too drunk with victory to absorb it. They went on and on with their excesses.

In the beginning the Russian war effort was almost hopeless. Stalin had wrecked the Red Army with his purges, and it was in no condition to fight. Leadership was the major problem. Battalion commanders and regimental commanders were afraid to lead, because if they made mistakes they expected to be relieved if not shot. So in the opening phases of battle the Germans won, and won, and won. But as several of the German generals said later, in their losses the Russians learned fast. And by autumn of 1942 Stalin had learned that if he wanted to survive he would have to begin trusting someone. In this change emerged Vasilevsky and Zhukov, Yeremenko, Chuikov, Rokossovsky, and other generals. The spirit of the Red Army remained the same: the Russian soldier was more Oriental than European; he was willing to subsist on a few crusts of bread for a week, to accept hardships that were totally foreign to western armies, and not only to survive but to fight very well.

I

The tales of partisan activity and the behavior of the Germans come from Sajer, Clark's *Barbarossa*, and Carell, on the German side, and Zhukov and Werth on the Russian. The Dwinger story is from Clark. The song "A People's Sacred War" is from *Russia at War, 1941–45*, by Vladimir Karpov, published in New York in 1987 by Vendome Press. The story of the battle for Moscow comes from Guderian, Werth, Clark, and Zhukov, and Stalin's mention of German atrocities is from one of his speeches.

I I

I depended on German historian Paul Carell for the assessment of the great change that came over the Eastern Front in the winter of 1942–43. I used the captured German records for the figures on divisional losses. The material on the Luftwaffe comes from *The Luftwaffe*, published by Times Books of New York, and materials in German archives in Freiburg. The material about Marshal Zhukov is from his own works and from Werth. The material about Guderian is from his book *Panzer Leader*. The material about Hitler's decisions is from the Keitel memoirs and Liddell Hart's *The German Generals Talk*.

The effect of the cold on the German panzer divisions is clearly illustrated in Guderian's accounts of his difficulties. The Clark book is the source of much of the material about Bock, and *The German Generals Talk* is another source.

I I I

Marshal Zhukov is the source for much of the material about the Russian move in the first Russian offensive. The activities of General Brauchitsch come from *Barbarossa* and from the Keitel memoirs; Guderian's remarks are from his own book. The Kluge incident is from the Keitel memoirs, as is the delineation of the Hitler position on retreat. The material about the Russian counterplans is from Zhukov. He was surprised and shocked when his opinion was asked and then ignored. But what he did not realize was that Stalin did not forget, and when he had been wrong, which was often, he attempted to rectify the situation without apology. Part of this section comes from Ericksson, part from Zhukov, part from Werth.

IV

The German Generals Talk is the source for the material about General Blumentritt. The Keitel memoirs were used for the discussions of the OKW and OKH plans. The Kleist remarks come from *The German Generals Talk*. The discussion of German morality in Russia comes from the Karpov book, *Russia at War,* and from glimpses shown by Sajer in his book about the German soldier. The discussions of the Russian offensives come from Zhukov. The material about Operation Blau comes largely from Carell. So does the story of General Stumme and the betrayal of the plan. Stalin's reaction is from Werth. The material about Paulus is largely from the Paulus book. The material about Chuikov is from his memoirs.

V

The note about Hitler's directive is from the Keitel memoirs, as is the description of the German strategy. I used Sajer for the basis of this tale of a German attack.

Hitler confided his feelings to the people around him. He was certain that the Russians would not last the summer. The material about the 62nd Russian Army is from Chuikov.

VI

The material about General Yeremenko comes from Werth, Clark and Blair, and Erickson. Hitler's attitude is revealed in the Keitel memoirs and the various conversations Liddell Hart had with German generals in *The German Generals Talk*. Part of the discussion of Yeremenko's first days in Stalingrad is from Carell. Craig also contributed here.

VII

A vivid pictorial history of the battle for Stalingrad is given in Karpov's *Russia at War.* General Richthofen's story is from parts of his diary printed in the Paulus book and from Craig. Stalin's watchword is from Zhukov. The German attack is described in detail in Carell. I also used the divisional papers of the captured records in the National Archives here. Chuikov described the scene carefully. The Stalin message is from Zhukov, as is the description of Russian counterattack. The September meeting of Hitler with Paulus is described by Keitel. Chuikov's planning is described in his book. He was surprised when the Germans beat him to the punch in the mid-September assault. The furious fighting in the city is well described in Chuikov and Craig and Carell. The material on the German soldier's feelings comes from Sajer. The story of the Tsaritsyn bunker is Chuikov. The story of Marshal Zhukov's counterattack in the northwest is from Zhukov. The account of the fighting in the grain elevator is from Carell and Werth, as is the story of the basement fortress. The notes about Marshal Goering are from Richthofen as quoted by Paulus.

VIII

The plans of Zhukov and Vasilevsky are from the Zhukov book, along with the story of the meetings with Stalin. "Every man a fortress" is from Chuikov. The story of Halder's dismissal and Schmundt's advancement is from Keitel. The talks of fighting in Stalingrad are from Erickson, Craig, and Chuikov. The discussions of German tactics at Stalingrad are from *The German Generals Talk*. The Stalingrad chronology of the battle is from Erickson. The story of the October fighting is from the Clark book and Werth. The story of the factory defenses is from Chuikov. The story of the Yeremenko-Chuikov encounter is from Chuikov. The Tania Chernova story is from Craig. The story of Vasili Zaitsev is from Craig and the Clark book and Carell.

IX

For this section I depended on Chuikov, Paulus, Karpov for the looks of things, and Werth. Several of the German generals in the Liddell Hart book had comments about the German way of fighting in Stalingrad. I used some of the anecdotes in the Craig book about street fighting. Hitler's attitude is clearly shown in the Keitel memoirs. The Sajer book provided the tale of the convoy bound for Stalingrad and the partisans. The stories of the Red October plant are from *Barbarossa*. Richthofen wrote about the troubles of the Luftwaffe. The tale of the German officer is from *Barbarossa*.

X

The Soviet offensive beginning comes from Zhukov and Werth. The Paulus book was a primary source. Richthofen's comments are from his diary. The Binder story is from Craig. Paulus messages are from his book. The account of Goering's visit to Rastenburg is from Keitel and *Barbarossa* and Carell. The Manstein plan is from Carell. The discussions within the Luftwaffe come from Richthofen's diary as quoted in Paulus.

XI

The Shapiro story is from Werth. The material about Zhukov is from his books. Richthofen is the source for the Luftwaffe material. I depended heavily on *Barbarossa*, Carell, and Paulus for the material about the 6th Army. I also used the divisional records of the captured German documents. The story of the Manstein plan is from Carell. For the material about Plan Saturn, I turned to Werth and Erickson. The material about the Russians fighting in Stalingrad is from Chuikov. Richthofen is the source for the Luftwaffe material. Rotundo is the source for the material about the Soviet air force. Chuikov is the source for the material on the German tenacity.

XII

The material on Manstein and his planes is from Carell and Erickson. I quoted Zhukov on Stalin, and Werth was the source for the material here on the Russian attack. Paulus is the source for the discussion on the 6th Army situation. The long series of messages between Paulus and Manstein is from Erickson, the captured German documents, Paulus, Blair, and *Barbarossa*. The story of Major Eismann's mission is from *Barbarossa*, Erickson, Carell, and Craig. The story of the starving soldiers is from Blair. The material on Hitler is from Keitel. The meanderings of Hitler are from *Hitler's Stalingrad Decisions*. The tales of German Christmas in Stalingrad are from Craig. The story of the Vatutin attack is from Zhukov.

XIII

The first part of this section comes from Werth, Carell, and *Barbarossa*. Blair is the source of the Biryuzov story. The material about Hitler is from

Keitel. The Manstein material is from Carell and *Barbarossa*. The progress of the Russian attack is detailed by Zhukov. The Russian ultimatum is in *Barbarossa*, and the Russian attack of January 10 is described from the Russian side in Werth and Zhukov, from the German in Carell. The letters from Germans are from Craig and Carell.

The fall of Pitomnik airfield is from Paulus and Craig and *Barbarossa*. The Gumrak story is from Carell, and *Barbarossa* and Craig. The tale of the odyssey of the correspondents is from Werth. The material about Hitler is from Keitel. The meeting of Manstein and Richthofen is from Richthofen's diary. The progress of the Russian offensive is detailed in Zhukov. The story of the Hollidt detachment's worries is from Carell. The material about the squeeze of the Germans is from *Barbarossa*.

XIV

The material about Fuehrer headquarters is from Keitel. The Paulus and Fuehrer interchanges are from Paulus's book and Keitel and Carell. The Zitzewitz story is from Carell and Craig. The material about the last days of the Germans in Stalingrad is from all sources, German divisional reports, Paulus's book, Craig, *Barbarossa*, Keitel, and Sajer.

INDEX

air defense
  Germany: *See* Luftwaffe (German
    Air Force)
  Soviet Union, 19, 57
air raids, 124–125, 135
American aid to Soviet Union, 239–
  240
Army Group Center (Germany), 70–
  73, 75
Army Group Don (Germany), 191,
  209

Barrikady factory, 122–123, 169, 172,
  175–176, 225
Belov, Gen. P.A., 283
Beria, Lavrenti, 21, 73
  SMERSH (Death to Spies) organi-
    zation, establishing, 91
Binder, Quartermaster, 193, 229, 245
Biryuzov, Gen. S.S., 238
Blumentritt, Gen. Guenthen, 85
Bock, Field Marshal Fedor von, 58,
  61–63, 69, 76, 96, 99
Bormann, Martin, 36
Borodino (steamer), 153

Brauchitsch, Field Marshal Walther
  von, 24, 68, 69
Budenny, Marshal Semyon, 40–41,
  47
Bulganin, Gen. Nikolai, 46

Carell, Paul, 55
casualties
  Germany, 37–38, 56, 161, 166,
    229, 232, 246, 254, 255, 276
  Soviet Union, 40, 92, 93, 165, 276
Caucasus, 86–88, 105, 232, 242, 243,
  252
Chernova, Tania, 170–171
Chistiakov, Gen. I. M., 206
Chuikov, Gen. Vasili, 100, 111–112,
  135, 140, 142–148, 152, 154,
  161–162, 164, 166, 169–170,
  182, 214, 228, 243
Conquest, Robert, 20

Dittmar, General, 284
Doer, General, 163
Don Front, 160
Don River, 98–101, 106–108, 196, 220

Winter Relief Campaign, 160
withdrawal from Stalingrad, refusal
to consider, 184–185, 191, 225–
227, 230–232, 245, 256
Hoepner, Gen. Erich, 43, 50
Hollidt, Gen. Karl, 209
Hollidt Force (Germany), 209
Hoth, Gen. Hermann, 45, 50, 112,
118, 134, 135–136, 190, 228,
237, 241–242, 254
Hube, Lt. Gen. Hans, 119, 132, 251

Jaenecke, Gen. Erwin, 252
Japan, 58, 138, 239
Jeschonnek, Gen. Albert, 191, 193,
197, 200
Jodl, Gen. Alfred, 24, 182, 191
Joseph Stalin (steamer), 153
Ju-52 aircraft, 79–80, 200, 206–207,
228, 248, 250

Keitel, Field Marshal Wilhelm, 23,
24, 29
Kharkov, 92–95, 280
Khrushchev, Nikita, 99, 100, 117,
120, 123, 132, 141, 143, 160
Kiev, 40, 47
Kleist, Field Marshal Paul von, 24,
31, 87–88, 99, 242, 280
assessing the Red Army, 283
Klin, 60, 61, 67
Kluge, Field Marshal Guenther von,
45, 70–71, 78
Koenigsberg Line (K-line), 75, 76–77,
78
Koestring, Gen. Ernst, 24, 29
Konev, Gen. Ivan, 43, 46, 283
Krylov, Gen. Nikolai, 142

Kube, Wilhelm, 35, 37
Kuebler, Gen. Ludwig, 76
Kuechler, Field Marshal Georg von,
76
Kurzbach, Gen. Walther Seydlitz, 195

Leeb, Field Marshal Wilhelm von,
61, 68, 75–76
Lelyushenko, Gen. Dmitry, 47
List, Field Marshal Wilhelm, 88
Lopatin, Gen. A. L., 101, 119, 121,
143
Luftwaffe (German Air Force), 21,
56–57, 79, 129, 142–143, 166,
183, 197, 199–201, 205, 220,
221–224, 240
airlift, carrying out, 79–80, 193,
226–227, 247
delivering supplies to Sixth Army,
200–201, 214, 247, 249–250

Mackensen, General von, 95, 96
Malandin, Lt. Gen. G. K., 46
Malenkov, Georgi, 18, 21, 73
Malinovsky, Lt. Gen. Rodion, 213
Malyshev, Vyacheslav, 122, 136
Mamayev Hill, 105–106, 145, 151,
155, 164, 287
Manstein, Field Marshal Fritz Erich
von, 191, 199, 209–210, 214–
215, 241–242, 249, 253–255,
263–264, 266
offer to resign, 242
relief expedition to Stalingrad, attempting, 218–233
Sixth Army breakout, trying to convince Hitler to order, 225, 230
three-phase operation plan, 210